DIRECTORY OF ILLUSTRATION 17

directoryofillustration·com

Portfolio On-Line

Art directors can now look at additional images from our participating illustrators on the web. Our Portfolio On-Line offers art buyers immediate access to artists' portfolios. Images are indexed for quick keyword searches by subject, style and artist's name.

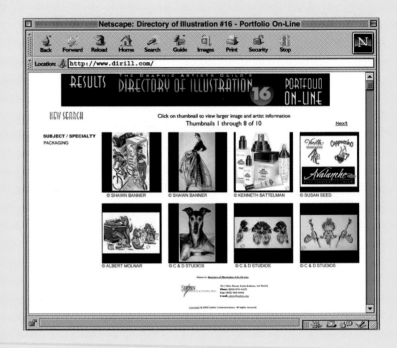

Directory of Illustration On-Line

Many of the pages in the Directory of Illustration #17 can also be found on the web. If an associate or client does not have a copy of the Directory of Illustration, our electronic version, via the internet, is a quick and easy alternative. Many of the pages have e-mail as well as direct links to the artist's personal site.

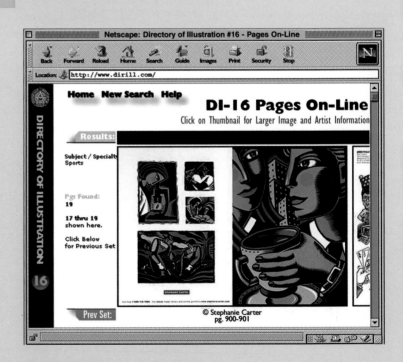

Published by:

Serbin Communications, Inc.
511 Olive Street
Santa Barbara, California 93101
(805) 963-0439
e-mail: admin@serbin.com

PUBLISHER/EDITOR
Glen Robert Serbin

VICE PRESIDENT/SOURCE BOOK DIRECTOR
Elizabeth Nebb Owen

MANAGING EDITOR, SOURCE BOOK DIVISION
Terry Bickmore

ACCOUNTANT, SOURCE BOOK DIVISION
Radana Khadilkar

MARKETING STAFF
Ellie Altomare   Jim Christen
Nancy Caldwell   Heather McGibbon
Sheila Cantillon   Annie Nicolletti
Beth Pierson

CIRCULATION & LIST COORDINATOR
Cathie Heckrotte

PRODUCTION MANAGER
Tamra Dempsey

TRAFFIC COORDINATOR
Barbara Kuhn

PRODUCTION STAFF
Annie Boissevain
Joseph Green
Theil Shelton

BOOK DESIGN
Kathleen Corby, Corby Design

PRODUCTION, PAGE DESIGN SERVICES
Terry Bickmore
Donald Henderson

ADMINISTRATIVE SUPPORT
Nella Principe-Nelson

PROOFING
Cynthia Anderson
David Compton
Julie Simpson

MANAGING EDITOR, MAGAZINE DIVISION
Julie Simpson

BOOKKEEPING
Ken Jurgensen

ACCOUNTING
Damitz, Brooks, Nightingale, Turner & Morrisset

GRAPHIC ARTISTS GUILD LIAISON EXECUTIVE DIRECTOR
Paul Basista

COVER ILLUSTRATION
Scott Wright, represented by
Dick Rutt & Associates, 843-238-9556
(See ad on pages 32-33)

COMPUTER DATABASE COORDINATOR
Debbie Mahterian

DIGITAL COLOR SERVICES
Digital Media Inc. USA
Grayphics Digital Imaging
Media Hippo

TYPOGRAPHER
Type Studio

SHIPPING & MAILING
Diversified Mailing Services, Inc.
Dahlgren's Mailing Services, Inc.
Blumenfield Marketing, Inc.

PRINTER
Toppan Printing Co., Ltd., Tokyo

FROM THE PUBLISHER

This year's Graphic Artists Guild's Directory of Illustration cover reflects the state of mind of today's commercial illustrator. Concerns regarding pricing, stock illustration, copyright enforcement, royalty free illustration and the internet are now simultaneously at the forefront. I want to thank our cover artist Scott Wright for working with me on this year's cover and doing an outstanding job!

In addition to the Directory of Illustration's printed edition, we also provide two internet services: our Portfolio On-line site and our Page On-line site. I invite you to explore directoryofillustration.com. Log on to review many of our advertiser's portfolios or locate links to their web sites.

Because of the extraordinary growth of the Directory of Illustration, we have been careful to review all submissions before final publication approval is granted. Many of the most respected artists and artist representative firms are featured in this year's Directory of Illustration.

This year's Directory of Illustration marketing, production and design staff worked together to bring us our best edition to date. I want to thank Elizabeth Owen, Terry Bickmore, Radana Khadilkar and Cathie Heckrotte for managing the entire project.

The core of the Directory of Illustration is the marketing team of Ellie Altomare, Nancy Caldwell, Sheila Cantillon, Jim Christen, Heather McGibbon, Annie Nicolletti and Beth Pierson. They all do an outstanding job of getting to know their clients and helping them design successful marketing plans. The Directory of Illustration is focused on building new business for our advertisers. I am proud of the professional standards and dedication our marketing group brings to this process.

My appreciation to our design and production team of Tamra Dempsey, Theil Shelton, Annie Boissevain, Joseph Green, Donald Henderson, Kathleen Corby and Barbara Kuhn. They once again produced an outstanding publication and kept the project on schedule.

We publish the Directory of Illustration book for the Graphic Artists Guild. I want to extend my appreciation for the help, advice and access that Paul Basista, the Executive Director of the Graphic Artists Guild has extended to me all year long. Thanks Paul!

This year I have noticed an increase in positive feedback communicated to us by our advertisers. This is significantly important news, because the Directory of Illustration is specifically designed to generate business for our illustrators.

The entire staff at Serbin Communications is proud to be associated with publishing the Directory of Illustration. I trust you will use and enjoy this year's 17th edition of the Graphic Artists Guild's Directory of Illustration.

Glen Robert Serbin
Publisher

The Directory of Illustration Volume 17 is published by Serbin Communications, Inc., 511 Olive Street, Santa Barbara, California 93101, 805-963-0439. e-mail:admin@serbin.com © 2000 by Serbin Communications, Inc. All Rights Reserved. "Directory of Illustration" is a trademark of Serbin Communications.

Copyright under International and Pan-American Copyright Convention. Printed in Japan ISBN 1-888318-13-9.

Graphic Artists Guild, 90 John Street, Suite 403, New York, New York 10038. 212-791-3400. e-mail: admin@gag.org

ARTISTS AND REPRESENTATIVES

ARTISTS AND REPRESENTATIVES

STYLE/TECHNIQUE INDEX

STYLE/TECHNIQUE INDEX

painterly

STYLE/TECHNIQUE INDEX

story boards/comps

technical

3-d collage

3-d computer

STYLE/TECHNIQUE INDEX

watercolor

SUBJECT/SPECIALTY INDEX

SUBJECT/SPECIALTY INDEX

architectural

book covers

SUBJECT/SPECIALTY INDEX

charts & maps

children

children's books & products

SUBJECT/SPECIALTY INDEX

corporate

SUBJECT/SPECIALTY INDEX

editorial

SUBJECT/SPECIALTY INDEX

fashion & cosmetics

food

historical

landscape

medical

SUBJECT/SPECIALTY INDEX

SUBJECT/SPECIALTY INDEX

SUBJECT/SPECIALTY INDEX

sports

wildlife

The Campaign For Illustration

Ironically, during one of the greatest economic booms in history, the illustration industry is in terrible shape. Commissions are fewer; deadlines are shorter;fees are lower. Creativity is valued less; competition is up from stock, royalty free and photographic images. Large media giants continue to be swallowed by even larger ones while illustrators are told it's illegal to compare their pricing with each other. Intellectual property, the currency of the new millennium, is becoming so valuable that more and more clients insist on work for hire or all rights contracts.

The ability to think visually is what distinguishes the professional illustrator from a client who picks and chooses images from a stock house or clip art from a royalty-free collection. When a client makes a choice from these types of alternative illustration sources, the unfortunate perception of the creative as a cut-and-paste "pair of hands" is reinforced. This devaluation of the creative process erodes the status of all creatives and diminishes the unique power that illustration provides in communicating ideas.

The fact remains we are all in this together, regardless of specialty, artistic style or client list and whether we are an art director or buyer. It is through the power of unity, organization and cooperation that we can achieve great things. With this in mind, the Guild has created the "Campaign for Illustration." Its focus—education, action, community—is an outline of programs designed to counter the formidable market trends taking place within the industry.

I. Education:

Not just graphic artists, but educators, students and clients need to be better informed about issues affecting the industry. For example, the biggest problem with stock is the contracts offered by stock houses. They lock up artists for too long. They control how the art is used. They negotiate the (too low) fees, and keep too much of a commission. Some believe that even stock sold by artists themselves compete with new commissions. Education is the key to addressing this issue. Here are a number of initiatives the Guild has executed and planned:

Educating the Industry

Educating Clients, many of whom are new, more conversant with the newer technology and alternative sources and unacquainted with the power that illustration provides in the communication process. The Guild is preparing a booklet, "Working with an Illustrator." Designed as a "leave-behind," the booklet will help clients better understand the value of illustration and make it easier for art buyers to commission illustration.

Guild News, our award winning bimonthly national newsletter contains articles that:

- Warned of the threats the stock houses pose; other articles explained how to do self-stock.

- Examined the graphic artist-rep relationship.
- Rated the major calls for entry.
- Analyzed the children's book market.
- Provide important copyright information to help graphic artists keep and control what they own.
- Alert graphic artists to the dangers of all-rights and work-for-hire contracts.

Contract Monitor, a bimonthly e-mail newsletter published by the Guild:

- Analyzed stock house contracts in detail.
- Will offer a "model" stock house agreement.
- Continues to alert graphic artists to the dangers of all-rights and work-for-hire contracts.

Handbook: Pricing & Ethical Guidelines, with nine editions since 1973, has been the first point of reference for graphic artists and buyers alike. The updated, expanded edition will be released in fall, 2000.

Campaign Against Royalty-Free highlights perhaps the most serious threat to graphic artists—the rising use of royalty-free images. Graphic artists who sell their work on a royalty-free basis lose control of their rights and effectively cut off all future revenue from those images. To that end, the Guild has launched an anti-royalty free campaign with ads to appear in Communication Arts, Step-by-Step Graphics and other trades.

II. Action

A Code of Fair Practice, newly updated, for the visual communications industry (with the Society of Illustrators (SI), the Advertising Photographers of NY (APNY), and the Society of Photographers and Artists Representatives (SPAR)).

Facilitate Graphic Artist Control by providing templates and instructions for creating a self-stock web site at little cost.

Promote (Good) Stock by aligning with graphic artist friendly/graphic artist controlled stock sites.

Increase Market Share. In some markets, the power of illustration is chosen only one out of five times. The Campaign for Illustration will seek to emphasize to decision-makers the benefits of original illustration.

Legal Defense. The Guild has committed up to $30,000 to support two major legal actions:

- Up to $20,000 to 18 medical illustrators to fight a publisher that has been routinely reselling works purchased on a one-time rights basis to foreign publications in at least 27 countries over a period of more than 20 years.
- Up to $10,000 to a photographer fighting an internet search engine that vacuums images and displays them on the World Wide Web without permission. The Guild also recently filed an amicus curae brief in support of the appeals process related to this case.

Pressure the US Postal Service to End Work for Hire. Under pressure from the Guild, the US Postal Service met with the Guild and reviewed its policies on contracts and compensation.

III. Community.

The Campaign for Illustration Needs YOU.

Only by working together will we be able to accomplish our goal of altering the current course that the illustration industry is taking. Through the combined efforts of its participants, the Campaign for Illustration will sustain the economic well being of illustrators and make them closer, stronger and more cohesive. The Campaign will also help more graphic artists keep, control and defend their rights.

Be an educator—spread the word.

To find out more about the Campaign and what you can do, please call, mail, or e-mail the Executive Director of the Graphic Artists Guild at 90 John Street, NY, NY 10038, phone # 212-791-3400, ext.106, e-mail: execdir@gag.org

S uccess means different things to different people. It is usually associated with achievements, which count for a lot, but the real success is how those achievements have helped those you work with on a daily basis.

Choosing the right creative collaboration begins that daily process. When you chose illustration, you commit to a collaborative approach to solving a problem that is built on a foundation of respect, trust, and a belief in the value of creativity. This approach develops a relationship that honors the profession and all those who contribute to it. In that sense, all those who take part in this creative process, whether they commission art or create it, are all part of the same community.

From the Guild's perspective, success is a philosophy built from a vital, active and connected community. The Guild's core purpose reflects this attitude — to be a strong community that empowers and enriches its members through collective action — and each of the Guild's successes is built from the power of our relationships.

The Directory of Illustration is your guide to a community of illustrators. When you choose an illustrator from this directory instead of an anonymous, ready-made stock illustration, you've made a decision to communicate the message your client wants to send with value, creativity and originality.

Success is a choice, so choose wisely. Now that you've made the right decision to use illustration, this book can help you find the right illustrator to realize your vision. Think of it as your creative community directory of problem solvers who are ready to help you discover ways to enhance yours and your client's success.

Jonathan Combs

National President, Graphic Artists Guild

A BETTER PLACE

WALTER HORTENS DISTINGUISHED SERVICE AWARDS

Hodges Soileau

2001

CALL FOR NOMINATIONS

MAKING THE PROFESSION

The **Walter Hortens** Distinguished Service Awards is your opportunity to nominate individuals who have put the visual communications industry first by consistently demonstrating their dedication to improving working conditions for all creators of graphic art and/or raising the standards for the entire industry. These awards are the only industry awards that recognize graphic artists and other individuals for their dedicated service to the industry. The Walter Hortens Distinguished Service Awards are presented in three categories:

• The **Professional Practices Award** recognizes an individual within the graphic communications industry who has demonstrated leadership or special achievements that improve working conditions for all creators of graphic art. Nominations for this award are open to all members of the visual communications industry.

• The **Outstanding Client Award** recognizes individuals or organizations that follow the principles outlined in the *Graphic Artists Guild Handbook, Pricing & Ethical Guidelines* and that represent the highest standards of ethical policy within their business practices. Nominations for this award are open to Guild members only.

• **Special Award for the Advancement of Creators' Rights** honors a prominent individual whose professional endeavors have advanced and safeguarded the rights of individual creators. This award is open to individuals outside the visual communications industry but who are in allied or related fields. Nominations for this award are open to everyone.

PREVIOUS WALTER HORTENS DISTINGUISHED SERVICED AWARDS WINNERS

PROFESSIONAL PRACTICES AWARD

Brad Holland 2000
DK Holland 1999
Milton Glaser 1998
Tad Crawford 1992

OUTSTANDING CLIENT

Steven Heller 2000
Robert Kanes 1999
Oxford Press University, ESL Department 1992

SPECIAL AWARD FOR THE ADVANCEMENT OF CREATORS' RIGHTS

Jonathan Tasini 2000
Marybeth Peters 1999

Above: Illustrator, Brad Holland (L), winner, Professional Practices 2000, Jonathan Combs (R), National President, Graphic Artists Guild. Below: Outstanding Client 2000, Steven Heller (R), Art Director, NY TIMES BOOK REVIEW, Paula Scher (L), Principal, Pentagram.

Below: Special Award for the Advancement of Creator's Rights 2000 winner, Jonathan Tasini (R), President, National Writers Union, Jonathan Combs (L), National President, Graphic Artists Guild.

WALTER HORTENS DISTINGUISHED SERVICE AWARDS 2001 NOMINATION FORM

Please return this form by December 31, 2000 to:

Walter Hortens Nominations | Graphic Artists Guild
90 John Street Suite 403 | New York, NY 10038 | fax 212.791.0333
This Nomination Form may also be downloaded from our
website at http://www.gag.org and emailed to pr@gag.org.

Nominees will be announced in Spring 2001; the award will be voted on by the Guild membership at that time. Award winners will be honored at a reception and dinner in New York City.

2001

Who are you nominating?

Name

Title

Organization

Address

City   State   Zip

Telephone

E-mail address

For which award are you nominating this individual? check one

☐ **Professional Practices**

☐ **Outstanding Client***

☐ **Special Award for the Advancement of Creators' Rights**

*Nominations open to Guild members only.

Why does this individual deserve this award?

Please attach a 500-word explanation of the individual's achievements or other criteria that make him or her deserving of this recognition.

Who are you?

Name of Nominator

Organization / Affiliation

Address

City   State   Zip

Telephone

E-mail address

CALL FOR NOMINA-TIONS

NOMINATIONS ARE DUE BY 12.31.2000

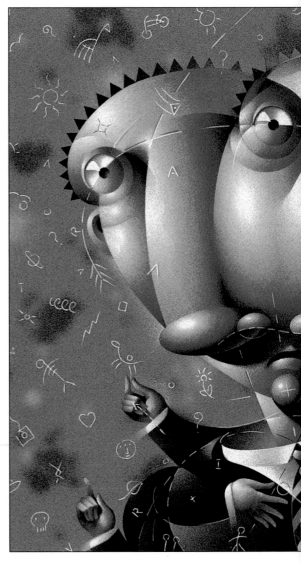

Interactive Weekly

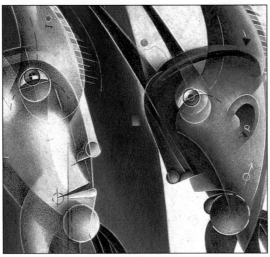

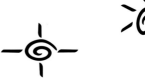

www.stwright.com

ST WRIGHT

Tel: (804) 353-8022
Fax: (804) 353-7601

Visit our web site for a more
comprehensive portfolio of:
*Illustrations, Icons, Concepts,
Identities & Logos.*

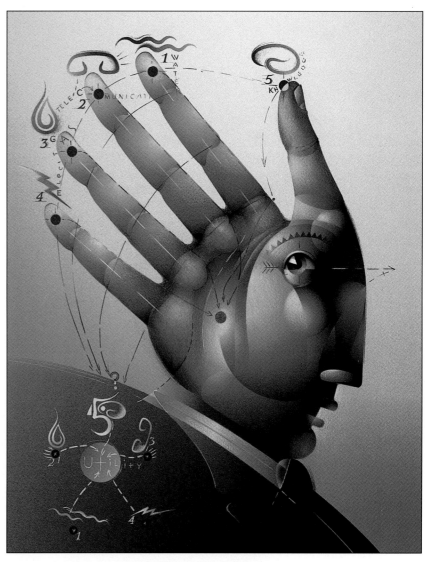

IBM

www.stwright.com
is pleased to announce the launch
of a stock collection of hundreds of images,
ideal for print and electronic mediums.

 Images are cataloged by subject
and can be cross referenced by
concept, making the site a
valuable tool for concept
development.

KEN JOUDREY

St. Martin's Press

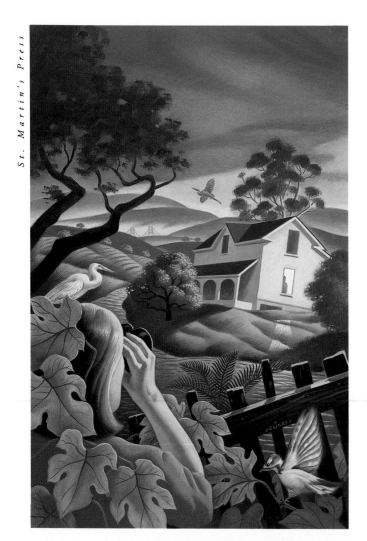

Dell Publishing

Landor Assoc.

Represented by
Day Yantis

Phone and Fax
619 479 2622
935 479 2622

CLIFF→KNECHT

ARTIST REPRESENTATIVE

Stock images available

CLIFF⊦KNECHT
ARTIST REPRESENTATIVE

309 WALNUT ROAD PITTSBURGH, PA 15202   PHONE 412 • 761 • 5666 FAX 412 • 761 • 4072

www.artrep1.com

Stock images available

CLIFF→KNECHT
ARTIST REPRESENTATIVE

309 WALNUT ROAD PITTSBURGH, PA 15202 PHONE 412 • 761 • 5666 FAX 412 • 761 • 4072

www.artrep1.com

Stock images available

Stock images available

CLIFF‣KNECHT
ARTIST REPRESENTATIVE

309 WALNUT ROAD PITTSBURGH, PA 15202 PHONE 412 • 761 • 5666 FAX 412 • 761 • 4072

www.artrep1.com

©2000 THE WALT DISNEY COMPANY

Stock images available

Stock images available

Stock images available

Stock images available

Stock images available

CLIFF→KNECHT
ARTIST REPRESENTATIVE

309 WALNUT ROAD PITTSBURGH, PA 15202   PHONE 412 • 761 • 5666 FAX 412 • 761 • 4072

www.artrep1.com

45

Stock images available

Stock images available

Stock images available

Stock images available

© Mead Johnson & Company

CLIFF‣KNECHT
ARTIST REPRESENTATIVE

309 WALNUT ROAD PITTSBURGH, PA 15202   PHONE 412 • 761 • 5666 FAX 412 • 761 • 4072

www.artrep1.com

Stock images available

Stock images available

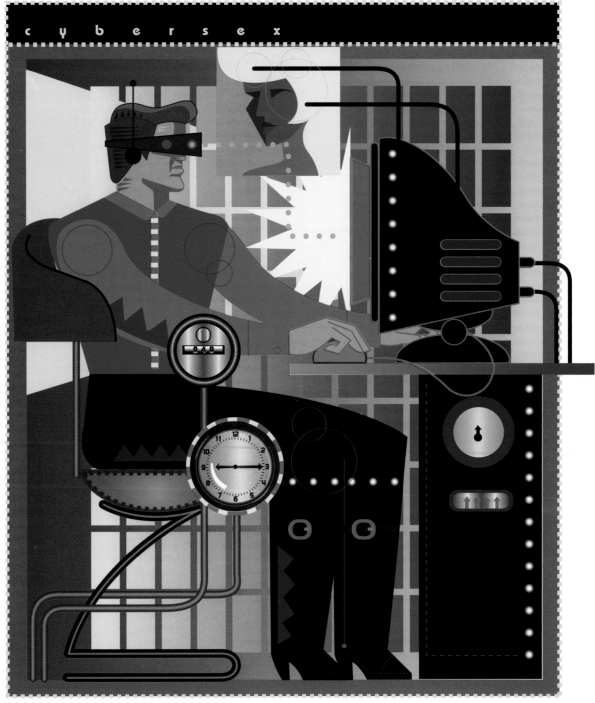

Stock images available

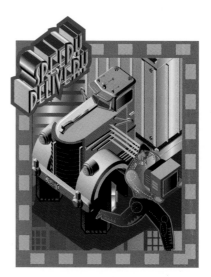

Stock images available

CLIFF·KNECHT
ARTIST REPRESENTATIVE

309 WALNUT ROAD PITTSBURGH, PA 15202   PHONE 412 • 761 • 5666 FAX 412 • 761 • 4072

www.artrep1.com

Stock images available

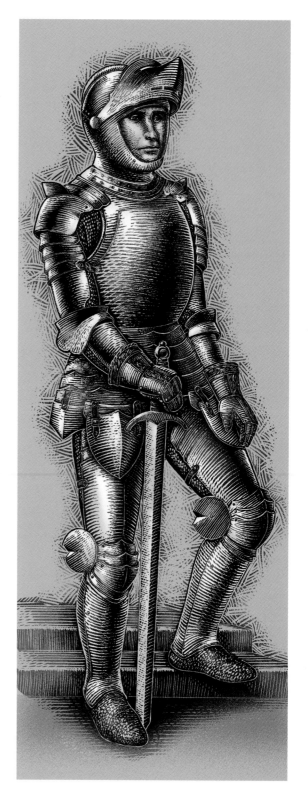

Stock images available

Stock images available

cindy REVELL

roy SCOTT

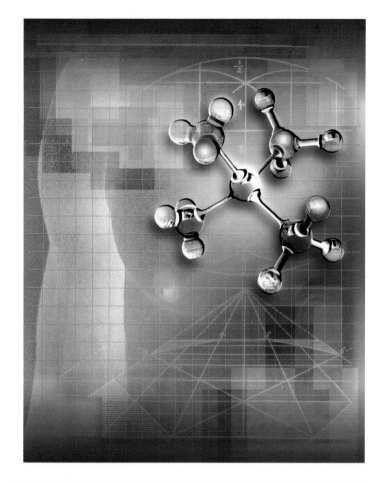

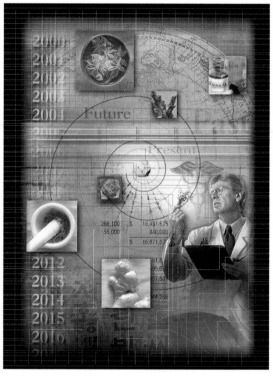

roy SCOTT

leif PENG

simon SHAW

jo TRONC

mike KERR

j.t. MORROW

harry MOORE

215.232.6666   fax 215.232.6585   www.deborahwolfeltd.com

DEBORAH WOLFE LTD
731 N 24th St., Philadelphia, PA 19130

patrick GNAN

marcia STAIMER

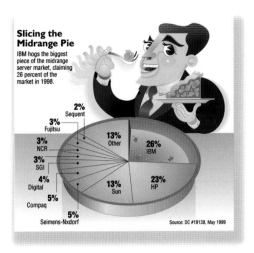

jo TRONC

nick ROTONDO

paine PROFFITT

lynn JEFFERY

215.232.6666   fax 215.232.6585   www.deborahwolfeltd.com

DEBORAH WOLFE LTD
731 N 24th St., Philadelphia, PA 19130

63

nancy HARRISON

chris VAN ES

simon SHAW

amy WUMMER

mark HEINE

felipe ECHEVARRIA

sharon & joel HARRIS

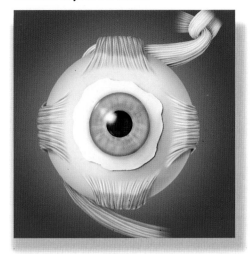

bruce GARRITY

richard WALDREP

simon SHAW

dave GARBOT

bob KAYGANICH

215.232.6666   fax 215.232.6585   www.deborahwolfeltd.com

DEBORAH WOLFE LTD
731 N 24th St., Philadelphia, PA 19130

CHARLIE HILL
DIGITAL ILLUSTRATION

CHARLIEHILL.COM

THE WILEY GROUP
415.442.1822
Fax.442.1823
david@thewileygroup.com

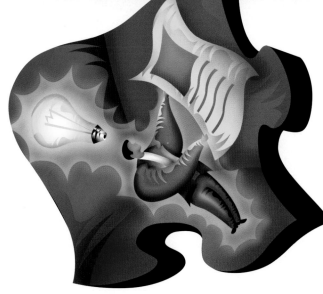

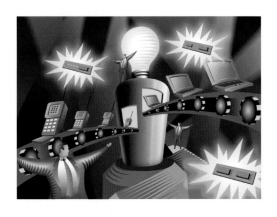

phone **415.442.1822**
fax **415.442.1823**

w
wiley represents

website address
www.wileyreps.com

phone 415.442.1822
fax 415.442.1823

wiley represents

website address
www.wileyreps.com

Richard Cowdrey

Shannon

new york 212.333.2551
los angeles 323.874.5700
washington dc 410.349.8669
london 011.44.207.636.1064

www.shannonassociates.com

Mendola
Artists

FEATURING
CHRIS DELLORCO

Portfolio online
MENDOLAART.COM

Telephone
212-986-5680

www.rowanbarnes-murphy.com

GARRY COLBY
ILLUSTRATOR

HAWAII

TOYS "Я" US

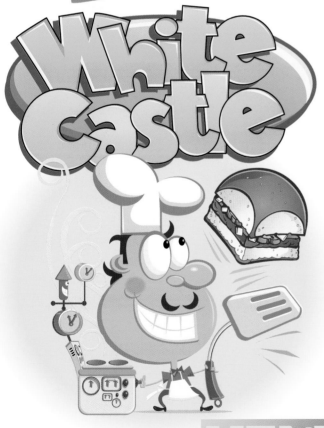

White Castle

DAVE HENDERSON

STEVE
CHORNEY
studio 805-688-4526 www.stevenchorney.com

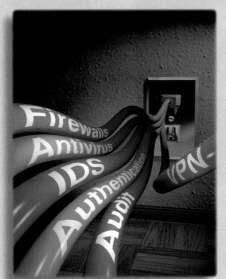

JiM TALBOT

MENDOLA LTD

420 LEXINGTON AVENUE
NEW YORK, NY 10170
TELEPHONE 212.986.5680
FAX 212.818.1246
EMAIL mendolaart@aol.com
view online portfolios at

WWW.MENDOLAART.COM

MENDOLA REPRESENTATIVES
ph 212.986.5680
Fx 212.818.1246

art by
Carole
Marchese

MARY ROSS

Derby 2000

RITA GATLIN REPRESENTS, INC.

USA 800.924.7881   **SF** 415.924.7881   **FAX** 415.924.7891   **WEB** www.ritareps.com

89

jon b e r k e l e y

rob b o l s t e r

linda b r o n s o n

stephen c o s t a n z a

danuta j a r e c k a

annette k r a u s

anne l a m b e r t

michael l o t e n e r o

bruce s a n d e r s

rod s a v e l y

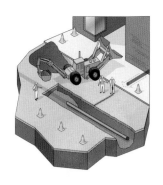

steve s t a n k i e w i c z

august s t e i n

Leighton & Company Inc.

A R T I S T S ' R E P R E S E N T A T I V E S

h t t p : / / w w w . l e i g h t o n r e p s . c o m

978 • 921 • 0887 phone

978 • 921 • 0223 fax

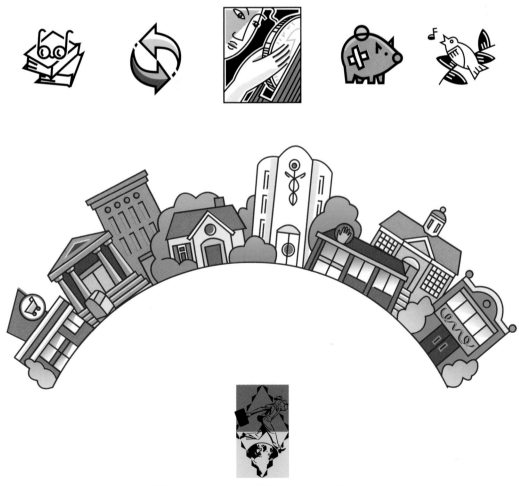

Leighton & Company Inc.
ARTISTS' REPRESENTATIVES
http://www.leightonreps.com

978 • 921 • 0887 phone

978 • 921 • 0223 fax

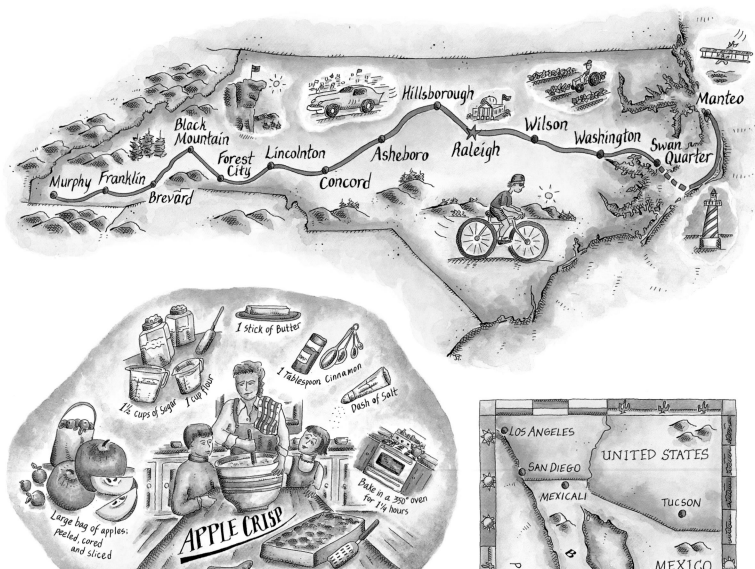

Leighton & Company Inc.
ARTISTS' REPRESENTATIVES
h t t p : / / w w w . l e i g h t o n r e p s . c o m

978 • 921 • 0887 *phone*

978 • 921 • 0223 *fax*

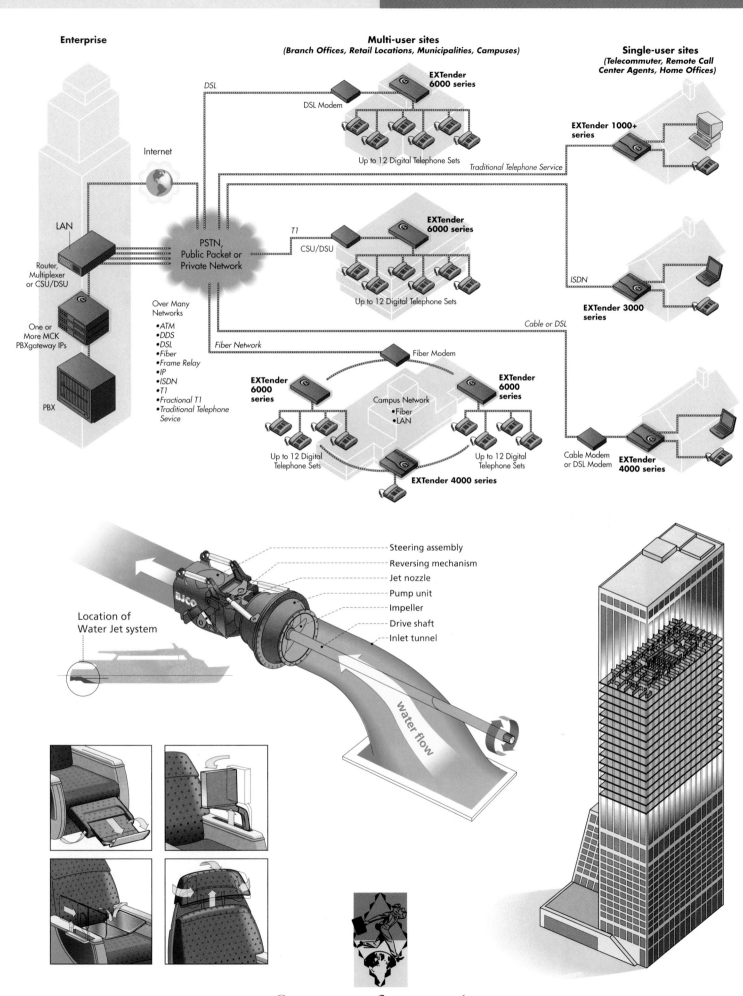

Enterprise

Multi-user sites
(Branch Offices, Retail Locations, Municipalities, Campuses)

Single-user sites
(Telecommuter, Remote Call Center Agents, Home Offices)

DSL

EXTender 6000 series

DSL Modem

Up to 12 Digital Telephone Sets

Internet

EXTender 1000+ series

LAN

Traditional Telephone Service

Router, Multiplexer or CSU/DSU

PSTN, Public Packet or Private Network

T1

EXTender 6000 series

CSU/DSU

Over Many Networks
- ATM
- DDS
- DSL
- Fiber
- Frame Relay
- IP
- ISDN
- T1
- Fractional T1
- Traditional Telephone Sevice

One or More MCK PBXgateway IPs

Up to 12 Digital Telephone Sets

ISDN

EXTender 3000 series

Cable or DSL

Fiber Network

Fiber Modem

PBX

EXTender 6000 series

EXTender 6000 series

Campus Network
- Fiber
- LAN

Cable Modem or DSL Modem

EXTender 4000 series

Up to 12 Digital Telephone Sets

Up to 12 Digital Telephone Sets

EXTender 4000 series

EXTender 4000 series

Location of Water Jet system

Steering assembly
Reversing mechanism
Jet nozzle
Pump unit
Impeller
Drive shaft
Inlet tunnel

water flow

978 • 921 • 0887 phone
978 • 921 • 0223 fax

Leighton & Company Inc.
ARTISTS' REPRESENTATIVES
http://www.leightonreps.com

in New York City call:
242 • 477 • 4229

Leighton & Company Inc.
ARTISTS' REPRESENTATIVES
http://www.leightonreps.com

978 • 921 • 0887 phone

978 • 921 • 0223 fax

WILLIAM SLOAN
THREE
236 West 26 Street, Suite 805
New York, NY 10001
TEL (212) 463-7025
FAX (212) 727-7961
e-mail: sloan@threeonline.com

Clientele includes:
Doubleday; Estée Lauder; Fortune;
Grey Entertainment; L'Oréal; Lucent;
MoMA; Eliran Murphy Group; Penguin
USA; St. Martin's Press; TBWA;
Uniworld

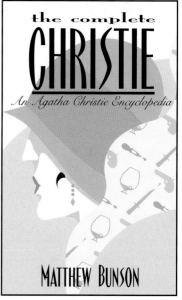

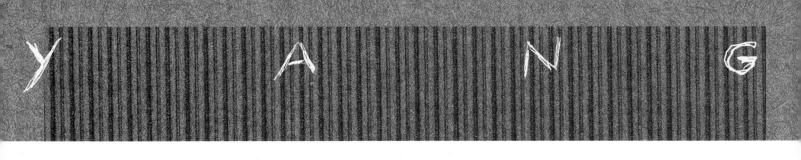

JAMES YANG/www.jamesyang.com is proudly represented by the DAVID GOLDMAN AGENCY
41 Union Square West-Suite 918, New York, NY 10003
Ph: 212-807-6627   Fax: 212-463-8175   www.davidgoldmanagency.com

Excuse me, Mr. Goldman, but it's happening again . . . he's animating.

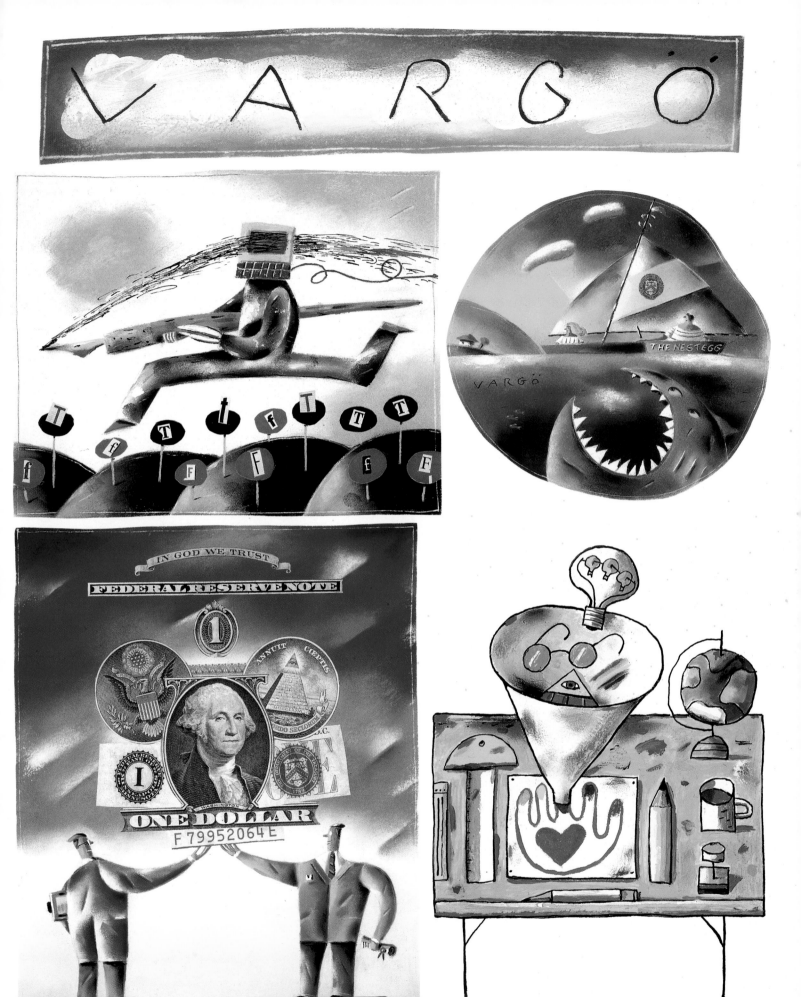

Nishan

WINTER SPRING SUMMER FALL

401K

NISHAN AKGULIAN is proudly represented by the DAVID GOLDMAN AGENCY
41 Union Square West-Suite 918, New York, NY 10003
Ph: 212-807-6627 Fax: 212-463-8175 www.davidgoldmanagency.com

TEOFILO OLIVIERI

TEOFILO OLIVIERI is Proudly Represented By the DAVID GOLDMAN AGENCY
41 Union Square West-Suite 918, New York, NY 10003
Ph: 212-807-6627 Fax:212-463-8175 www.davidgoldmanagency.com

rosemary fox

Doug Panton

dougpanton.com

IN CANADA • 416.920.5612

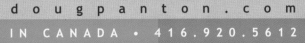

Represented by

irmeliholmberg.com

212.545.9155

ERIC BOWMAN

"FOXGLOVES"/OIL

"PANCHO VILLA"/OIL

LISA HENDERLING

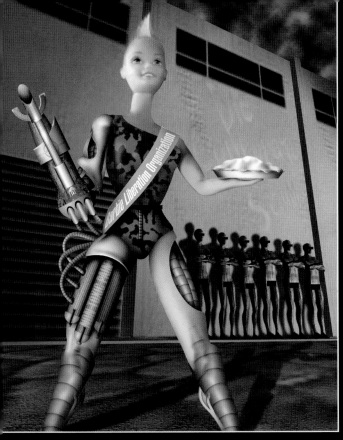

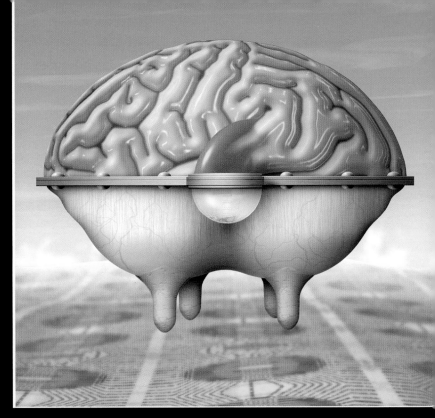

Serving clients in New York City: (212) 889-8777 • Fax (212) 447-1475 • E-mail: gt@artcoreps.com • Web: www.artcoreps.com

DALE STEPHANOS

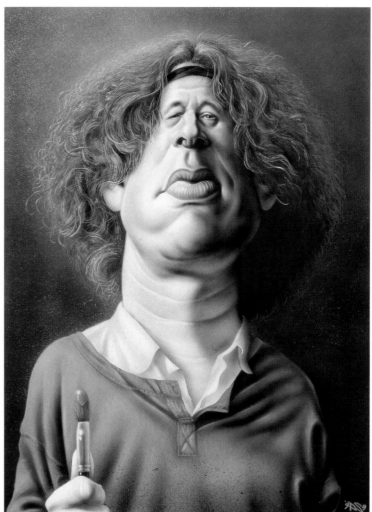

ARTCO

Serving clients in New York City: (212) 889-8777 • Fax (212) 447-1475 • E-mail: gt@artcoreps.com • Web: www.artcoreps.com
Outside New York City: (203) 222-8777 • Fax (203) 454-9940 • E-mail: jp@artcoreps.com • Web: www.artcoreps.com

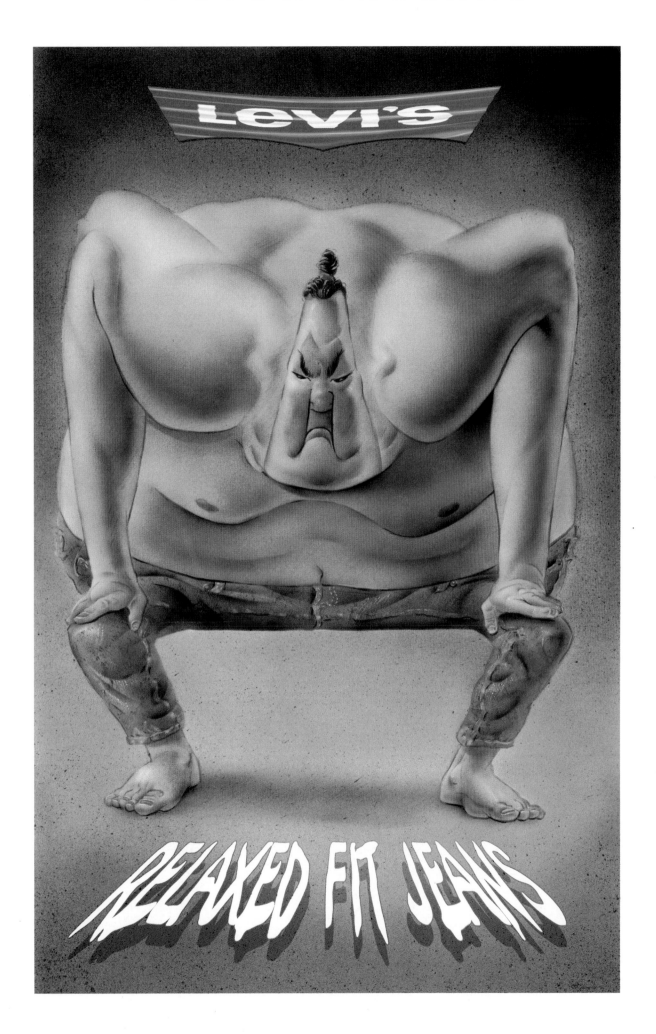

◆Koralik

Koralik Associates
represents **ILENE ROBINETTE**
Tel: 312 944 5680   Fax: 312 421 5948

◆Koralik

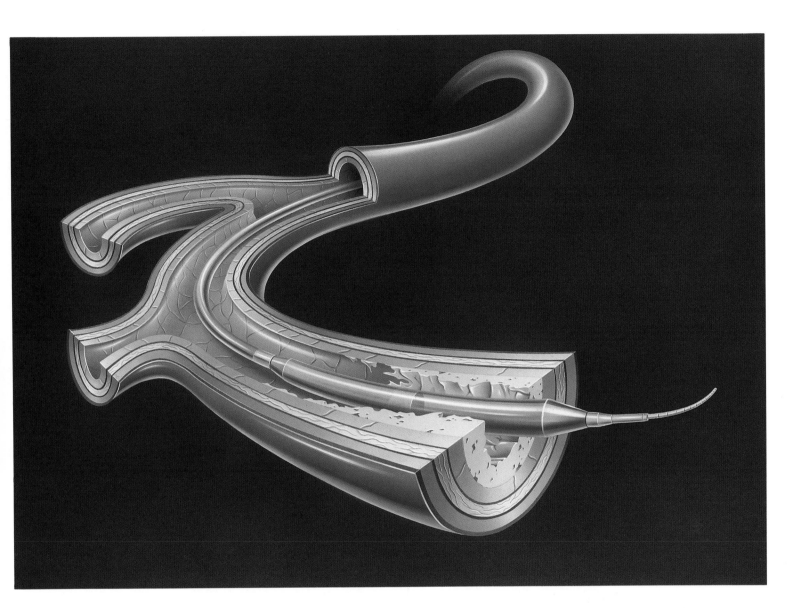

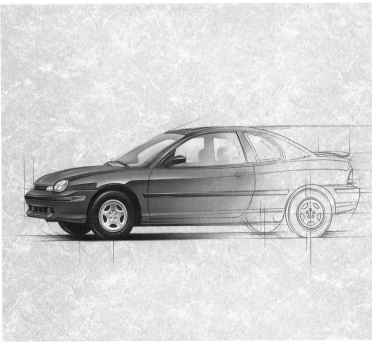

•Koralik

Koralik Associates
represents **PAMELA EKLUND**
Tel: 312 944 5680   Fax: 312 421 5948

clients include:

shedd aquarium

disney

nickelodeon

sega

archie comics

marvel comics

d.c. comics

acclaim

homage studios

top cow

©John G. Shedd Aquarium

BOOKMAKERS LTD.

DAVID J. BROOKS

P.O. Box 1086, 40 Mouse House Road, Taos, NM 87571 • (505)776-5435 • Fax(505)776-2762
email: bookmakers@newmex.com • website: bookmakersltd.com

BOOKMAKERS LTD.

JUDITH MITCHELL

LYDIA HALVERSON

MARSHA SERAFIN

P.O. Box 1086, 40 Mouse House Road, Taos, NM 87571 • (505)776-5435 • Fax(505)776-2762
email: bookmakers@newmex.com • website: bookmakersltd.com

BOOKMAKERS LTD.

KATHI McCORD

KAREN PELLATON

SUSAN BANTA

P.O. Box 1086, 40 Mouse House Road, Taos, NM 87571 • (505)776-5435 • Fax(505)776-2762
email: bookmakers@newmex.com • website: bookmakersltd.com

Roc Goudreau
Digital Illustration

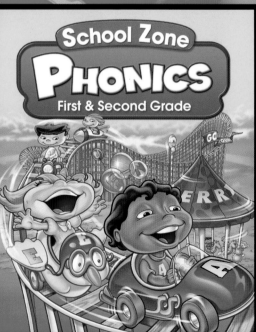

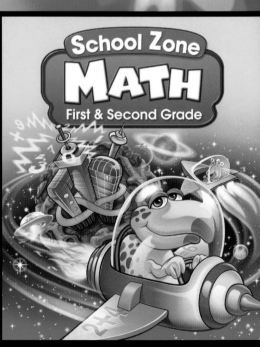

Represented by Pat Heroux Goudreau
Portfolio: www.pgreps.com

Phone: 413.967.9855
pgreps@mediaone.net

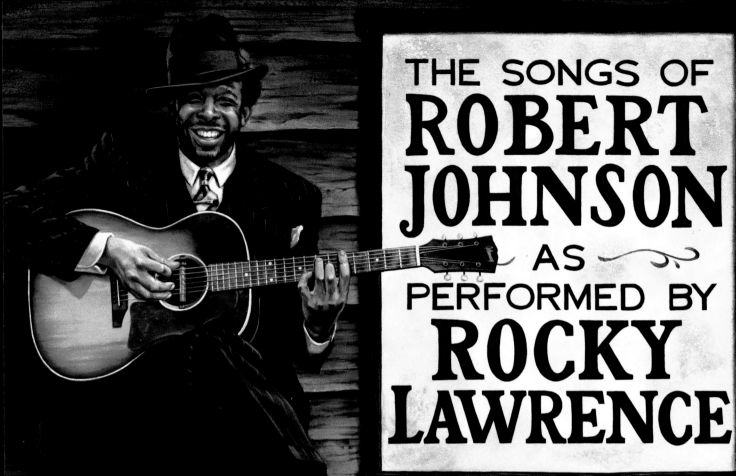

THE SONGS OF ROBERT JOHNSON
AS
PERFORMED BY
ROCKY LAWRENCE

Rich Lynes

Chuck Primeau

Gary LaCoste

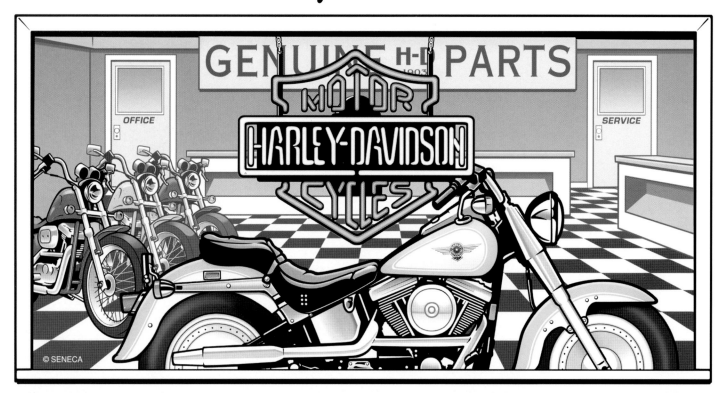

images created in Photoshop

Represented by Pat Heroux Goudreau
Portfolio: www.pgreps.com

PG REPRESENTATIVES
VISUAL COMMUNICATION

Phone: 413.967.9855
pgreps@mediaone.net

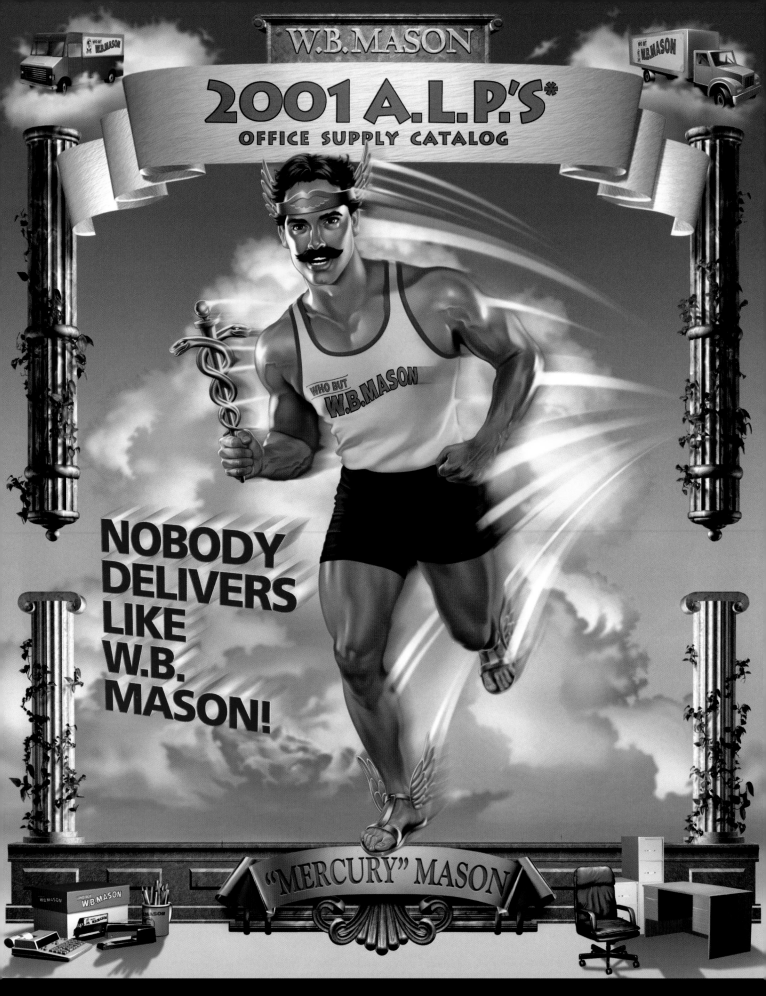

SUSAN WELLS & ASSOCIATES
ARTIST REPRESENTATIVE

5134 Timber Trail South
Atlanta, GA 30342-2148
(404) 255-1430 Voice
(404) 255-3449 Fax
(888) 255-1490 Toll-Free

www.swell-art.com

Elaine Dillard

Chad Cameron

Ted Burn

Alex Hackworth

Mark Andresen

Dave Clegg

Lynne Riding

Matt Phillips

Colin Poole

Contact us for your free copy of our
"Rainy Day Activity Book"
for designers and art directors.

The greens are hardly green…

the fairways are rarely fair…

Creekside

and the balls are barely legal…

is for elephant

What color is art?

Get Well Soon

Pour It On

d e l u x

Presenting vanity cabinets with a whole new dimension.

Elaine Dillard

Chad Cameron
www.chadcameron.com

Ted Burn
www.tedsart.com

REPRESENTED BY SUSAN WELLS & ASSOCIATES
(888) 255-1490 www.swell-art.com

Alex Hackworth

REPRESENTED BY SUSAN WELLS & ASSOCIATES
(888) 255-1490 www.swell-art.com

Alex Hackworth

REPRESENTED BY SUSAN WELLS & ASSOCIATES
(888) 255-1490 www.swell-art.com

Innovative

Expert

Proactive

Personal

Objective

Mark Andresen

REPRESENTED BY SUSAN WELLS & ASSOCIATES
(888) 255-1490 www.swell-art.com

Mark Andresen

Dave Clegg
www.daveclegg.com

REPRESENTED BY SUSAN WELLS & ASSOCIATES
(888) 255-1490 www.swell-art.com

Dave Clegg
www.daveclegg.com

REPRESENTED BY SUSAN WELLS & ASSOCIATES
(888) 255-1490 www.swell-art.com

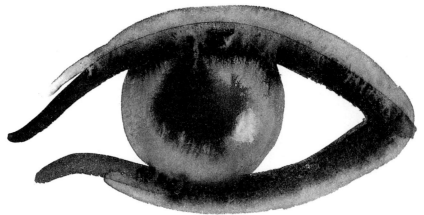

Lynne Riding

REPRESENTED BY SUSAN WELLS & ASSOCIATES

(888) 255-1490 www.swell-art.com

Lynne Riding

REPRESENTED BY SUSAN WELLS & ASSOCIATES

(888) 255-1490 www.swell-art.com

Matt Phillips

REPRESENTED BY SUSAN WELLS & ASSOCIATES
(888) 255-1490 www.swell-art.com

Matt Phillips

REPRESENTED BY SUSAN WELLS & ASSOCIATES
(888) 255-1490 www.swell-art.com

COLIN POOLE
1 - 800 - 808 - 5005

Colin Poole

REPRESENTED BY SUSAN WELLS & ASSOCIATES
(888) 255-1490 www.swell-art.com

COLIN POOLE
1-800-808-5005

Colin Poole

MARSHALL WOKSA
www.dimensioncreative.com
TEL (952) 892-8474
FAX (952) 892-8475
e-mail: jkoltes@dimensioncreative.com

Representation: Dimension
Joanne Koltes

C.A. NOBENS ILLUSTRATION & DESIGN, INC.
www.dimensioncreative.com
TEL (952) 892-8474
FAX (952) 892-8475
e-mail: jkoltes@dimensioncreative.com

Representation: Dimension
Joanne Koltes

Augustina's day began
with friends and lemon cake.
They read their favorite stories, swam,
and sailed on Big Clear Lake.

C.A. Nobens

M.F. DUNWORTH

Studio **708.484.7201**
Fax *708.484.7202*
mfdunworth@ameritech.net
www.dimensioncreative.com

Midwest Rep **Joanne Koltes**
952.892-8474 fax 952.892.8475
jkoltes@dimensioncreative.com

Serving New York City and the World for Over 70 Years

Web
www.aareps.com

Stock
www.repstock.com

e-mail
info@aareps.com

353 West 53rd Street #1W, New York, NY 10019 phone 212.682.2462

© Warner Bros.

© 4Kids Entertainment/Nintendo of America

© M&M Mars

© Disney

© Cartoon Network

Serving the U.S. and the World for 80 Years

Business Concepts

info@aareps.com
Tel: (212) 682-2462

American Artists

http://www.aareps.com
Fax: (212) 582-0090

Business Concepts

Serving the U.S. and the World for 80 Years

On-Star Site Development

FREE GAS

DDITIONAL BENEFITS

VER PLEASE

SAVINGS AHEAD

FREE SERVICE

NEW CAR BUYING

TRAVEL BENEFITS

FREE TOWING

Domino Sugar Website

Domino SUGAR

Baking School

Info Center

Historical Society

Recipe Library

Fun House

Dottie Domino's Place

Serving the U.S. and the World for 80 Years

153

Food & Still Life

info@aareps.com
Tel: (212) 682-2462

American Artists

http://www.aareps.com
Fax: (212) 582-0090

Food & Still Life

Serving the U.S. and the World for 80 Years

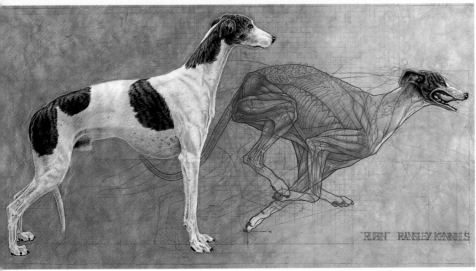

Serving the U.S. and the World for 80 Years

info@aareps.com

Tel: (212) 682-2462

http://www.aareps.com

Fax: (212) 582-0090

American Artists

 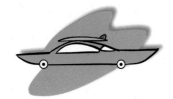 

JOHN HOLM

American Artists

tax.cch.com

ANDY ZITO

info@aareps.com

Tel: (212) 682-2462

http://www.aareps.com

Fax: (212) 582-0090

American Artists

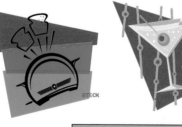

JIM STECK

info@aareps.com
Tel: (212) 682-2462

American Artists

http://www.aareps.com
Fax: (212) 582-0090

JIM EFFLER

Greg Copeland

K&K Studios, Inc.
Tel: (612) 338-9138
Fax: (612) 338-9148

See also: *Workbook 19, American Showcase 22, Directory of Illustration 16, CA Image 2000*

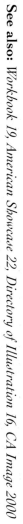

©2000 ErinM

erinm.com

Erin Marie Mauterer   51 Ascot Drive   Ocean, NJ 07712   800 258 9287   Fax 732 922 4330

erinm.com

ERIN MARIE MAUTERER   51 ASCOT DRIVE   OCEAN, NJ 07712   800 258-9287   FAX 732 922-4330

PIRANHA

TIVADAR BOTE

Represented by Adrienne Arbour at PIRANHA p: 416.410.9828 f: 416.588.9800 www.piranha.ca adrienne@piranha.ca

TERRY WIDENER

represented by MICHÈLE MANASSE

Simon & Schuster

Private Collection

Harcourt Inc.

© 2001 Terry Widener

ph.215.862.2091 fax.215.862.2641 e-mail.mmanasse@new-work.com web.www.new-work.com

BARBARA QUINN

New Work
ILLUSTRATION

Represented by MICHÈLE MANASSE

Governing Magazine Supplement

Strategic Communications

Proctor & Gamble

Food Marketing Institute

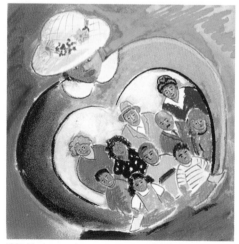
ICFA Management

© 2001 Barbara Quinn

ph 215.862.2091 fax 215.862.2641 e-mail mmanasse@new-work.com web www.new-work.com

Tingas-Hill design

America's Community Banker

American Spectator

SMZ Advertising

© 2001 Matthew Trueman

First United Methodist Church of Dallas

Unpublished

Houghton Mifflin

Private Collection

© 2001 Leslie Stall

ph.215.862.2091 fax.215.862.2641 e-mail.mmanasse@new-work.com web.www.new-work.com

Celebrity International   © 2001 Geneviève Leloup

Kleinert's   © 2001 Geneviève Leloup

CAROL INOUYE   represented by MICHÈLE MANASSE

S is for...   © 2001 Carol Inouye

"The Stresses of Working Mothers"

REED SPRUNGER

digital illustration

portfolio on line www.jaewagoner.com

JAE WAGONER 310 392 4877

CHRISTINA A. TUGEAU
Representing:

Martha Avilés

Jason Wolff

Wayne McLoughlin

Christina A. Tugeau   203 • 438 • 7307

CHRISTINA A. TUGEAU
Representing:

Melissa Iwai

Keiko Motoyama

Jeremy Tugeau

Christina A. Tugeau 203 • 438 • 7307

John Kanzler

Lisa Carlson

Christina A. Tugeau 203 • 438 • 7307

CHRISTINA A. TUGEAU
Representing:

Teri Sloat

Meryl Treatner

Stacey Schuett

CHRISTINA A. TUGEAU
Representing:

Susan Simon

Cheryl Kirk Noll

Ann Barrow

Christina A. Tugeau 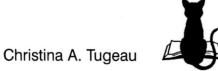 203 • 438 • 7307

CHRISTINA A. TUGEAU
Representing:

Larry Day

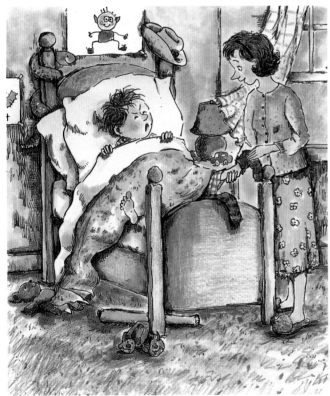

Heather Maione

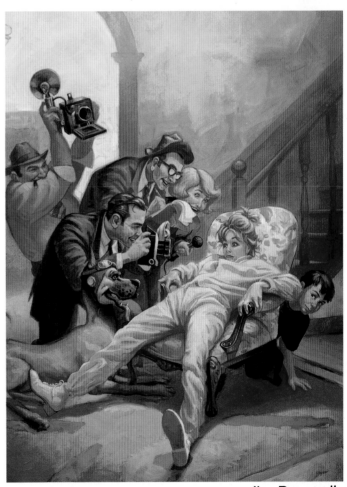

Jim Bernardin

Christina A. Tugeau   203 • 438 • 7307

Priscilla Burris

Sarah Beise

Karen Stormer-Brooks

Lauren Klementz-Harte

Daniel Powers

Carla Golembe

Frank Sofo

PAUL KRATTER
Represented by:
Christina A. Tugeau
110 Rising Ridge Road
Ridgefield, CT 06877
TEL (203) 438-7307

Christina A. Tugeau   203 • 438 • 7307

CRAIG BROWN

alias: FARMER BROWN

Christina A. Tugeau   203·438·7307

**MICHEL STONG
ILLUSTRATION**
655 Cherry Street
Santa Rosa, CA 95404
TEL (707) 575-0749
FAX (707) 575-0749 *51
e-mail: mstong@metro.net
Representation: Melissa Mackey

michel stong

r e p r e s e n t e d   b y

MELISSA MACKEY
1 . 8 0 0 . 8 4 7 . 5 1 0 1

PHIL & JIM BLISS

IN WESTERN USA
CALL
WILLIAMS GROUP WEST
800-847-5101

VIEW OUR PORTFOLIO AT:
WWW.DIR ILL.COM

EVERYWHERE ELSE
CALL
PHILIP BLISS STUDIO
716-377-9771

J.F. MARTIN
TEL (800) 847-5101
Representation: Melissa Mackey/
Planet Rep.

J.F. MARTIN
TEL (800) 847-5101
Representation: Melissa Mackey/
Planet Rep.

GIRAFFICS GRAPHICS

3041 DUNDEE LN, MOUND, MN 55364

952-472-4344 Phone/Fax

MARGO DE PAULIS, ILLUSTRATOR & DESIGNER

▶ Logos & corporate identity
▶ Web icon design & illustration
▶ Retail signage & packaging
▶ Editorial & educational illustration

email: margod@earthlink.net

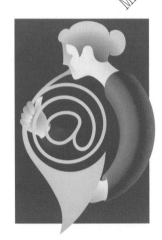

Scotty B's RESTAURANT

spirit of the red horse

Primary Ink

TASTE OF THE LAKES

RICK STROMOSKI

The Penny & Stermer Group
East Coast: TEL (212) 505-9342
West Coast: TEL (520) 708-9446

Please visit our web site:
www.pennystermergroup.com
or e-mail: carollee@primenet.com

**PLEASE CALL US...
WE'D LIKE TO WORK
WITH YOU...
THANK YOU!**

JOANNA BORRERO
P.O. Box 442
Bearsville, New York 12409
TEL/FAX (914) 679-9656
Representation: The Penny and
Stermer Group

The Penny & Stermer Group
East Coast: TEL (212) 505-9342
West Coast: TEL (520) 708-9446

Please visit our web site:
www.pennystermergroup.com
or e-mail: carollee@primenet.com

**PLEASE CALL US...
WE'D LIKE TO WORK
WITH YOU...
THANK YOU!**

TOM PAYNE

The Penny & Stermer Group
East Coast: TEL (212) 505-9342
West Coast: TEL (520) 708-9446

Please visit our web site:
www.pennystermergroup.com
or e-mail: carollee@primenet.com

**PLEASE CALL US...
WE'D LIKE TO WORK
WITH YOU...
THANK YOU!**

JOHANSEN NEWMAN

LIZ SANDERS AGENCY
TELEPHONE: (949) 495-3664 FACSIMILE: (949) 495-0129 WWW.LIZSANDERS.COM

JOHANSEN NEWMAN

Liz Sanders Agency

Telephone: (949) 495-3664   Facsimile: (949) 495-0129   www.lizsanders.com

CATS AND JAMMERS STUDIO

TOM PANSINI

NEWPORT/BALBOA

LIZ SANDERS AGENCY

TELEPHONE: (949) 495-3664   FACSIMILE: (949) 495-0129   WWW.LIZSANDERS.COM

OCTAVIO DIAZ

LIZ SANDERS AGENCY

R.S. ROGERS

200

DON MARGOLIS
TEL (847) 498-8936
FAX (847) 498-8946
e-mail: nodsilogra@aol.com

Represented by
LANGLEY AND ASSOCIATES
TEL (312) 782-0244
FAX (312) 782-1535
e-mail: artrepsjl@aol.com

KEITH D. SKEEN
3228 Prairie Drive
Deerfield, WI 53531
TEL (608) 423-3020
FAX (608) 423-9531
e-mail: kskeen@chorus.net

To view more work:
www.wilson-zumbo.com
Represented in Chicago by
Langley & Associates
TEL (312) 782-0244

Clients include:
IBM, Simon & Schuster, Oxford
University Press, McDougal-Littell,
Access, Milwaukee, Timex, Southwest
Airlines *Spirit*, *Eating Well*, *Better
Homes & Gardens*, Computer World.

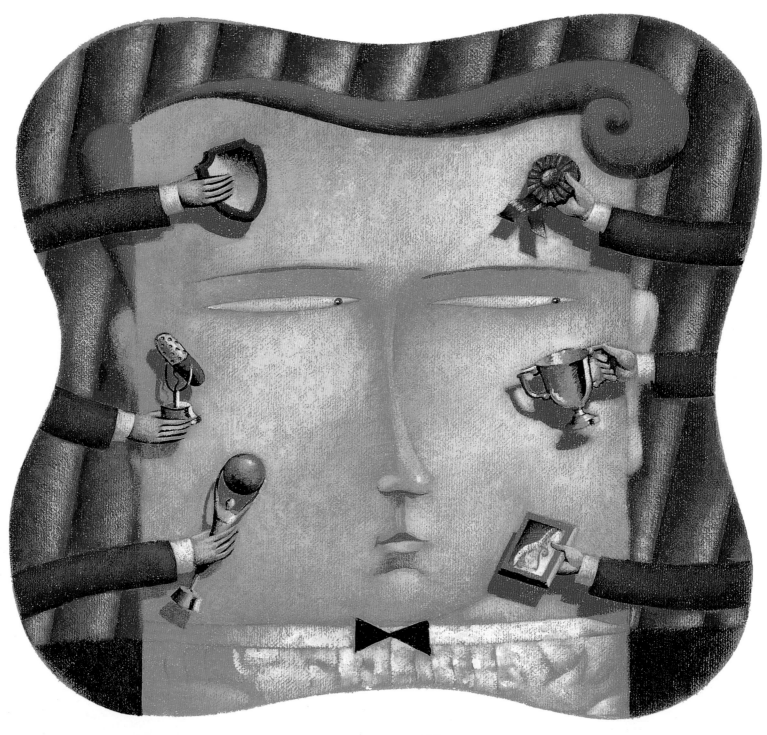

VINCENT CHIARAMONTE
920-19th Street
Rockford, IL 61104
TEL (815) 963-2887

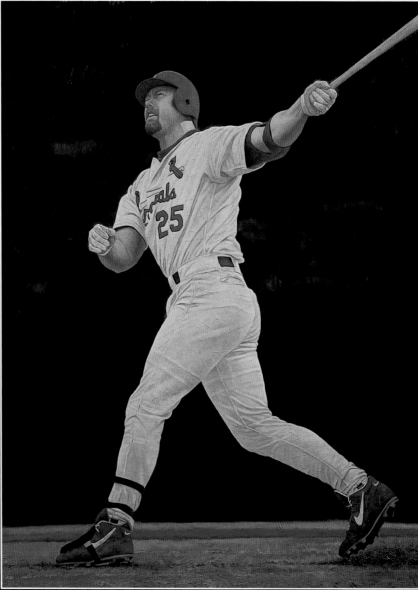

ROSE MARY BERLIN

GREG HARRIS

BEN MAHAN

2-D Cross Highway, Westport, CT 06880
Ph:(203) 454-4210, Fax:(203) 454-4258, E Mail:CMartreps@aol.com

STEVE HENRY

2-D Cross Highway, Westport, CT 06880
Ph:(203) 454-4210, Fax:(203) 454-4258, E Mail:CMartreps@aol.com

EILEEN HINE

2-D Cross Highway, Westport, CT 06880
Ph:(203) 454-4210, Fax:(203) 454-4258, E Mail:CMartreps@aol.com

DIANE TESKE HARRIS
Marion Moskowitz Represents, Inc.
315 East 68th Street
New York, NY 10021
TEL/FAX (212) 517-4919

RogEr RotH

Marion Moskowitz Represents Inc.
315 East 68th Street • New York 10021
Tel. / Fax 212-517-4919

American Banker

Wall Street Journal

Poster / Group Publishing, Inc.

Grey Advertising

2000 © Roger Roth

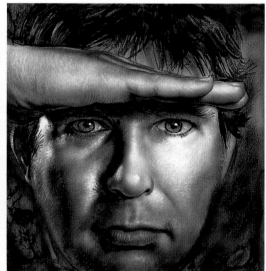

www.illusionrep.com

PIFKO

MEUNIER

www.illusionrep.com

www.illusionrep.com

ROBERTS

PHILIBERT

www.illusionrep.com

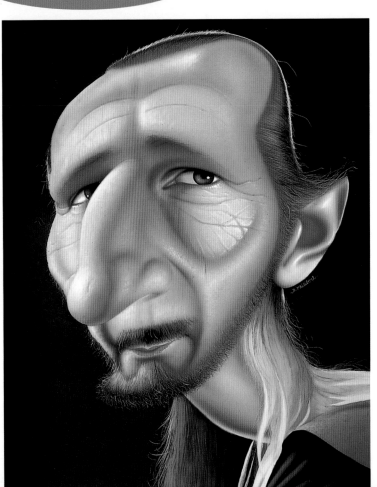

www.illusionrep.com

BEAUREGARD

ESCALMEL
digital illustration

www.illusionrep.com

EGGER

HENRY

GALLOWITZ

LAROSE

www.illusionrep.com

NINON

MALÉPART

www.illusionrep.com

Spiderwebart

Artists' Representatives • 973-770-8189 • fax 973-770-8626
http://www.spiderwebart.com

Greg & Tim Hildebrandt

----------------------------**MARK ROMANOSKI**----------------------------   **NELSON DeCASTRO**

Greg & Tim Hildebrandt

--------------------ALEX HORLEY--------------------   --------------------PETER AMBUSH--------------------

DAVE AIKINS

LET'S DRAW! STUDIO · PHONE/FAX: 614·844·6433

 illustrators  photographers designers stock art

wendy wassink-ackison

david aikins

michael bonilla

robert brünz

doug chaffee

robbin cuddy

jake ellison

judy hand

bill fox

fred grigg

alfred kamajian

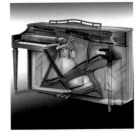
misty maxwell

jeanine kinchelo

corrie maritz

chuck marshall

duane orlemann

jack pennington

randy rogers

mark rose

john sledd

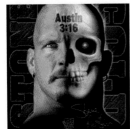
tommy thomson

kevin torline

christina wald

jim williams

jonn q. wright

*Please visit one of our many websites designed to satisfy all your creative needs. **The Rep on The Net!***

Rep - Bob Berendsen   (513)   **861·1400**   fax 861-6420   *Your Global Resource*

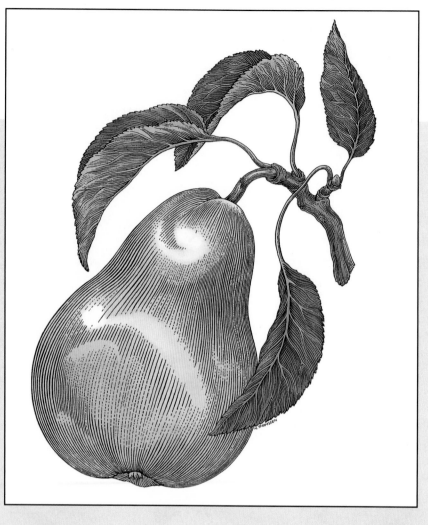

KATE THOMSSEN

651.698.9129

REPRESENTED BY JANET VIRNIG

952.926.5585

WWW.THEISPOT.COM

RICK ALLEN · WOODBLOCKS
218.727.3706

CREATIVE CONNECTION, INC.
P.O. Box 253, 614 Stillwater Road
Gibson Island, MD 21056
TEL (410) 360-5981
FAX (410) 255-8889
e-mail: creativeinc@erols.com

Client List: Recycled Paper Products, This End Up, Kid's Décor, Marian Heath Greeting Cards, Paper Magic, Inscribe, U.S. Can. Also in Directory of Illustration 14 and 16.

JESSICA SPORN

Client List: Art Resources, Dimensions, Butz Gaskins. **EDIE HOPKINS**
Also in Directory of Illustration 16.

Client List: Conimar Corp., Converting Inc., JCA, Inc. **LORRAINE RYAN**
Also in Directory of Illustration 14.

CREATIVE CONNECTION, INC.
P.O. Box 253, 614 Stillwater Road
Gibson Island, MD 21056
TEL (410) 360-5981
FAX (410) 255-8889
e-mail: creativeinc@erols.com

Client List: Ceaco, Doubleday, Woman's World, World Wildlife Fund, Leanin' Tree, McGraw Hill, Oxmoor House, San Francisco Music Box Co. Also in Directory of Illustration 13, 14, 15 and 16.

PARKER FULTON

Client List: Woman's Day, Kimberly Clark, Prudent, The Bradford Exchange. Also in Directory of Illustration 13, 14 and 16.

JULIA JONES

CAROL ZUBER-MALLISON
maps • charts • information graphics

www.zmgraphics.com
www.brookeco.com

AGENT
Brooke & Co.
4911 West Hanover
Dallas, Texas, USA 75209
TEL (214) 352-9192
FAX (214) 350-2101
e-mail: brooke7 @airmail. net

STUDIO
ZM Graphics
2340 Edwin Street
Fort Worth, Texas, USA 76110-6634
TEL (214) 906-4162
FAX (817) 924-7784
e-mail: mallison@startext.net

▲ Map for ExxonMobil

▼ Cross section of Fort Worth's new Bass Performance Hall for Magnolia Media

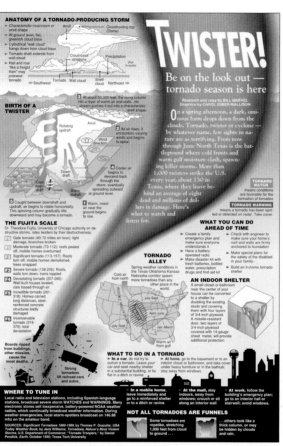

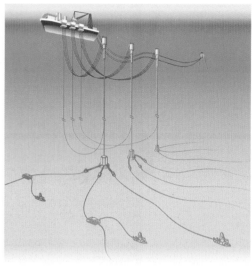

▲ Diagram of deep-water drilling for ExxonMobil

◀ Full-page infographic on tornado season for *The Dallas Morning News*

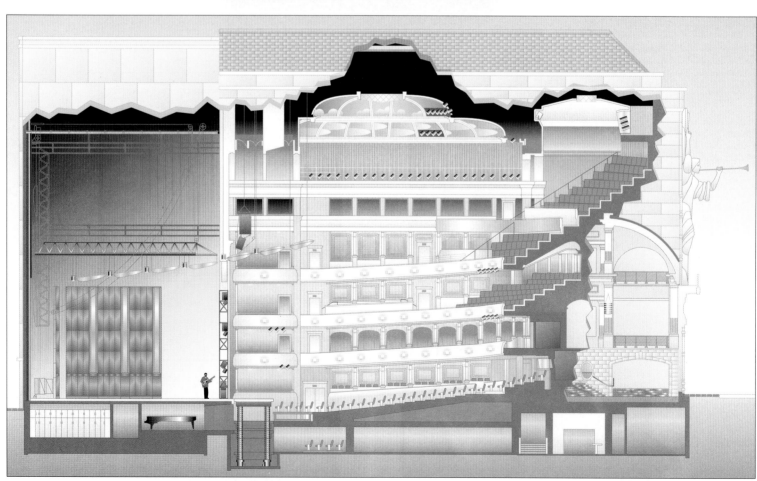

WENDY WRAY
Represented by: Morgan Gaynin Inc.
TEL (212) 475-0440
FAX (212) 353-8538

*Step
by
Step
Art*

Robert Sauber

Represented by Morgan Gaynin inc. (212) 475-0440 www.morgangaynin.com

Robert Sauber

Represented by Morgan Gaynin inc. (212) 475-0440 www.morgangaynin.com

marcburckhardt 512.458.1690 *www.marcart.net*

burckhardt 512.458.1690 www.marcart.net

ANITA GRIEN
155 East 38th Street
New York, NY 10016
TEL (212) 697-6170
FAX (212) 697-6177
e-mail: agrien@aol.com
www.anitagrien.com

Representing:
Jerry McDaniel
Alan Neider
Hal Just
Dolores Bego

Also Representing:
Fanny Mellet Berry
Julie Johnson
Mona Mark
Don Morrison
Alan Reingold

Jerry McDaniel

Alan Neider

Hal Just

Dolores Bego (digital art)

ANITA GRIEN
155 East 38th Street
New York, NY 10016
TEL (212) 697-6170
FAX (212) 697-6177
e-mail: agrien@aol.com
www.anitagrien.com

Representing:
Alan Reingold
Fanny Mellet Berry
Mona Mark
Julie Johnson

Also Representing:
Dolores Bego
Hal Just
Jerry McDaniel
Don Morrison
Alan Neider

Alan Reingold

Fanny Mellet Berry (digital art)

Mona Mark

(digital art)

Julie Johnson

RUTGERS MAGAZINE

PC WORLD

TIME DIGITAL

THE NEW YORK TIMES

SF MAGAZINE

THE WASHINGTON POST

PSYCHOLOGY TODAY

BUSINESS WEEK

THE WALL STREET JOURNAL

KIPLINGER.COM

MSN.UNDERWIRE.COM

LA TIMES

CONSUMERS DIGEST

FORBES

CHRISTOPH HITZ · PHONE (800) 558 3623 · HTTP://WWW.HITZ-ILLUSTRATION.COM

*PRODUCT ILLUSTRATION
*CHARACTER DEVELOPMENT
*HUMOROUS ILLUSTRATION
*PACKAGING ILLUSTRATION
*FOOD ILLUSTRATION

before

after

JAE SHIM
105 Nonesuch Place
Irving, TX 75061
TEL/FAX (972) 986-0947
e-mail: jshim9494@aol.com

Hughes Electronics Annual Report

http://members.aol.com/jshim9494

JAE SHIM
105 Nonesuch Place
Irving, TX 75061
TEL/FAX (972) 986-0947
e-mail: jshim9494@aol.com

Hughes Electronics

Hughes Electronics

Cellular Communication

Deloitte & Touche

http://members.aol.com/jshim9494

237

Stacy Peterson

rep:
Lori Nowicki
& Associates
212:243:5888 | lori@lorinowicki.com
www.lorinowicki.com | fax: 212:243:5955

rep: **Lori Nowicki**
& Associates

fax: 212:243:5955 | lori@lorinowicki.com | 212:**243:5888**
www.lorinowicki.com

rep: Lori Nowicki
& Associates
212:243:5888 | lori@lorinowicki.com | fax: 212:243:5955
www.lorinowicki.com

JUI ISHIDA

MIKE WEPPLO

NORA KOERBER

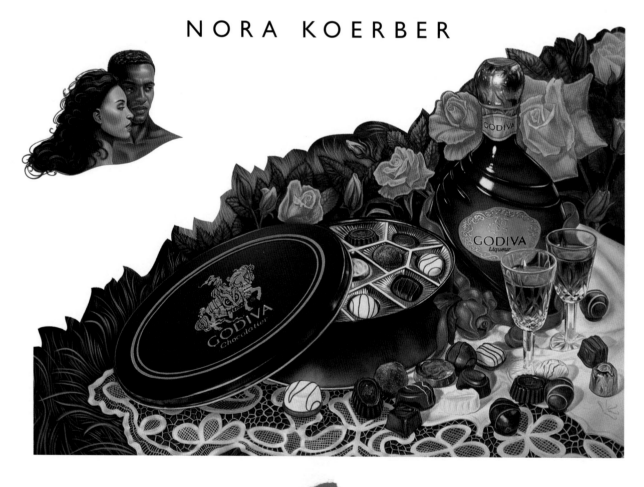

409 N. Pacific Coast Hwy. #474 Redondo Beach, CA 90277   Phone: 310.540.5958 E-mail: carrie@dasgrup.com

www.dasgrup.com

GARY GLOVER

RAY GOUDEY

409 N. Pacific Coast Hwy. #474 Redondo Beach, CA 90277

Phone: 310.540.5958 E-mail: carrie@dasgrup.com

www.dasgrup.com

Mike **CARROLL**

Organic Valley Dairy

Digital

Chicago Tribune

Digital

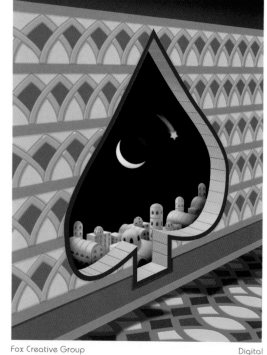

Fox Creative Group

Digital

P 503.658.7070
f 503.658.3960
www.christineprapas.com

christine prapas ----------------------------------- **represented by**

244

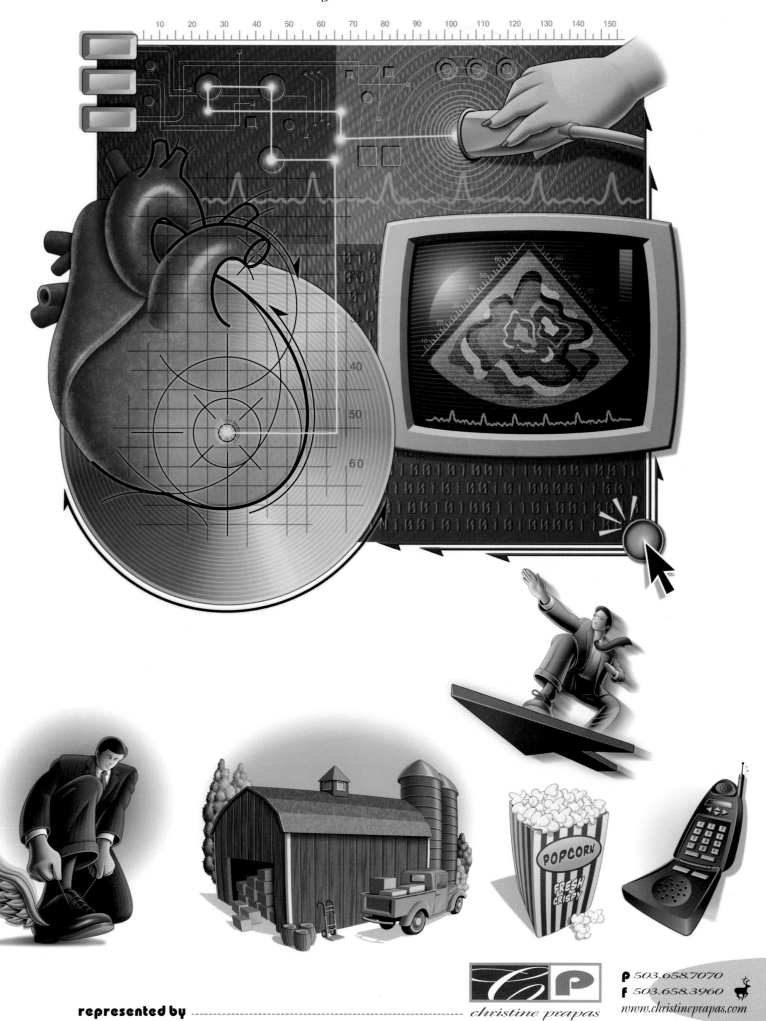

POPCORN

FRESH CRISPY

represented by ---

christine prapas

p 503.658.7070
f 503.658.3960
www.christineprapas.com

KEVIN O'MALLEY

ELIZABETH WOLF

KA BOTZIS

WENDY SMITH

BRIDGET STARR TAYLOR

NEECY TWINEM

Melissa Turk
THE ARTIST NETWORK

phone (845) 368-8606 / fax (845) 368-8608   9 babbling brook lane / suffern, new york 10901

JOE LeMONNIER

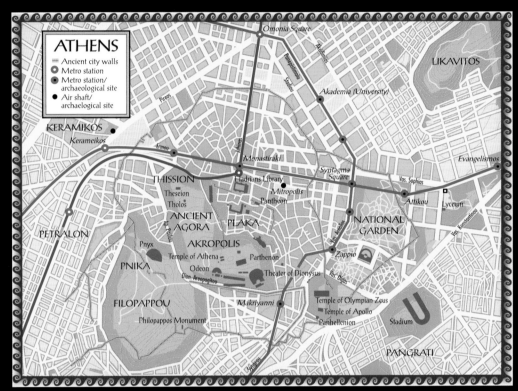

ATHENS

- ▬ Ancient city walls
- ◎ Metro station
- ◉ Metro station/ archaeological site
- ● Air shaft/ archaeological site

KERAMIKOS
Kerameikos
LIKAVITOS
Panepistimiou
Akadimias
Stadiou
Piraios
Akademia (University)
Ermou
Athinas
THISSION
Monastiraki
Hadrians Library
Syntagma Square
Evangelismos
Theseion
Mitropolis
Vas. Sophias
Tholos
Pantheon
Attikou
Lyceum
ANCIENT AGORA
PLAKA
NATIONAL GARDEN
PETRALON
Pnyx
AKROPOLIS
Temple of Athena
Parthenon
Zappio
PNIKA
Odeon
Dion. Areopagitou
Theater of Dionysus
Leof. Olgas
FILOPAPPOU
Makriyanni
Temple of Olympian Zeus
Temple of Apollo
Panhellenion
Stadium
Philopappos Monument
PANGRATI

Grand Comoro
Réunion
Tanjona Bobaomby
Antsiranana
Mayote (Fr.)
Nosy Be
Mozambique Channel
Mahajanga
Cape St-André
Sofia
Bemarivo
Betsiboka
Antongil Bay
Nosy Boraha
Antananarivo
Antsirabe
Mania
Mangoky
INDIAN OCEAN
Toliara
Onilahy
Tropic of Capricorn
Tôlanâro (Fort Dauphin)
Tanjona Vohimena

0 — 200 mi
0 — 300 km

Caracas
NORTH ATLANTIC OCEAN
GUYANA
VENEZUELA
SURINAME
FR. GUIANA
Bogotá
Georgetown
Paramaribo
Cayenne
COLOMBIA
Equator
Quito
ECUADOR
Amazon River
PERU
BRAZIL
Lima
L. Titicaca
BOLIVIA
Brasília
La Paz
Sucre
PARAGUAY
São Paulo
Rio de Janiero
CHILE
Asunción
ARGENTINA
URUGUAY
SOUTH ATLANTIC OCEAN
Santiago
Mt.Aconcagua
Buenos Aires
Montevideo
SOUTH PACIFIC OCEAN

SOUTH AMERICA
- ● Capital city

0 — 600 Miles
0 — 900 Kilometers

Falkland I. (Br.)
Drake Passage
Tierra del Fuego

ALASKA
Anchorage
Valdez
Chenega
Cordova
Seward
Bligh Reef
Cook Inlet
Homer
Prince William Sound
Dillingham
Jack's Bay
Shelikof Strait
Bristol Bay
OIL SPILL BOUNDARY
Kodiak
Bering Sea
Gulf of Alaska
Ivanof Bay

0 — 200 Miles

Melissa Turk
THE ARTIST NETWORK

phone (845) 368-8606 / fax (845) 368-8608   9 babbling brook lane / suffern, new york 10901

24 hours a day 7 days a week 365 days a year

Tim Tucker

Victoria Brzustowicz

Victoria Brzustowicz

Laurie J. McCall

Laurie J. McCall

Tim Tucker

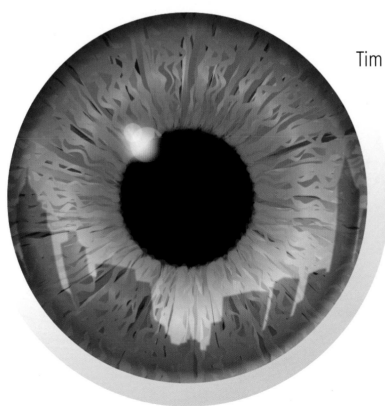

Tim Tucker

BRIAN BEHNKE

Lisa Freeman Inc • 317-920-0068, fax 317-923-9906 • lisa@lisafreeman.com • www.lisafreeman.com

250

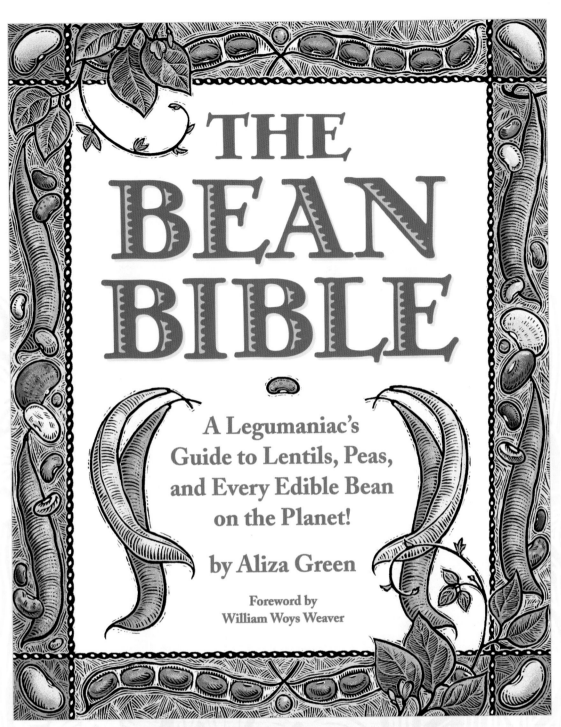

THE BEAN BIBLE

A Legumaniac's
Guide to Lentils, Peas,
and Every Edible Bean
on the Planet!

by Aliza Green

Foreword by
William Woys Weaver

SARA LOVE

Lisa Freeman Inc   •   317-920-0068, fax 317-923-9906   •   lisa@lisafreeman.com   •   www.lisafreeman.com

DEBORAH MELMON

SHELTON LEONG

SHARON MORRIS
ASSOCIATES
Artist Representative

phone 415.362.8280 • fax 415.362.8310 • email smasf@aol.com
See also Graphic Artists Guild Directory #10, #11, #12, #13, #14, #15, #16 and www.dirill.com

Tim Jessell

TEL 918 749 9424   FAX 918 749 5165   www.suzannecraig.com

EAST: STUDIO 405 377 3619   jessell@ionet.net   www.timjessell.com

SUZANNE CRAIG REPRESENTS
INCORPORATED

GENEVIEVE MEEK
6207 Orchid Lane
Dallas, TX 75230
TEL (214) 363-0680
FAX (214) 692-9337
Representation: Suzanne Craig
Represents

Clients include: Big Red Chair Books, a division of Lyrick Publishing; Harcourt Brace; Triton Oil; Raytheon; American Airlines; Central and Southwest Services; Genie Industries; Ziff-Davis Publishing; Assoc. of Certified Fraud Examiners; Frito-Lay; American Floral Services.

SUZANNE CRAIG
REPRESENTS
INCORPORATED

TEL 918 749 9424   FAX 918 749 5165

WWW.SUZANNE CRAIG .COM

GIL ADAMS
3103 South Madison Ave.
Tulsa, Oklahoma 74105
drawbrush@earthlink. net

Suzanne Craig Represents
Phone (918) 749-9424
Fax (918) 749-5165
www.suzannecraig.com

Specializing in conceptual solutions for
corporate, financial, editorial and
advertising illustration.

SUZANNE CRAIG REPRESENTS
INCORPORATED

helenravenhillrepresents

tel 816 333 0744 fax 816 333 0745 web ravenhill.net

doug bowles

r

helenravenhillrepresents

tel 816 333 0744 fax 816 333 0745 web ravenhill.net

darryl shelton

{www.levycreative.com}

JONATHAN WEINER

ROBERTO PARADA

DAVID RANKIN

ALAN DINGMAN

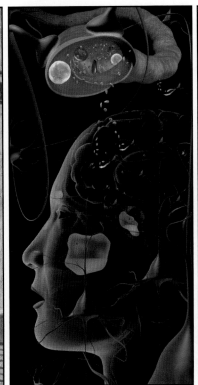

DOUG STRUTHERS

SHANE EVANS

OREN SHERMAN

MAX GRAFE

TIM OKAMURA

THOMAS FLUHARTY

{212} 687 6463 Tel   {212} 661 4839 Fax   www.levycreative.com

DAVID DANZ

Represented by
SANDY DANZ
TEL (530) 622-3218
FAX (530) 622-4346
Email: danzart@jps.net
www.jps.net/danzart

SEE THE WORKBOOK TO VIEW ADDITIONAL WORK

Bill Thomson Illustration

Represented By: Molly Birenbaum
203.272.9253   FAX: 203.272.7188
mbreps@sprintmail.com

Studio:
860.621.5501
billt@megahits.com

Also see Illustrators 42 and Communication Arts Illustration Annual 2000.

Linda Howard Bittner

Specializing in fun & educational projects for kids!

Wilkinson
STUDIOS, LLC

Linda Howard Bittner is represented by Wilkinson Studios exclusively for all educational, trade book and children's market publishing work. Please contact the artist directly for all other markets.

901 West Jackson Blvd. Suite 201 Chicago IL 60607 Phone: 312.226.0007 Fax: 312.226.0404

LINDA HOWARD BITTNER

LET'S DO SOMETHING WILD!

REGGIE HOLLADAY
730 Rosada Street
Satellite Beach, FL 32937
TEL (321) 779-0373
FAX (321) 779-0373
Representation: Wilkinson Studios, LLC

Wilkinson STUDIOS, LLC

901 West Jackson Blvd. Suite 201 Chicago IL 60607 telephone 312.226.0007 facsimile 312.226.0404

CD Hullinger Illustration

815.744.6053
cdilustr8@aol.com

CD Hullinger is represented by Wilkinson Studios, LLC exclusively for all educational, trade book and children's market publishing work. Please contact the artist directly for all other markets.

901 West Jackson Blvd. Suite 201, Chicago, IL 60607 Phone: 312.226.0007 Fax:312.226.0404

IN CASE OF
EMERGENCY
CALL
LEE STOKES

photography: steve mchugh · curtis johnson

MacTech Magazine™

Formerly MacTutor

FOR MACINTOSH PROGRAMMERS

DECEMBER 1993 • VOLUME 9, NO. 12

BACKGROUND PROCESSING ISSUE

IN THIS ISSUE!

Getting Started:
Color QuickDraw, Part II

Programmers' Challenge:
Present Packing

A Piece of Apple π

THINK Top 10:
Code Resources and
the A4 World

Jörg's Folder: Apple Event
Handlers in MacForth

The Pascal Programmer's
Guide to Understanding 'C'

Running in the Background

Outlining the Art Class
Tools Menu

The "Re" Decade

And more!

$5.85 US
$6.95 Canada
ISSN 1067-8360
Printed in U.S.A.

DAN ROSANDICH
906-482-6234 (VOICE or FAX)

See: Directory of Illustration #10, RSVP #19,
RSVP #25, RSVP #01 and Workbook #16

Virginia Journal of
Education

JANUARY 1997

Humor in the Classroom

• Carpe Diem in Herndon
• Getting More From Professional Development
• How to Have a Bully-Free School

CAR SMARTS
ACTIVITIES FOR KIDS ON THE OPEN ROAD

ED SOBEY

McGraw-Hill

DANIELS & DANIELS
14 South Madrid Avenue
Newbury Park, CA 91320
TEL (805) 498-1923
FAX (805) 499-8344
e-mail: Ariaart@aol.com
Representaion: BeauDaniels.com

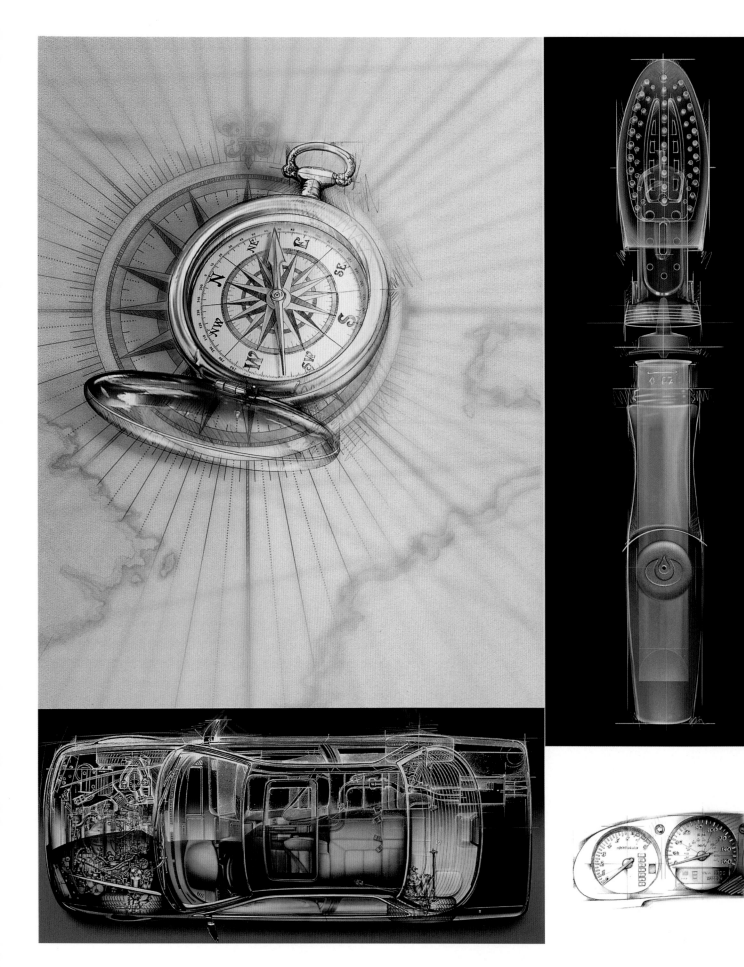

DANIELS & DANIELS
14 South Madrid Avenue
Newbury Park, CA 91320
TEL (805) 498-1923
FAX (805) 499-8344
e-mail: Ariaart@aol.com
Representaion: BeauDaniels.com

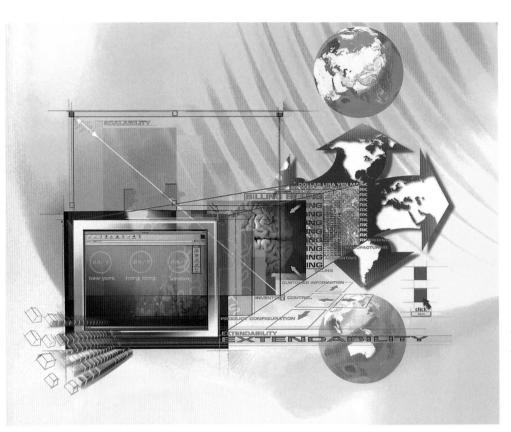

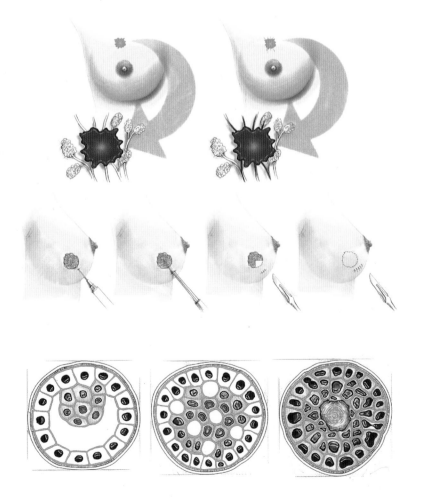

WARREN **Gebert**

DIGITAL OR TRADITIONAL

(845) 354-2536   WWW.WARRENGEBERT.COM

©JW'99

HOM²

STUDIO
805 374 9634
818 880 1524

JOHN and PHILLIP HOM

TRADITIONAL AND DIGITAL ILLUSTRATION

FAX
805 374 9647
818 880 1525

ZITA ASBAGHI

(718) 275-1995

ZITA ASBAGHI
125-10 Queens Blvd., Apt. #1023
Kew Gardens, New York 11415
TEL (718) 275-1995

MARGARET SPENGLER

2668 17TH STREET

SACRAMENTO, CA 95818

916 • 441 • 1932

FAX 916 • 441 • 3490

KENNETH SPENGLER

2668 17TH STREET

SACRAMENTO, CA 95818

916 • 441 • 1932

FAX 916 • 441 • 3490

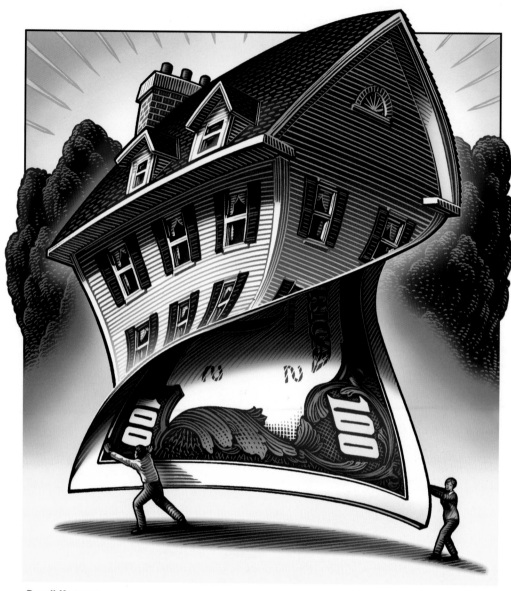

Bozell Kamstra

Mutual Funds Magazine

Supply Chain Management Review

Mutual Funds Magazine

On-line portolio: and selection of stock images: http://www.jmacdonald.com

US News & World Report

Windows Magazine

Architectural Digest

US News & World Report

dOUgLaS aNdELiN

415.927.1945

For additional samples see: GAG 8 through 16, Alternative Pick 1, 2, 3 & Showcase 22.23

dOUgLaS aNdELiN
415.927.1945

For additional samples see: GAG 8 through 16, Alternative Pick 1, 2, 3 & Showcase 22,23

LISA FALKENSTERN

Dell Publishing

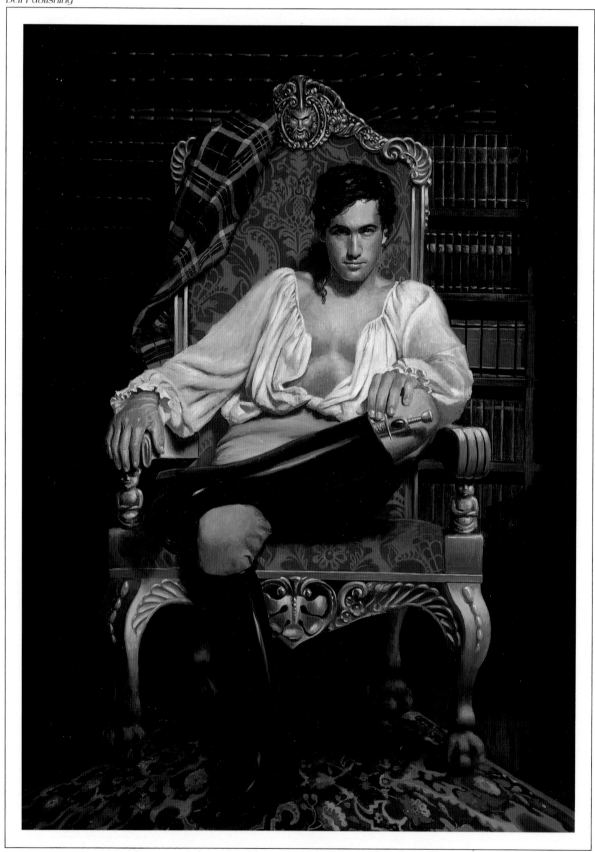

To view more work, see Graphics Artists Guild Directory of Illustration Vol. 12-15.

904 RAVINE ROAD, CALIFON, NJ 07830
Phone: (908) 832-5789 Fax: (908) 832-2445 Email: lisamilt@interactive.net

LISA FALKENSTERN

Califon Graphics

To view more work, see Graphics Artists Guild Directory of Illustration Vol. 12-15.

904 RAVINE ROAD, CALIFON, NJ 07830
Phone: (908) 832-5789 Fax: (908) 832-2445 Email: lisamilt@interactive.net

Lisa McLeod

For client list and portfolio please call:
678.584.5556 voice 678.584.5222 fax
or visit www.lisamcleod.com
P.O. Box 451202   Atlanta, GA 31145

W1

W2

W3

W4

W5

W6

W7

W8

W9

Christine Mau
TEL/FAX 920·751·4217

Christine Mau
TEL/FAX 920·751·4217

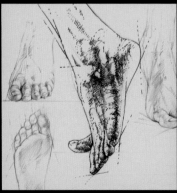

201 E 87th Street
New York, NY 10128

Nenad Jakesevic

http://members.aol.com/nenadj/

212-831-4634
Fax 212-831-4930

BARRY FITZGERALD   785 841 2983

GARRY NICHOLS

TEL 317.861.6550 ■ FAX 317.861.6552 ■ E-MAIL GNICHOLSIL@AOL.COM ■ WWW.GNICHOLSILLUSTRATION.COM
3094 WEST 200 SOUTH, GREENFIELD, IN 46140

WILLIAM COOK
3804 E. Northern Pkwy.
Baltimore, MD 21206
TEL/FAX (410) 426-1130

See also Directory of Illustration
Vol. 13 to 16 for additional work

FUTURE ADDITION · MARYLAND SCIENCE CENTER

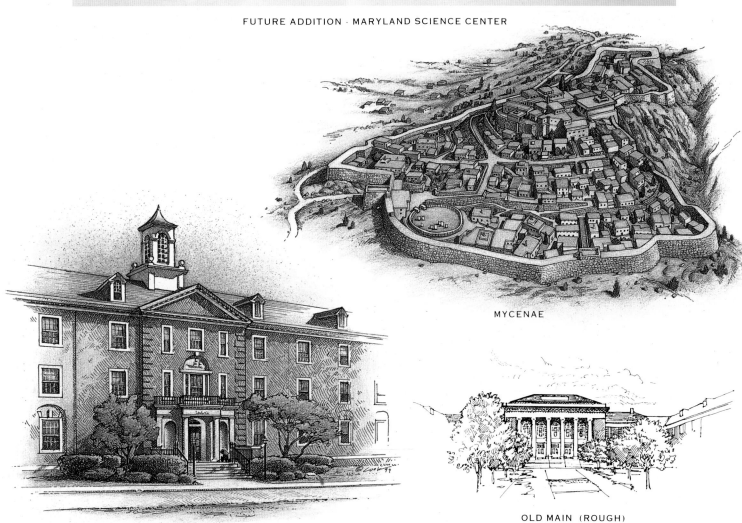

MYCENAE

OLD MAIN (ROUGH)

CHASE HALL · USCGA

GARRY NICHOLS

TEL 317.861.6550 ■ FAX 317.861.6552 ■ E-MAIL GNICHOLSIL@AOL.COM ■ WWW.GNICHOLSILLUSTRATION.COM

3094 WEST 200 SOUTH, GREENFIELD, IN 46140

Patrick Corrigan > Illustration
phone > 1.207.780.6467
email > patrickc@javanet.com

...or, direct smoke signals towards
portland, maine.

for more samples,
see directory of illustration
numbers 15 and 16.

201 E 87th Street
New York, NY 10128

Sonja Lamut

http://members.aol.com/slamut/

212-831-4634
Fax 212-831-4930

joyce wynes • *illustrator*

P: 704.442.9323   F: 704.442.1267   E: joyce@wynesdesynes.com   W: wynesdesynes.com

LA Times • Diversion Magazine • Atlantic Monthly Magazine • Silver Burdett & Ginn
Chicago Tribune • National Restaurant Magazine • Christian Parenting Magazine
Games Magazine • Prime Times Magazine • MacMillan Publishing • Scholastic, Inc.
Consumer Reports Magazine • General Learning Corp • TV Online
Various Magazines in France, Germany and Japan

L.A. Times - Oscars

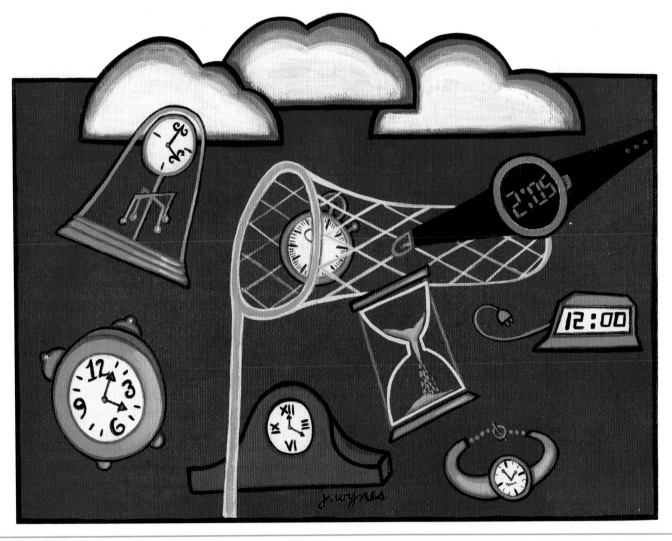

MARIA RENDON
tel. 626.794.5195
fax. 626.794.7538

LIGHTBRIDGE

w w w . m a r i a r e n d o n . c o m

HARPER'S

THE AMERICAN LAWYER

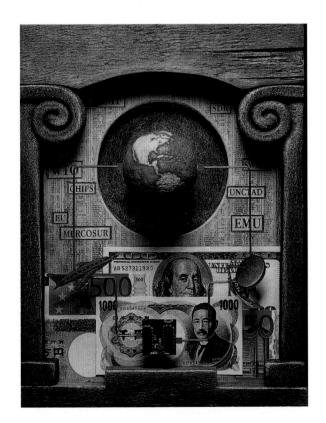

MC-GRAW HILL HIGHER EDUCATION

FARMERS INSURANCE GROUP

Tom Stanley is @ 1741 Prospect Avenue in Santa Barbara, Ca 93103 (805) 687-1223 *also see D of I #16.

MICHAEL LETZIG
437 W. 22nd Street, #3
New York, NY 10011
TEL/FAX (212) 627-3959
e-mail: mletzig@aol.com

For additional samples go to
www.dirill.com

C MICHAEL DUDASH

32 Hurdle Road, Moretown, Vermont 05660 USA ph. 802-496-6400 fax: 802-496-5108
dba/Mission House Artworks E-MAIL: *michael@cmdudash.com* WEB-SITE: *http://www.cmdudash.com*

STOCK-ILLUSTRATION AVAILABLE - PEOPLE, SPORTS, LANDSCAPES, CHRISTIAN, MISC (DIGITALLY CUSTOMIZED ON REQUEST)

TARZAN - Aladdin Books

"As an award winning ARTIST and ILLUSTRATOR for the past 23 Years, Michael has produced over 1,000 paintings & illustrations for galleries, magazine & art publishers, advertising agencies, design firms, film companies & corporations. He has over 200 book covers to his credit as well. Some of his clients include: The Readers Digest, US Postal Service, TV Guide, the United Nations, Sports Illustrated, Disney Studios, Universal Pictures, MGM/UA, Time/Life, Bantam/Doubleday/Dell and Warner Bros."

JOSEPH & MARY ON THE WAY TO BETHLEHEM - Zondervan Publishing House

IN HIS ARMS - C. Michael Dudash / Mission House Artworks

THE QUIET LITTLE WOMAN - Honor Books

ULYSSES S. GRANT - Bantam Books

304

Studio 608 236 0022
Portfolio
Stock Catalog
earlkeleny.com

earl KELENY

illustration

Vincent McIndoe 416.967.2840 fax 416.967.5414 www.vince.on.ca webmaster@vince.on.ca

Giora Carmi

illustrator and writer of children's books

82 Wayne Street #6
Jersey City NJ 07302
Phone and Fax:
201-985-1697
E-mail:
gioracarmi@peoplepc.com

Published Books
And Shira Imagined
A Journey to Paradise
Daddy's Whiskers
Deena the Damselfly
Happy Thanksgiving
Like a Maccabee
Little Red Riding Hood
Mr. Snow's New Home
My First 100 Hebrew Words
Night Farm
Rabbit Trouble and the Green Magician
The Chanukkah Tree
The Chanukkah Guest
The Greatest of All
The Jolly Woodchuck
The Little Menorah Who Forgot Chanukkah
The Miracle of the Potato Latkes
The Mouse in The Wainscot
The Old Woman and Her Pig
The Rooster Prince
The Worst Best Day Ever

Selected Publishers
Contemporary Books
Crown Publishers
Holiday House
Jewish Publication Society
McGraw Hill
Pitspopany
as well as
The Wall Street Journal
The New York Times

GREG•NEWBOLD

801.268.2209 • 1231 EAST 6600 SOUTH, SALT LAKE CITY, UT 84121

GREG·NEWBOLD

801.268.2209 • 1231 EAST 6600 SOUTH, SALT LAKE CITY, UT 84121

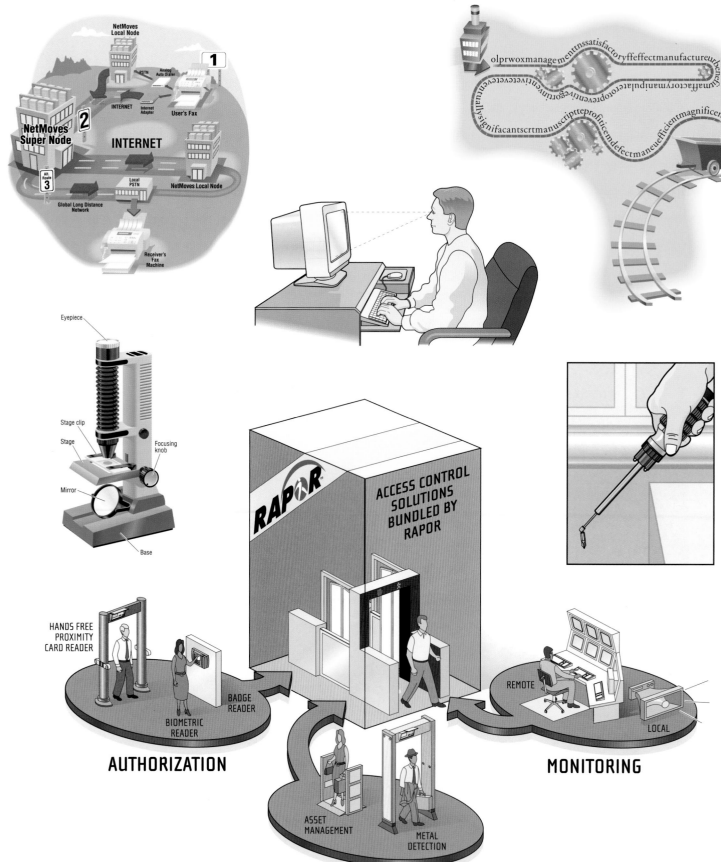

NetMoves Local Node

1

PSTN | Analog Auto Dialer

INTERNET | Internet Adapter | User's Fax

NetMoves Super Node

2

INTERNET

Alt. Route **3**

Local PSTN

NetMoves Local Node

Global Long Distance Network

Receiver's Fax Machine

olprwoxmanagementtnssatisfactoryffeffectmanufactureurbeneﬁ...

...mmaffactorymanipulatetmicrooperoverevenueorutriuvevestcevent...

... allysignifacantscrtmanuscriptteproﬁtcendefectmaneuefficientmagnificent

Eyepiece

Stage clip

Stage

Focusing knob

Mirror

Base

RAPOR®

ACCESS CONTROL SOLUTIONS BUNDLED BY RAPOR

HANDS FREE PROXIMITY CARD READER

BADGE READER

BIOMETRIC READER

AUTHORIZATION

ASSET MANAGEMENT

METAL DETECTION

SCREENING

REMOTE

LOCAL

MONITORING

Spring | Waterfall | **RIVER SYSTEM**

Tributary

Natural Levée

Estuary

Meander | Delta

Floodplain

Oxbow Lake

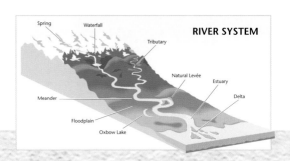

TFC

AWS | B | C

NATIONAL BUSINESS CUSTOMER

REGIONAL BUSINESS CUSTOMER

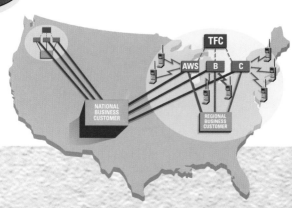

COLIN
HAYES
ILLUSTRATOR
(425) 338-5452
colinhayes@aol.com

ASTRID DININNO
457 John Joy Road
Woodstock, New York 12498
TEL (845) 679-7929
FAX (845) 679-8357
e-mail: astrid@netstep.net

Additional Samples:
Directory of Illustration #14–16
American Showcase 22, 23

For Stock Illustration:
Stock Illustration Source Vols. 5–8
Online Samples/Stock Available:
www.images.com

RICK NASS
4130 Barlow Road
Cross Plains, WI 53528
TEL/FAX (608) 798-3500
rnass@hotmail.com

CARICATURE AND HUMOROUS
ILLUSTRATION

Over twenty years experience
creating artwork for editorial,
advertising and corporate clients
nationwide.

See Directory of Illustration 13, 15, 16.

RICK NASS
4130 Barlow Road
Cross Plains, WI 53528
TEL/FAX (608) 798-3500
rnass@hotmail.com

CARICATURE AND HUMOROUS
ILLUSTRATION

Over twenty years experience
creating artwork for editorial,
advertising and corporate clients
nationwide.

See Directory of Illustration 13, 15, 16.

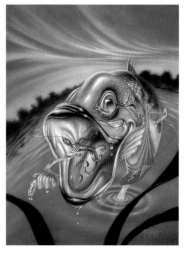

LUSTRATIONS & DESIGN BY

D A N T É

MUSARRA

EMAIL: SAXMAN2K@HOTMAIL.COM

TEL 714.542.5093

FAX 714.542.2110

HAL LOSE

8019 Anderson Street
Philadelphia, PA 19118
TEL/FAX (215) 248-3056

Three-dimensional illustration using paper sculpture, marbled papers, monotypes and etchings.

Conceptual work with a touch of Fine Art.

If you would like to see more samples, just call me.

Online samples—
http://www.sisstock.com

Clients in USA/Europe/Japan

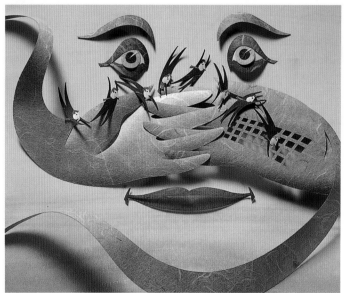

mspress.microsoft.com

Where do you want to go today?

DamanStudio

888.213.6852

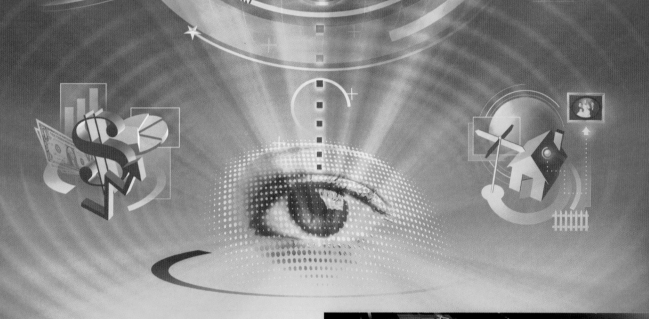

DamanStudio

888.213.6852
Bothell, Washington

Assigned & Stock Illustration for All Media

DAVID WESTWOOD STUDIO

Santa Monica, CA
TEL (310) 828-6694
FAX (310) 829-3021
e-mail: DAWestwood@aol.com
www.davidwestwood.com

Clients include:
American Express, Disney, EMI, FILA, Fox, Gucci, Honda, IBM, Isuzu, Kia, Mazda, MCA/Universal, Mattel, Nestlé, Paramount, Revlon, Sanrio, Sony, Technicolor, 3M, Westinghouse

Member Graphic Artists Guild

Print Advertising, Packaging, Editorial, TV, Video, Film, Software, Website, CD-ROM

318

BARBARA GRIFFEL
23-45 Bell Boulevard
Bayside, NY 11360
TEL/FAX (718) 631-1753
e-mail: Barb24G

Clients include: The New York Times, Newsday, QVC Publishing, Guess?, Rodale Press, Penguin Putnam Inc., Dupont, Creative Homeowners Press, The Franklin Mint, Jones N.Y. Sport, i. natural, Macy's, Bugle Boy, Chelsea Nites, Fashion Center BID and Hearst Publications.

Additional samples of my work can be found in the Directory of Illustration #14 and on www.dirill.com. or call for portfolio.

Specialties: Fashion, beauty, accessories, lifestyle, home furnishings and food.

Mascara

Lipstick

Foundation

Blush

319

BARBARA GARRISON

12 East 87th Street
New York, NY 10128
TEL (212) 348-6382
FAX (212) 423-9220

Selected Clients:
- Boyds Mills Press
- Carnegie Hall Stagebill
- Dial Children's Books
- Dutton Children's Books
- 4walls.com
- Harcourt-Brace

- Macmillan/McGraw Hill
- Marian Heath Cards
- Mondo Publishing
- Simon & Schuster
- Schurman Fine Papers
- UNICEF
- Woman's Day

See Also:
RSVP# 13–25

Member of:
- Graphic Artists Guild
- SCBWI
- Society of Illustrators

GARY OVERACRE

3 8 0 2   V i n e y a r d   T r a c e ,   M a r i e t t a ,   G e o r g i a   3 0 0 6 2   7 7 0 - 9 7 3 - 8 8 7 8

CATHY GENDRON
Represented by:
JoAnne Schuna
TEL (651) 631-8480
FAX (651) 631-8426

PETER GROSSHAUSER
13 South Raleigh
Helena, MT 59601
TEL/FAX (406) 443-3762
e-mail: grosshauser@mcn.net

Brian Jensen

rkbStudios
illustration & graphic design

612.339.7055

www.rkbstudios.com

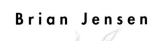

PATRICK KELLEY
1040 Veto Street NW
Grand Rapids, MI 49504
TEL/FAX (616) 458-5925

For additional work see:
Directory of Illustration #12–16
RSVP Vol #23, 24, 25
Spectrum 6 The Best in Contemporary
Fantastic Art

Client list available upon request.

SAMMY SILBERSTEIN
13825 Cumpston Street
Sherman Oaks, CA 91401
TEL (818) 787-5866
FAX (818) 787-8346
e-mail: ddogdesign@earthlink.net
www.theispot.com/artist/sammysil

Clientele includes:
GTE, California Lottery,
Sm@rt Reseller, Guideposts for Teens,
Wall Street Journal Europe

See thispot.com for
**additional work, or call
for portfolio and samples**

**TAYLOR STAMPER
ILLUSTRATION**
888-4STAMPER
Taylor@stamperillustration.com

Clients include:
Oxford University Press
Hewlett Packard
Greenwire Consulting
Granite Street Vintners
And more.

See additional work in the Directory
of Illustration vol. 14 and 15 and
American Showcase vol. 23 or visit
www.stamperillustration.com
for full online portfolio.

Member Graphic Artists Guild

Nickelodeon

MacAddict

Pittsburgh

EMERGENCY PHONE NUMBERS

PREPAID PHONE CARD

MEDICAL ALERTS

Honda of America

Honey

CTW

Computer Illustrations
Computer Graphics
Photo Manipulations
Photo Illustrations

Manipulations Inc.
1-800-723-4754 Fax 330-867-9728

SI HUYNH
5353 Dewar Road
Nanaimo, B.C. Canada V9T 5G1
TEL (250) 758-2504
FAX (250) 758-2534
e-mail: Shdesign@home.com

PORTFOLIO AVAILABLE ONLINE @

W W W . S I H U Y N H . C O M

GRAND CLASSIC

JULY 7-9, 2000

LAKE GENEVA, WIS.

WISCONSIN REGION CLASSIC CAR CLUB OF AMERICA, INC.

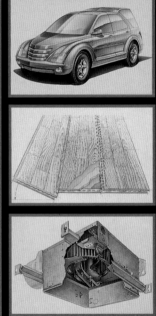

TOM SIEBERS
10182 WHITNALL COURT
HALES CORNERS, WI 53130
414 425 6405   FAX 414 425 6730
E-MAIL tsiebers@execpc.com   www.tomsiebers.com

GEORGE WITHAM
12 Reagan Road
Townsend, MA 01469
TEL (781) 533-2005
FAX (781) 533-3155
e-mail:
George_Witham@millipore.com

Areas of Specialization:
In addition to these unique
"imaginative" rock creations, custom
designs can be painted on rocks.

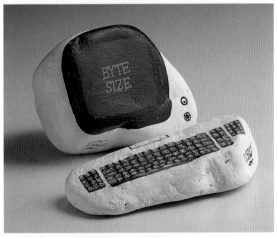

**NANCY LANE
ILLUSTRATION**
10 Glendale Road
Ossining, NY 10562
TEL (914) 944-0565
FAX (914) 944-0535
e-mail: NELane10@aol.com

Clientele includes: ASPCA, Harcourt
Brace, Juvenile Diabetes Foundation,
The Hampton-Brown Company,
EcoTerra, Standard Publishing,
The Benefactory.

Member: Graphic Artist's Guild,
Society of Children's Book Writers
and Illustrators

See Directory of Illustration #14, 15
and 16 for additional work.

Lisa Blackshear

(212) 387-8138

"Pets with Personalities Like Their Owners" --Pets Magazine

"Family Fun Logo" --Tupperware.com

"Who Wants to be a Millionaire" --Charlotte Magazine

"Employee Theft" --Inc. Magazine

"For a Healthy Pregnancy--Eat Your Veggies" --Disney Online

"Reading to Baby" --Family.com

"Russia Launches Siberian Sun Satelite" --Newsweek

"Mayo vs. Yogurt" --Good Housekeeping

"Apple's Steve Jobs" --MacAddict

KENNETH BATELMAN

1-888-532-0612

batelman.com

Digital Illustration for use in advertising, textbooks, editorial, products & packaging, technical, covers & interiors of books & magazines, info-graphics, illustrated charts & maps, internet

All art created using Adobe Illustrator

Clients:
McGraw Hill, Macmillan, Harcourt Brace, Silver Burdett Ginn, Inc., Prentice Hall, Scholastic, Simon & Schuster, Allstate, Young & Rubicam, Newsweek, Revlon, Businessweek, Reader's Digest, Clinique, Woman's Day, Popular Science, Mayo Clinic, Coca-Cola

Additional work samples:
Black Book
American Showcase
New Media Showcase
Stock Illustration Source
California Image
Book Production Buyer's Guide
www.theispot.com

BRUCE VAN PATTER

128 S. 17th. Street
Lewisburg, PA. 17857

570-524-9770

Clients include: McDonald's,
Scholastic, Crayola, MasterCard,
Children's Television Workshop,
Houghton Mifflin, *Ranger Rick*,
Ringling Bros. Circus

Holmes
in
Hawaii

JUDE MACEREN

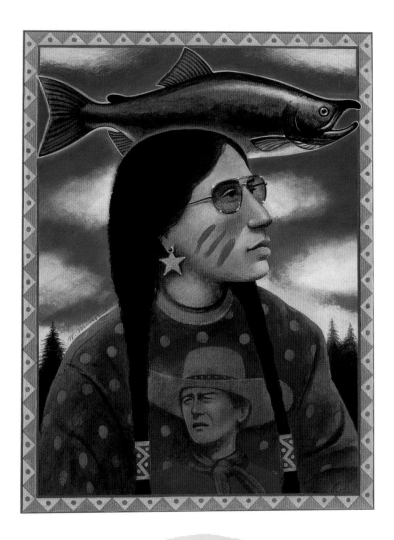

Visit Wendell Minor at minorart.com

ROB DUNLAVEY
8 Front Street
South Natick, MA 01760
TEL (508) 651-7503
FAX (508) 651-8344
WEB www.robd.com

Specializing in hand-crafted digital images for editorial, corporate, children's and educational clients for use in print and electronic media.

See past Directories of Illustration for samples or visit my web portfolio.

ROB DUNLAVEY
8 Front Street
South Natick, MA 01760
TEL (508) 651-7503
FAX (508) 651-8344
WEB www.robd.com

Specializing in hand-crafted digital images for editorial, corporate, children's and educational clients for use in print and electronic media.

See past Directories of Illustration for samples or visit my web portfolio.

MARTY NORMAN
162 Scenic Drive
Southington, CT 06489
TEL (860) 621-7507

Additional Samples:
The Stock Illustration Source Vol. 7
or www.images.com and
Portfolio On-Line: www.dirill.com

Mark Schroeder
DIGITAL ILLUSTRATION

Airbrush
Line drawings
Photo illustration
Retouching

1021 Sherman St.
Alameda CA 94501
510/814.7382
Fax 510/814.7351
mark@markschroeder.com
www.markschroeder.com

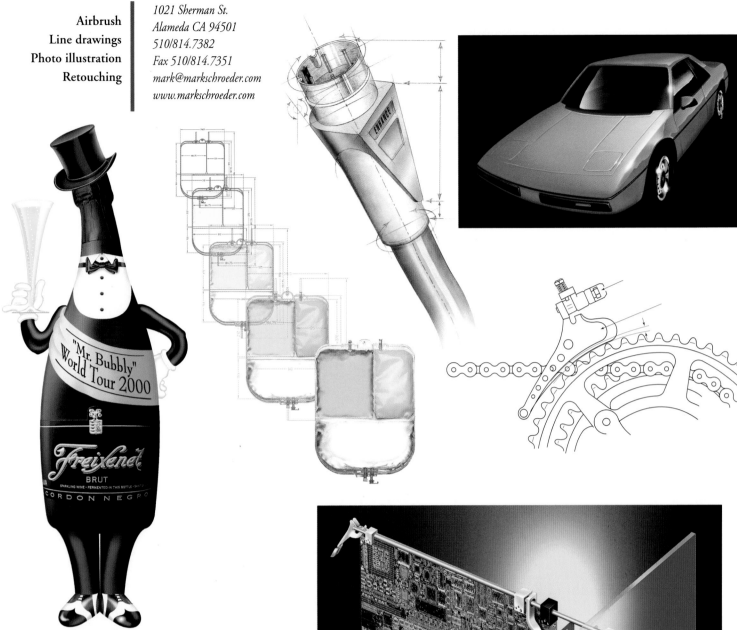

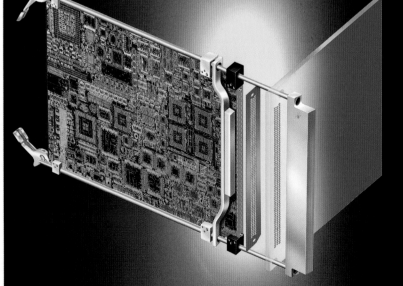

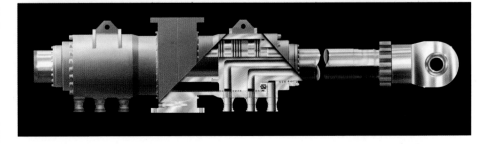

Member: San Francisco Society of Illustrators   Clients Include: Fujitsu, Kingsford Charcoal, Bio Rad, Del Monte, Clorox, Ortho, Chevron, Blue Star Lines, Amtrak, Peterbuilt, Hewlett Packard, Galoob Toys, Seagate, Skidmore, Owings, & Merrill, Applied Materials, National Semiconductor, IBM, Gloria Ferrer, Paul Masson, Freixenet

ANDREW PLEWES ILLUSTRATION
508-402 W. Pender Street
Vancouver, B.C. Canada V6B 1T6
TEL/FAX: (604) 687-2127

Work shown includes: Hanniford Brothers Bakery, Tetley Teas, Mama Mia Pastas, English Bay Swim Club, A&W Root Beer, Captain Highliner Foods, Schneiders Foods.

Clientele includes: Billboard Magazine, Toblerone, Cadbury, Kraft General Foods, McDonalds, Harcourt Brace

ANNIE BISSETT
SPECIALIZING IN INFORMATION GRAPHICS

www.anniebissett.com
for more samples
1-800-515-1060

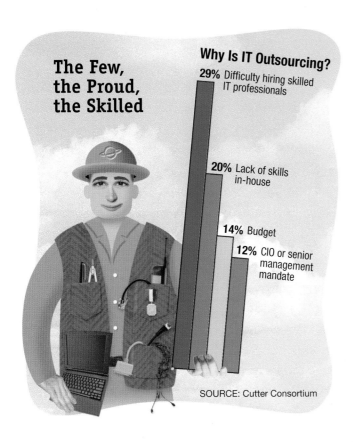

The Few, the Proud, the Skilled

Why Is IT Outsourcing?
29% Difficulty hiring skilled IT professionals

20% Lack of skills in-house

14% Budget

12% CIO or senior management mandate

SOURCE: Cutter Consortium

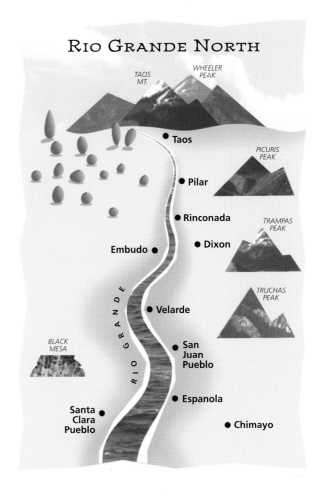

RIO GRANDE NORTH

TAOS MT.
WHEELER PEAK
Taos
PICURIS PEAK
Pilar
Rinconada
TRAMPAS PEAK
Dixon
Embudo
TRUCHAS PEAK
RIO GRANDE
Velarde
BLACK MESA
San Juan Pueblo
Espanola
Santa Clara Pueblo
Chimayo

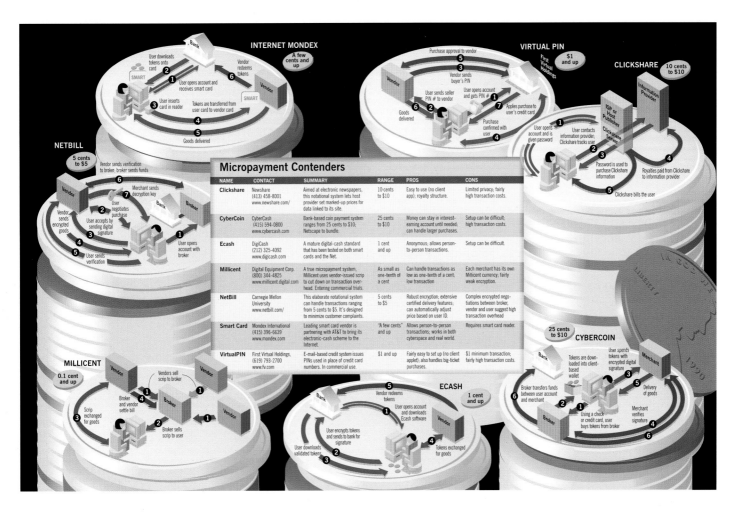

Micropayment Contenders

NAME	CONTACT	SUMMARY	RANGE	PROS	CONS
Clickshare	Newshare (413) 458-8001 www.newshare.com/	Aimed at electronic newspapers, this notational system lets host provider set marked-up prices for data linked to its site.	10 cents to $10	Easy to use (no client app); royalty structure.	Limited privacy; fairly high transaction costs.
CyberCoin	CyberCash (415) 594-0800 www.cybercash.com	Bank-based coin payment system ranges from 25 cents to $10; Netscape to bundle.	25 cents to $10	Money can stay in interest-earning account until needed; can handle larger purchases.	Setup can be difficult; high transaction costs.
Ecash	DigiCash (212) 325-4092 www.digicash.com	A mature digital-cash standard that has been tested on both smart cards and the Net.	1 cent and up	Anonymous; allows person-to-person transactions.	Setup can be difficult.
Millicent	Digital Equipment Corp. (800) 344-4825 www.millicent.digital.com	A true micropayment system, Millicent uses vendor-issued scrip to cut down on transaction overhead. Entering commercial trials.	As small as one-tenth of a cent	Can handle transactions as low as one-tenth of a cent; low transaction	Each merchant has its own Millicent currency; fairly weak encryption.
NetBill	Carnegie Mellon University www.netbill.com/	This elaborate notational system can handle transactions ranging from 5 cents to $5. It's designed to minimize customer complaints.	5 cents to $5	Robust encryption; extensive certified delivery features; can automatically adjust price based on user ID.	Complex encrypted negotiations between broker, vendor and user suggest high transaction overhead
Smart Card	Mondex International (415) 396-6639 www.mondex.com	Leading smart card vendor is partnering with AT&T to bring its electronic-cash scheme to the Internet.	"A few cents" and up	Allows person-to-person transactions; works in both cyberspace and real world.	Requires smart card reader.
VirtualPIN	First Virtual Holdings, (619) 793-2700 www.fv.com	E-mail-based credit system issues PINs used in place of credit card numbers. In commercial use.	$1 and up	Fairly easy to set up (no client applet); also handles big-ticket purchases.	$1 minimum transaction; fairly high transaction costs.

INTERNET MONDEX — A few cents and up
User downloads tokens onto card
User opens account and receives smart card
User inserts card in reader
Tokens are transferred from user card to vendor card
Goods delivered
Vendor redeems tokens
Bank
SMART

VIRTUAL PIN — $1 and up
First Virtual Holdings
Purchase approval to vendor
Vendor sends buyer's PIN
Vendor
User sends seller PIN # to vendor
User opens account and gets PIN #
Goods delivered
Applies purchase to user's credit card
Purchase confirmed with user

CLICKSHARE — 10 cents to $10
Information Provider
ISP or Host Publisher
Clickshare Server
User opens account and is given password
User contacts information provider; Clickshare tracks user
Password is used to purchase Clickshare information
Royalties paid from Clickshare to information provider
Clickshare bills the user

NETBILL — 5 cents to $5
Vendor sends verification to broker, broker sends funds
Merchant sends decryption key
Vendor
Vendor sends encrypted goods
User negotiates purchase
User accepts by sending digital signature
User sends verification
User opens account with broker
Bank
Broker

MILLICENT — 0.1 cent and up
Vendor
Vendors sell scrip to broker
Broker and vendor settle bill
Scrip exchanged for goods
Broker sells scrip to user
Broker

ECASH — 1 cent and up
Vendor redeems tokens
Bank
User opens account and downloads Ecash software
User encrypts tokens and sends to bank for validation
User downloads validated tokens
Tokens exchanged for goods
Vendor

CYBERCOIN — 25 cents to $10
Bank
Tokens are downloaded into client-based wallet
User spends tokens with encrypted digital signature
Merchant
Broker transfers funds between user account and merchant
Using a check or credit card, user buys tokens from broker
Delivery of goods
Merchant verifies signature
Broker

Tom Klare

(858)565-6167   fax(858)569-7577

tomklare@aol.com

©2000

Tom Klare
(858)565-6167   fax (858)569-7577
tomklare@aol.com

Steve Feldman Illustration/Design

Tel/Fax (661) 945-5966 • 1402 W. Jackman St. • www.stevefeldman.com
Lancaster CA 93534

more work in Directory of Illustration 16 pg.407

Marian Heibel Richardson

616-394-1291

JOHN DYESS
703 Josephine Ave.
St. Louis, MO 63122
TEL/FAX (314) 822-2893

I bring 35 years of experience to this profession of illustration. I am a visual problem solver having worked with a vast variety of clients.

This recent group of images uses both traditional and digital methods combining typography, texture, photography and drawing. The original base art or collage, is created essentially in black and white with color being added in various media. The overall theme is one of portraiture and biography with layers of emotions and history represented in textural elements.

I welcome the opportunity to provide further information or samples. View more of my work at www.portfolios.com.

Raphael Montoliu
1(800) 652-1785

EARTH DAY 2000

CLEAN ENERGY NOW !

Robert Stroleny

Alter Image Illustration

359 E. Rosedale Ave. Milwaukee, WI 53207   ph: (414) 747-0425   alterim@execpc.com

ALFRED RAMAGE
Silent Sounds Studio
5 Irwin Street
Winthrop, MA 02152
TEL (617) 846-5955
FAX same, call first
e-mail: ramageart@aol.com

Representation:
ispot.com/portfolios.com

Digital Illustrator

1 Whales over oil...
2 The real Glass Ceiling
3 "Coke it's Universal"

Jan Stamm

tel/fax 619.280.6205   email jan@simplenet.com   website www.jan.simplenet.com

Debbie Komadina # Huntsman

[voice] 480•893•2850 [e-mail] designer@amug•org

(808) 572-6571 Fax (808) 572-1285
wertheim@maui.net   www.annew.com
4150 Hana Highway
Haiku, Maui, HI 96708

ANNE
WERTHEIM

ANNE
WERTHEIM

(808) 572-6571 Fax (808) 572-1285

wertheim@maui.net   www.annew.com

4150 Hana Highway

Haiku, Maui, HI 96708

**EILEEN STARR
MODERBACHER
STUDIO STAR**

2637 Mc Gee Avenue
Berkeley, CA 94703
TEL (510) 848-0901
FAX (510) 848-2926
e-mail: eileen@studio-star.com

Web: www.studio-star.com

Clientele includes:
Sun Microsystems, Microsoft, McKinsey
& Co., Phone Works, USENIX, Morgan
Kaufmann, Blackwell Science, Inc., Fort
Mason Center, Bookbuilders West,
TeleTriage Systems, Maschinenfabrik

Andritz, Austria, AVL List GmbH
MatrixArts International 2000
Exhibition: Woman Consuming/
Woman Consumed, Sacramento, CA
April 5–April 29, 2000
Blazing Apple, Spinning Tops–20″ × 26″
medium–tempera

Call for portfolio or references.
Visit our hi-tech web and print
partnership at www.star-group.com

TOM BŌLL

MINNEAPOLIS, MINNESOTA

TEL 952.942.6119

AMY L. WASSERMAN
6 Country Lane
Pelham, MA 01002
TEL (413) 253-4664
FAX (413) 253-7667

Clients include: Children's Television Workshop, *Ladies Home Journal*, Little Brown & Co., Motorola, MasterCard, *Money*, Nickelodeon, Putnam Publishing, *Smithsonian*, *Sports Illustrated for Kids*, *Time*, *Woman's Day*

Please see Directory of Illustration #16 pages 300–301 for additional samples.

AMY L. WASSERMAN
6 Country Lane
Pelham, MA 01002
TEL (413) 253-4664
FAX (413) 253-7667

Clients include: Children's Television Workshop, *Ladies Home Journal*, Little Brown & Co., Motorola, MasterCard, *Money*, Nickelodeon, Putnam Publishing, *Smithsonian*, *Sports Illustrated for Kids*, *Time*, *Woman's Day*

Please see Directory of Illustration #16 pages 300–301 for additional samples.

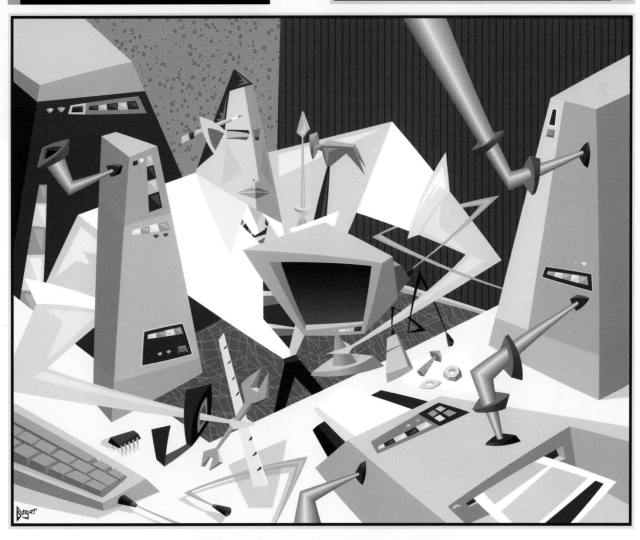

609 ▸ 397 ▸ 3737

LISA HOLLEY
P.O. Box 3
Sun Valley, Idaho 83353
TEL (208) 622-9122
FAX (208) 622-5657
e-mail: lisaholley_studio@yahoo.com
www.lisaholley.com

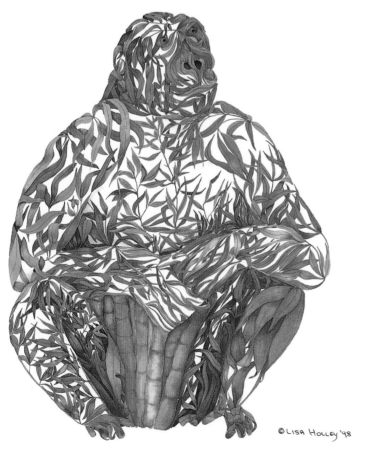

NED SHAW STUDIO

Voice: 812-333-2181
Fax: 812-331-0420
www.nedshaw.com
nshaw@kiva.net

©2000 Ned Shaw
Portions © Synopsys

TRIPLE
·PLAY·
DESIGN

Eric Kittelberger
Illustrator

1772 Bramblebush NW
Massillon, Ohio 44646

Telephone
330.830.0893

Facsimile
330.830.0879

E-Mail
eric@TriplePlayDesign.com

Internet
www.TriplePlayDesign.com

Triple Play Design

Phone 330 830-0893   Facsimile 330 830-0879

Mike Moran · Humorous Illustration ·
39 Elmwood R.D. Florham Park NJ 07932
973·966·6229   www.illustrators.net/moran

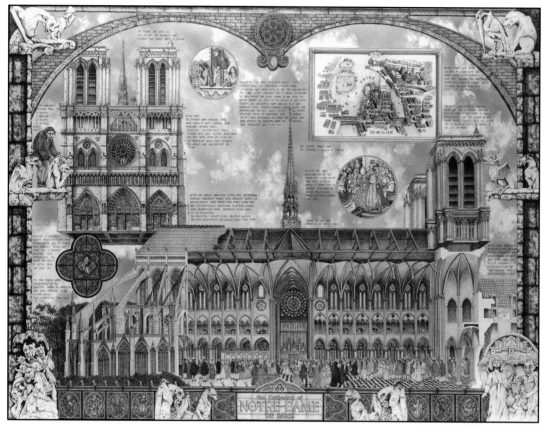

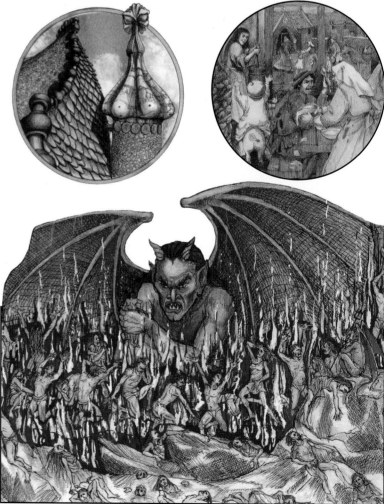

www.qadigital.com

Designed entirely by our in-house team of over 40 illustrators, our extraordinary high-definition digital illustrations have attracted the attention of numerous companies in advertising, publishing, corporate and editorial markets.

With a portfolio of more than 10,000 high-quality product, medical and technical illustrations, and 3D designs and animations, as well as extensive experience in custom illustrations for major accounts, QA Digital can meet any customer-specific requirement.

Clients include BBDO, Saatchi & Saatchi, Team One Advertising, Mazda, Bell South, Polygram, Simon & Schuster and Wieden & Kennedy.

QA DIGITAL

P 1.888.350.0047 **>** 1.514.350.0047 **> F** 1.514.499.3010 **>** info@qadigital.com

ANIMALS
ARCHITECTURE
ASTRONOMY
CAMPING
CLOTHING
COMMUNICATIONS
CREATIVE ACTIVITIES

DO-IT-YOURSELF
ENERGY
FARMING
FLAGS
FOOD
GARDENING
GEOGRAPHY

HEALTH & SAFETY
HOUSE & FURNITURE
HUMAN BEING
INDOOR GAMES
MEASURING DEVICES
MUSICAL INSTRUMENTS
OFFICE SUPPLIES

OPTICAL INSTRUMENTS
PERSONAL ARTICLES
SCHOOL
SPORTS
SYMBOLS & ROADSIGNS
TRANSPORTATION
WEAPONS

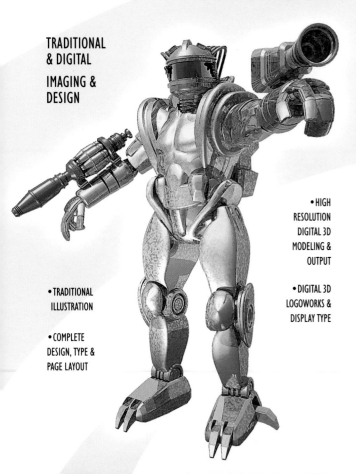

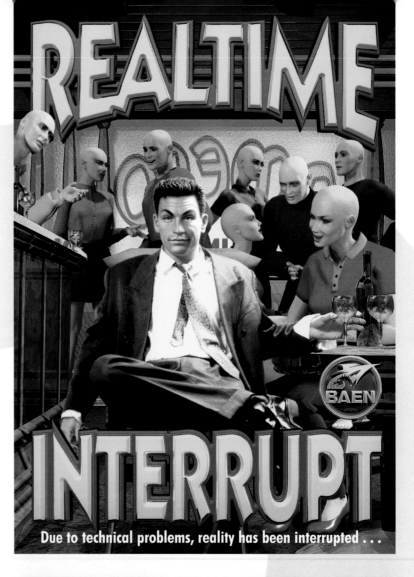

BILL LATTA
Latta Art Services
536 Wilson Drive
Mt. Juliet, TN 37122
TEL/FAX (615) 758-8369
www.members.home.net/las

Digital illustrations: Contemporary and historical perspectives, technical illustrations, illustrated maps, statistical charts, diagrams, cut-a-ways, reconstructions, and games.

Areas of Specialization: A resource for accuracy of historical periods of western civilization; illustration and graphic design consultant.

Member: Graphic Artists Guild

See also: *Directory of Illustration 14* (p. 362); *DI 15* (p.217); and *DI 16* (p. 286)

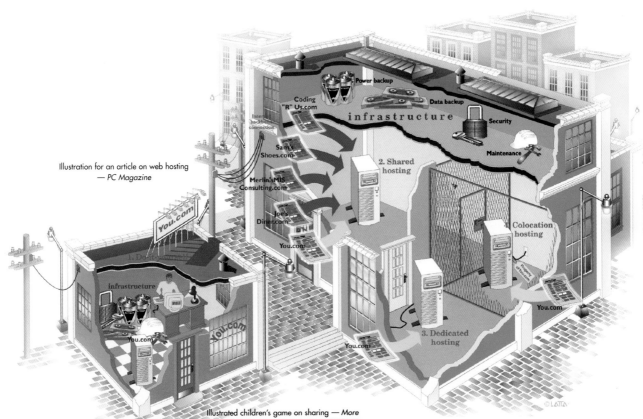

Illustration for an article on web hosting — *PC Magazine*

Illustrated children's game on sharing — *More*

Illustration for an article on ancient warfare — LifeWay

Illustration for a travel promotion — HHBC

Juke box illustration used with a children's game — *Adventure*

LATTA
Art Services
www.members.home.net/las

BILL LATTA
(615) 758-8369

OH BOY,

COME AND GET IT!

**ANATOL WOOLF
ILLUSTRATION**
495 Chestertown Street
Gaithersburg, MD 20878
TEL (301) 527-1757
FAX (301) 527-0014
e-mail: a.woolf@ix.netcom.com

Clientele includes:
Washington Post, Washington Times,
Chronicles, Legal Times, National
Geographic Traveler, Policy Review,
Cricket Magazine.

See more Illustrations at:
http://www.netcom.com/~a.woolf

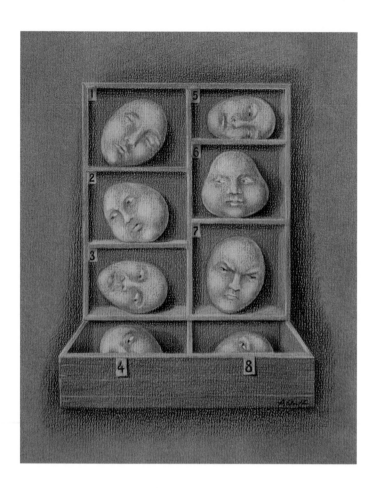

**MONA CARON
ILLUSTRATION**
San Francisco, CA
TEL/FAX (415) 255-8488
e-mail: mona@bok.net
www.monacaron.com

JOHN BERG
110 Cottage St.
Buffalo, NY 14201
TEL (716) 884-8003
FAX (716) 885-4281

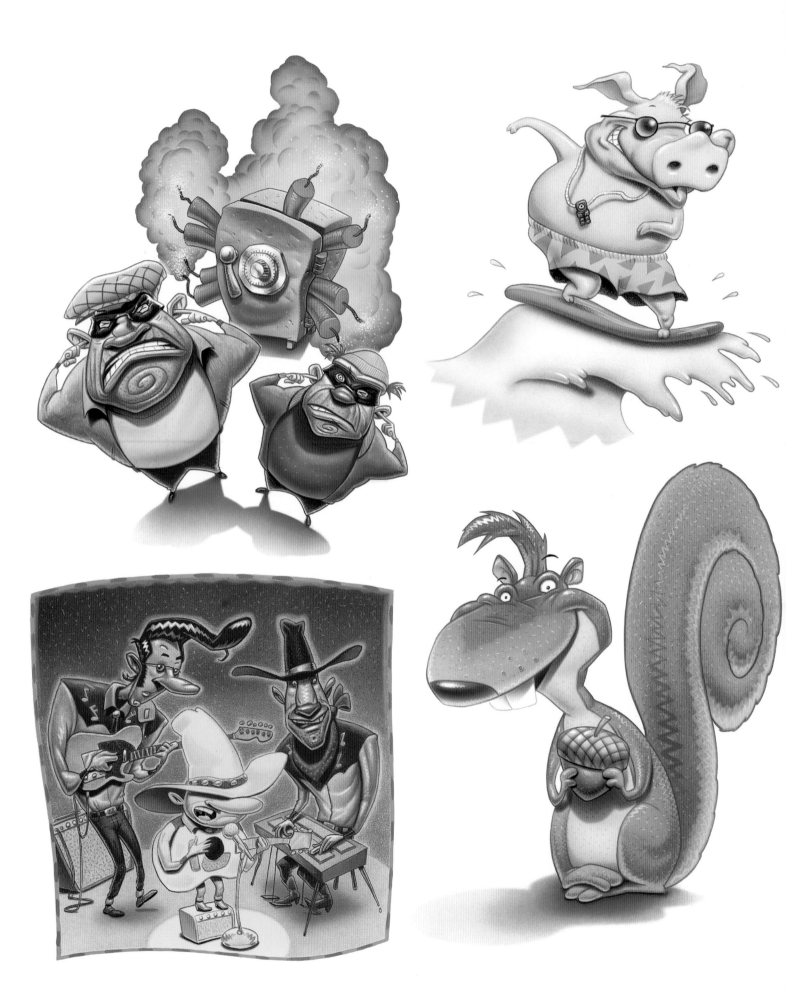

JOHN BERG
110 Cottage St.
Buffalo, NY 14201
TEL (716) 884-8003
FAX (716) 885-4281

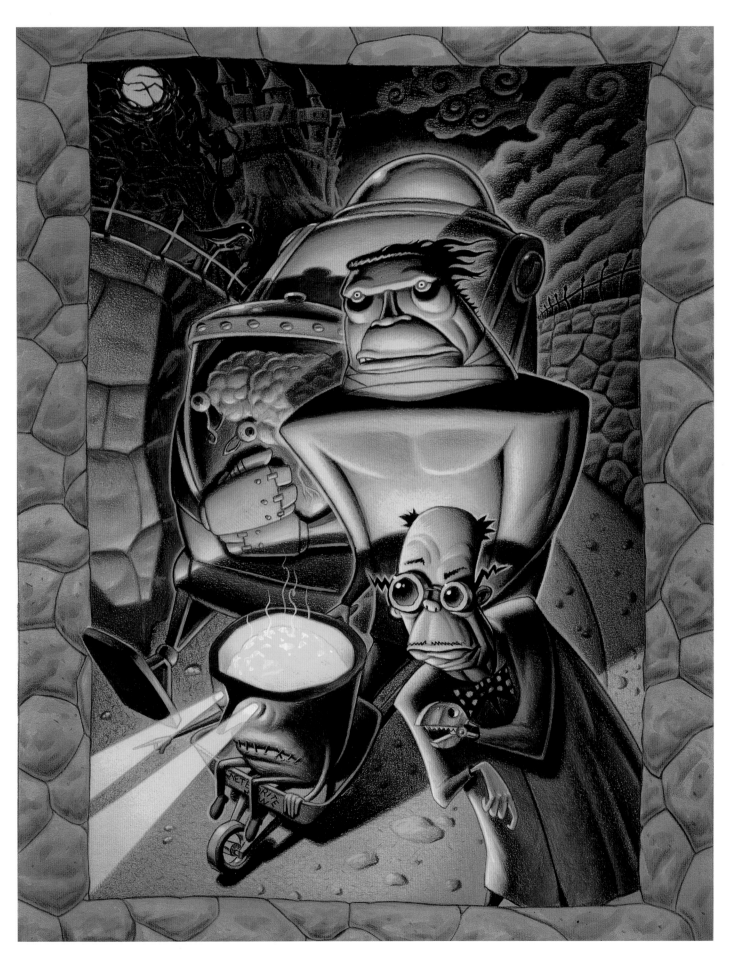

INGO FAST

WWW.INGOFAST.COM

TEL (718) 387-9570
FAX (718) 387-5970

INGO FAST

WWW.INGOFAST.COM

TEL (718) 387-9570
FAX (718) 387-5970

Nationwide Insurance

Rainlight umbrella-flashlight

Enron-PGE

Morley Capital

Oregon Garden

ellen mueller

phone
707·778
6 2 2 1

address
3 1 4
eleventh
street
petaluma
ca 94952

Susan Sanford

Studio/Editorial : 510-208-5581

Email: ssanford@ncal.verio.com

www.theispot.com/artist/sanford

STUDIO ARTISTICO/
DEBORAH SCHILLING

P.O. Box 546408
Miami Beach, Florida 33154
TEL/FAX (305) 861-5233
e-mail: sartist@bellsouth.net

Specializing in:
Book/Book Covers, Children's Books,
Animals & Nature, Editorial,
Products and more…

Illustrations in:
Pastel, Colored Pencil/Watercolor Mix,
Pen & Ink/Wash, Pencil.

Clients include:
Harcourt Brace & Company, *Orlando,
Florida*
Monotype Composition, *Baltimore, MD*
Univision "Sabado Gigante", *Miami, FL*
Biodoron Inc., *Hollywood, Florida*
Computerbanc Inc., *Miami, Florida*
Brain Wash, *San Francisco, California*

RestEz Inc., *Miami, Florida*
Caran S. Inc., *Miami, Florida*

Additional work can be seen in
Directory of Illustration #16 and
www.dirill.com

STEPHEN FOSTER
847-835-2741 studio
847-835-2783 fax
For samples or animation reel:
800-944-1109
www.do-dah.com

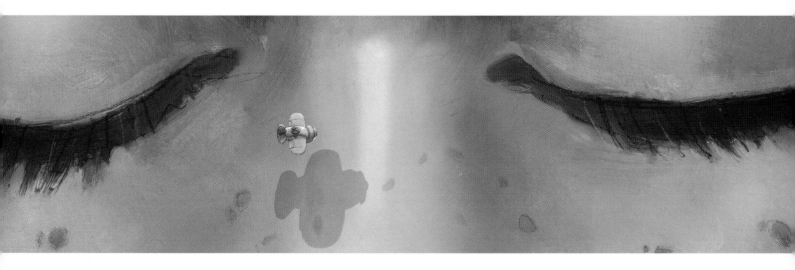

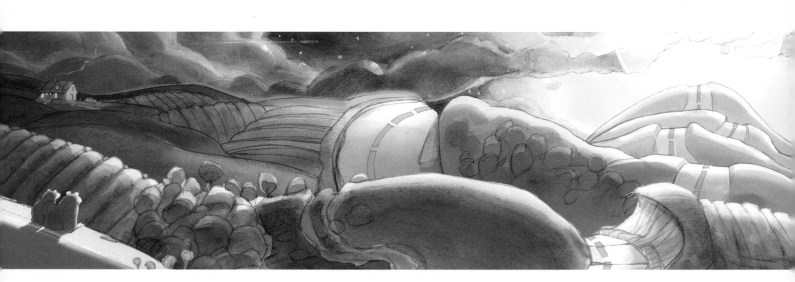

STEPHEN FOSTER
847-835-2741 studio
847-835-2783 fax
For samples or animation reel:
800-944-1109
www.do-dah.com

MIKE HARPER
15 Waverly Place
Red Bank, NJ 07701
TEL (732) 741-0552

Additional work may be seen in the
Directory of Illustration Vol. #14, #15,
and #16, American Showcase Vol.
#20, #21, #22, #23.

MIKE HARPER
15 Waverly Place
Red Bank, NJ 07701
TEL (732) 741-0552

Additional work may be seen in the
Directory of Illustration Vol. #14, #15,
and #16, American Showcase Vol.
#20, #21, #22, #23.

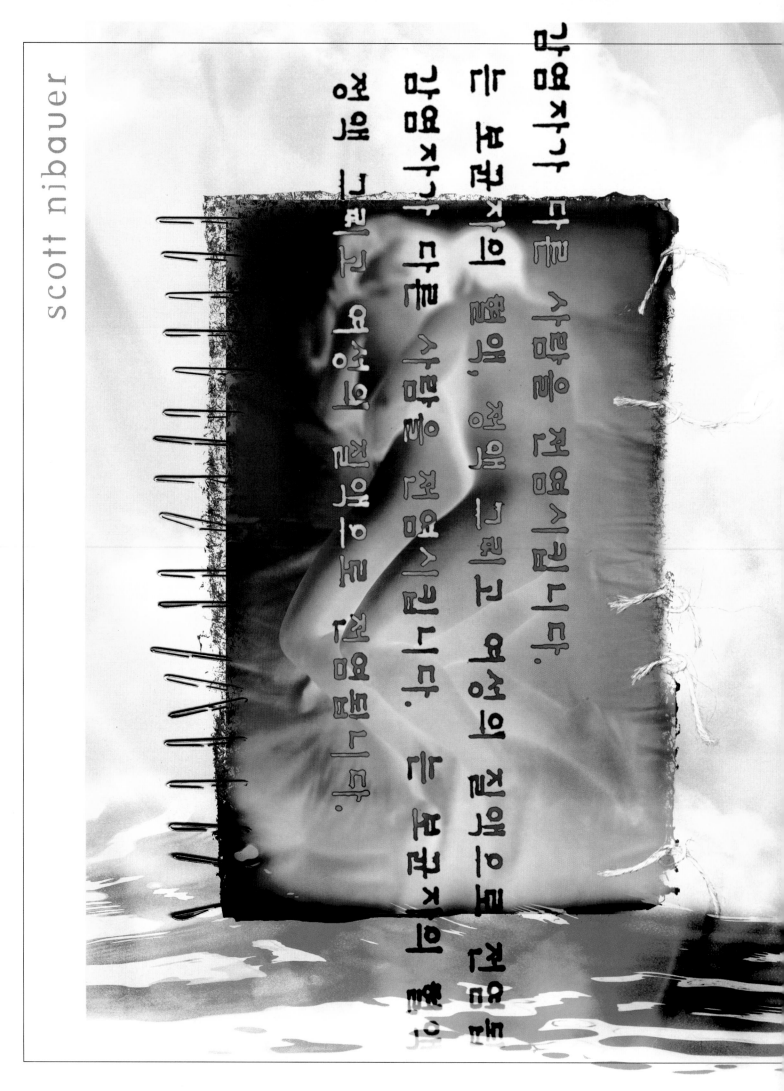

감요자가 다른 사람을 계획시킵니다.

눈 눈꺼풀 자의 별의, 정액 눈꺼풀 여성의 침대으로 전 감요자가 다른 사람을 계획시킵니다.

감요자가 다른 사람을 계획시킵니다. 눈 눈꺼풀 자의 별의 정액 눈꺼풀 여성의 침대으로 전 정액 그리고 여성의 침대으로 계획됩니다.

scott nibauer

Scott Nibauer's ability to compose complex visual montages

originates from his experience as a still photographer and film

director. From photographing lions in South Africa and dolphins

in Mexico, to top-notch CEO's, lab assistants and factory workers,

Scott always finds something wild, strange and magnificent

wherever he shoots. He weaves these images into unique

stories that challenge creative boundaries.

301 cherry street . philadelphia, pa 19106

1.800.726.3988 . 215-238-9917 fax

www. peoplepix.com . nibauer@peoplepix.com

LIEN NIBAUER
PHOTOGRAPHY

JOANNE HUS

CREATIVE SERVICES
126 HOYT STREET, 1J
STAMFORD, CT 06905

(203) 316-9248

JHUSCS@AOL.COM

MEMBER:

GRAPHIC ARTISTS GUILD
CONN. ART DIRECTORS' CLUB

CLIENTS INCLUDE:

BURSON MARSTELLER
CHASE MANHATTAN BANK
CHESEBROUGH-POND'S USA
DUPONT PUERTO RICO
GE CAPITAL

HOFFMANN-LA ROCHE
PABLO CASALS MUSEUM
ROCHE MOLECULAR SYSTEMS
SANOFI PHARMACEUTICALS

JOANNE HUS

CREATIVE SERVICES
126 HOYT STREET, 1J
STAMFORD, CT 06905
(203) 316-9248
JHUSCS@AOL.COM

MEMBER:
GRAPHIC ARTISTS GUILD
CONN. ART DIRECTORS' CLUB

CLIENTS INCLUDE:
BURSON MARSTELLER
CHASE MANHATTAN BANK
CHESEBROUGH-POND'S USA
DUPONT PUERTO RICO
GE CAPITAL

HOFFMANN-LA ROCHE
PABLO CASALS MUSEUM
ROCHE MOLECULAR SYSTEMS
SANOFI PHARMACEUTICALS

www.go-global.com

MATTHEW AMBRE
743 W. Brompton
Chicago, IL 60657
TEL (773) 935-5170
FAX (773) 935-5748

Clientele includes:
Ameritech, Motorola, Sears, Whirlpool,
CNA, Olive Garden Restaurants.

www.johnnelson.com

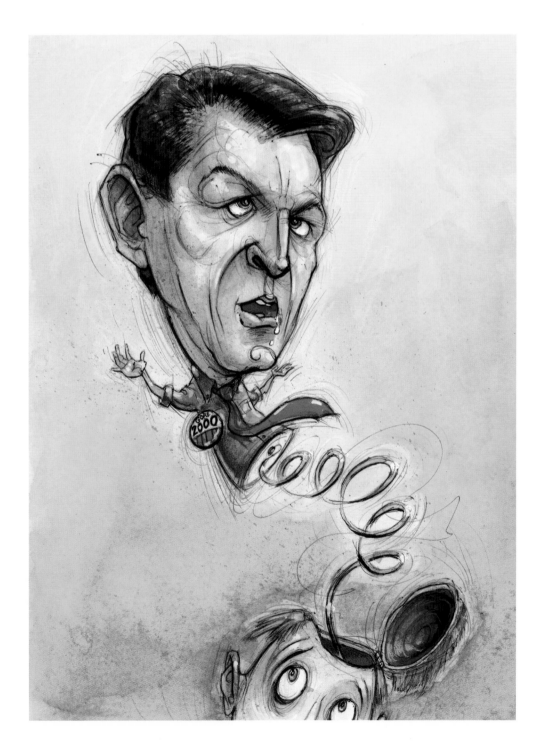

DENNY BOND
6481 Miriam Circle
East Petersburg, PA 17520
TEL/FAX (717) 569-5823
e-mail: bond004@msn.com
dennybondillustration.com

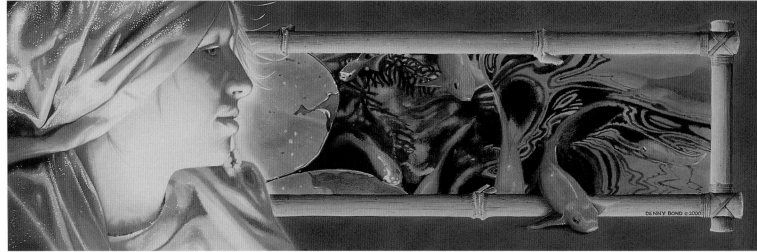

**EILEEN ROSENFELD
ILLUSTRATION**
33-52 Crescent St., Apt. 7B
Astoria, New York 11106
TEL/FAX (718) 956-3930
e-mail: Astoriart@aol.com

Client List:
Caswell Massey, JC Penney,
Lenox Brands, Conimar Corp.,
Hausenware, Converting Incorp.,
US CAN, Bertle's CAN

See Directory of Illustration #16 for
additional work or call for portfolio.

GREG RUHL

40 ALEXANDER STREET PH.9 TORONTO, ONTARIO, CANADA, M4Y 1B5

TEL (416) 928-1997 FAX (416) 928-9382

143 W. Montgomery Avenue,
North Wales, PA 19454–3411
e-mail: sitndyno@sprynet.com

Clients include: Pitney Bowes,
Springhouse Corporation, The
Local Government Environmental
Assistance Network, Johnson &
Johnson, Bauer Publishing Co.,
Philadelphia Newspapers, Ohio
Casualty, Philadelphia Gas Works,
American Hospital Association, and The Education Center
Awards include: The Business Card Museum, *PRINT'S Regional
Design Annual, The Artist's Magazine,* Neographics Franklin Award,
Neenah Paper-Text and Cover Paperworks Competition

Also See Directory of Illustration #13–16 for additional work.

Member: Graphic Artists Guild

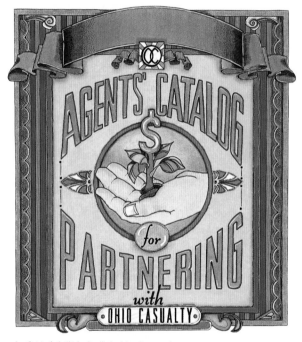

Cover illustration for the Ohio Casualty publication, *Pointers.* Cover story explores ways
that Ohio Casualty associates and independent insurance agents can grow together.

Illustration for the article "Sound Advice for Home Buyers," in which recommendations
are given regarding the various housing options available at every stage of life.

Artwork for the article "The Caregiving Connection—Making the Right Decision,"
confronting the question of when to place your loved one in an assisted living facility.

For the article "Adding Insult to Injury," regarding violence inflicted against people with disabilities by their caregivers.

VINCENT A. CANNINO
713 Archer Road
Winston-Salem, NC 27106
TEL (336) 760-3099
FAX (336) 774-0675
e-mail: vcannino@aol.com

Clientele includes:
Old Salem, Inc.:
"Herr Kater's ABC und Bilder-Buch"
(Mister Cat's ABC & Picture-Book)

SCOTT GETCHELL
617 661 0658
www.scottgetchell.com

403

Better Homes and Gardens

Anne Cook • 96 Rollingwood Drive • San Rafael, CA 94901
Tel. 415·454·5799 • Fax 415·454·0834 • akcart@aol.com

Anne Cook

Illustration using
a variety of
techniques with
textiles and
stitchery

96 Rollingwood Drive, San Rafael, CA94901
Tel. 415·454·5799 Fax 415·454·0834
akcart @ aol.com

CYNTHIA FAGGIANO

30 River Street
Methuen, MA 01844
TEL (978) 687-4413
FAX also available—call for info.

Illustration in Color or Black & White.
- Fashion
- Children's Books
- Cover Art
- Posters
- Magazines
- Books
- Costume Design

B.F.A. (Illustration), Massachusetts
College of Art, Boston.
All outfits below are by Cynthia.
© Cynthia Faggiano 2000

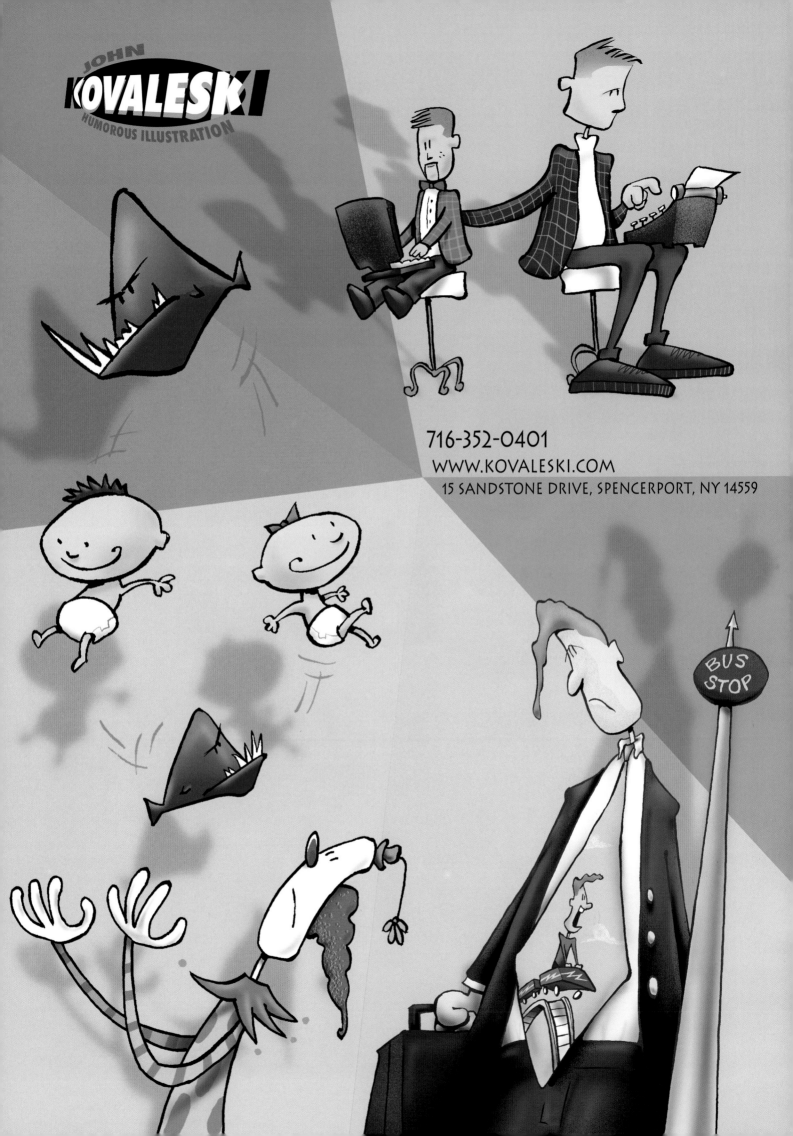

716-352-0401
WWW.KOVALESKI.COM
15 SANDSTONE DRIVE, SPENCERPORT, NY 14559

JOHN LAMBERT
1911 E. Robin Hood Ln.
Arlington Hts., IL 60004
TEL/FAX (847) 873-0065
e-mail: lambertart@home.com

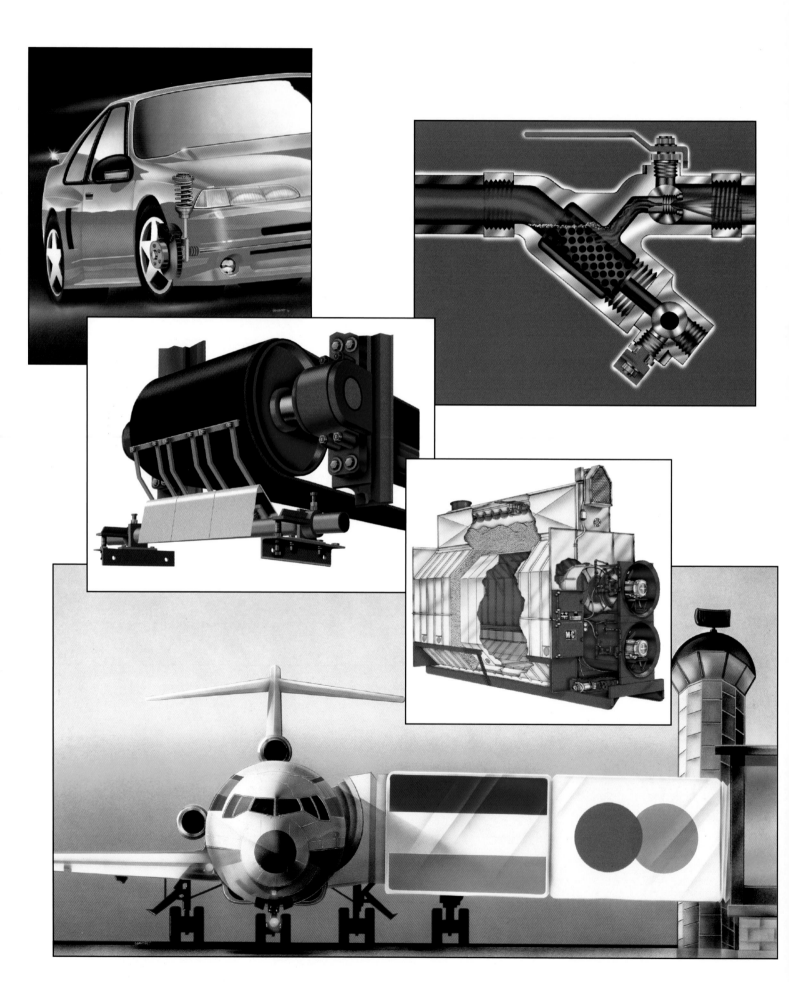

kathleen
o'malley

815 GLENWOOD LANE • GLENVIEW • IL • 60025-4021

847·729·5311
FAX 847·729·5347

ERIC RIDER
www.ewik.com • rider@ewik.com
800.763.3947 • San Jose. CA

christine joy pratt

christinejoypratt.com phone & fax: (808) 591-8879

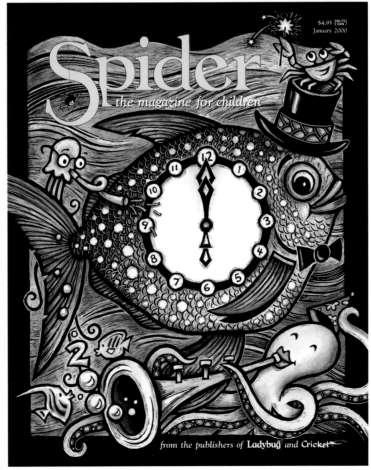

Jeff Grunewald • Digital Illustration

Architectural, Retail and Trade Show Visualization
Technical Illustration • Conceptual Illustration

773-281-5284

www.jeffgrunewald.com

Jeff Grunewald • Digital Illustration

Architectural, Retail and Trade Show Visualization
Technical Illustration • Conceptual Illustration

773-281-5284

www.jeffgrunewald.com

laurie luczak

phone/fax 212.251.9694 | online portfolio @ www.laurieluczak.com | email: laurieluczak@aol.com

NANCY WOLFF
100 W. 87th Street, #1D
New York, NY 10024
TEL/FAX (212) 873-6183

PETER WALLACE
23 Crown St.
Milton, MA 02186
TEL/FAX (617) 696-6023

Clients include: PepsiCo, Columbia House, *Boston Globe, Boston Herald, TV Guide, Ski Magazine, Field & Stream, Infoworld, Sales & Marketing Management, Vegetarian Times,* Cahners, Scholastic Inc., Children's Television Workshop, *Chickadee,*

National Geographic World, Boys' Life, Book of the Month Club.

Additional work can be seen in Directory of Illustration 14, 15, 16.

416

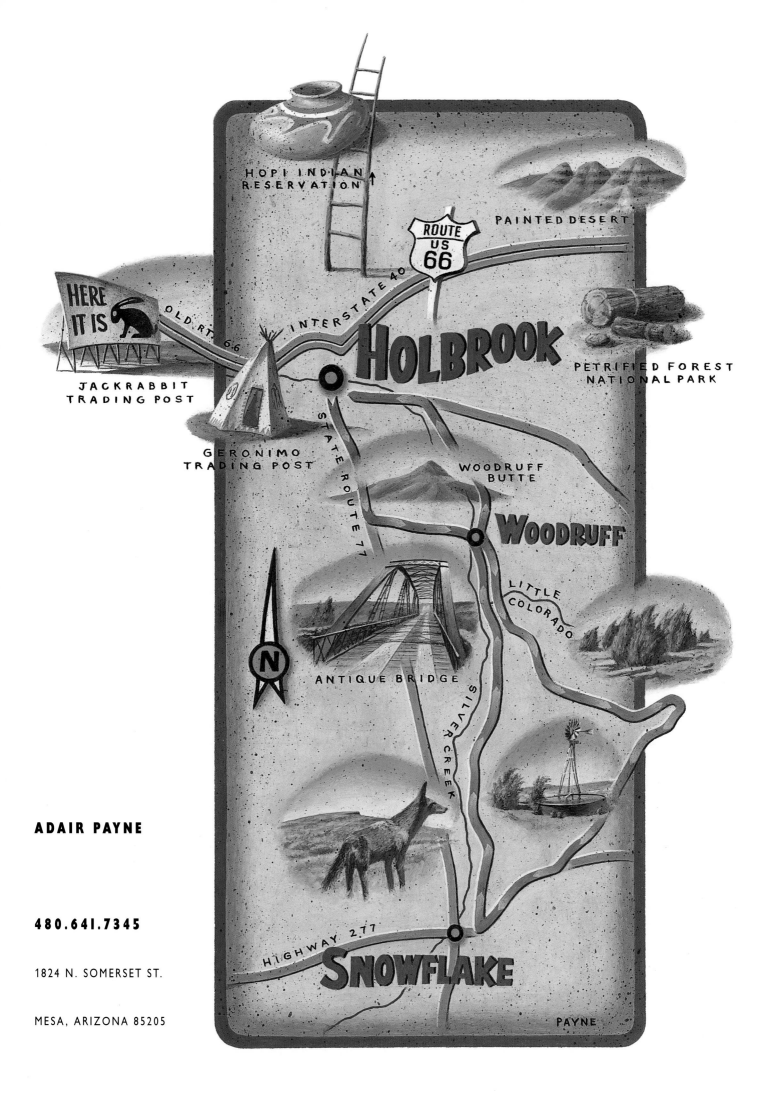

HOPI INDIAN RESERVATION

PAINTED DESERT

ROUTE US 66

INTERSTATE 40

HERE IT IS

OLD RT. 66

HOLBROOK

PETRIFIED FOREST NATIONAL PARK

JACKRABBIT TRADING POST

STATE ROUTE 77

GERONIMO TRADING POST

WOODRUFF BUTTE

WOODRUFF

LITTLE COLORADO

ANTIQUE BRIDGE

N

SILVER CREEK

HIGHWAY 277

SNOWFLAKE

PAYNE

ADAIR PAYNE

480.641.7345

1824 N. SOMERSET ST.

MESA, ARIZONA 85205

TED WILLIAMS
5118 Twitchell Road
Rushville, NY 14544
TEL (716) 554-5373
FAX (716) 554-4162
e-mail: whcom@earthlink.net

Specializing in original, digitally created illustrations for advertising, editorial, book publishing and corporate events.

Samples available upon request.

Clients include: McGraw Hill, Don Morris Design, Houghton-Mifflin, Kirchoff/Wohlberg, Friedman/Fairfax Publishers, Metro Books, Oxford University Press, Bozell, Jacobs, Kenyon & Echkardt, Inc., Vandamere Press, *Skyways*, U.S. Air Force, Air National Guard, Xerox, Kodak, General Motors, and Corning Incorporated.

For additional samples of work see Directory of Illustration #14,15 & 16 and www.studioillustrators.com

418

LINDA BILD
TEL (319) 444-9962
e-mail: LBild16658@aol.com

Clientele: Children's Press–a Division of Grolier Publishing, Fox Kids Studios, Harcourt Brace School Publishers, Lowell House Juvenile, McGraw Hill, McClanahan Publishing, Scott Foresman Addison Wesley, Sound Source Interactive, Universal Studios, Warner Bros. Interactive Entertainment.

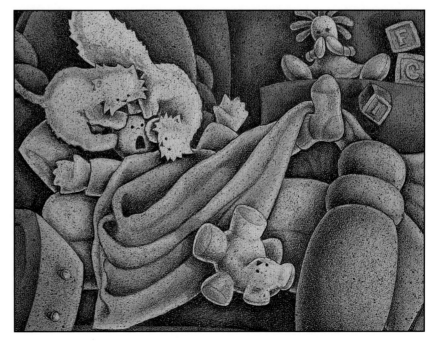

**TOMOKO WATANABE
ILLUSTRATION**

1285 Cresthaven Drive
Pasadena, CA 91105
TEL/FAX (323) 344-9612
e-mail: tomocat@pacbell.net

Society of Illustrators NY
Student Competition Award

Member: Graphic Arts Guild
SCBWI

Also See:
Picturebook '98 & '99
www.tomocat.com

Cinderella/ Oil on wood

Oil on wood

Oil on wood

**TOMOKO WATANABE
ILLUSTRATION**
1285 Cresthaven Drive
Pasadena, CA 91105
TEL/FAX (323) 344-9612
e-mail: tomocat@pacbell.net

Society of Illustrators NY
Student Competition Award

Member: Graphic Arts Guild
SCBWI

Also See:
Picturebook '98 & '99
www.tomocat.com

Greeting Card

Greeting Card

IAN BOTT
8520 Calle Cristobal
San Diego, CA 92126
TEL (858) 689-9420
FAX (858) 547-9823
e-mail: ianbott@aol.com

Portfolio, further samples
and comprehensive client
list available upon request.

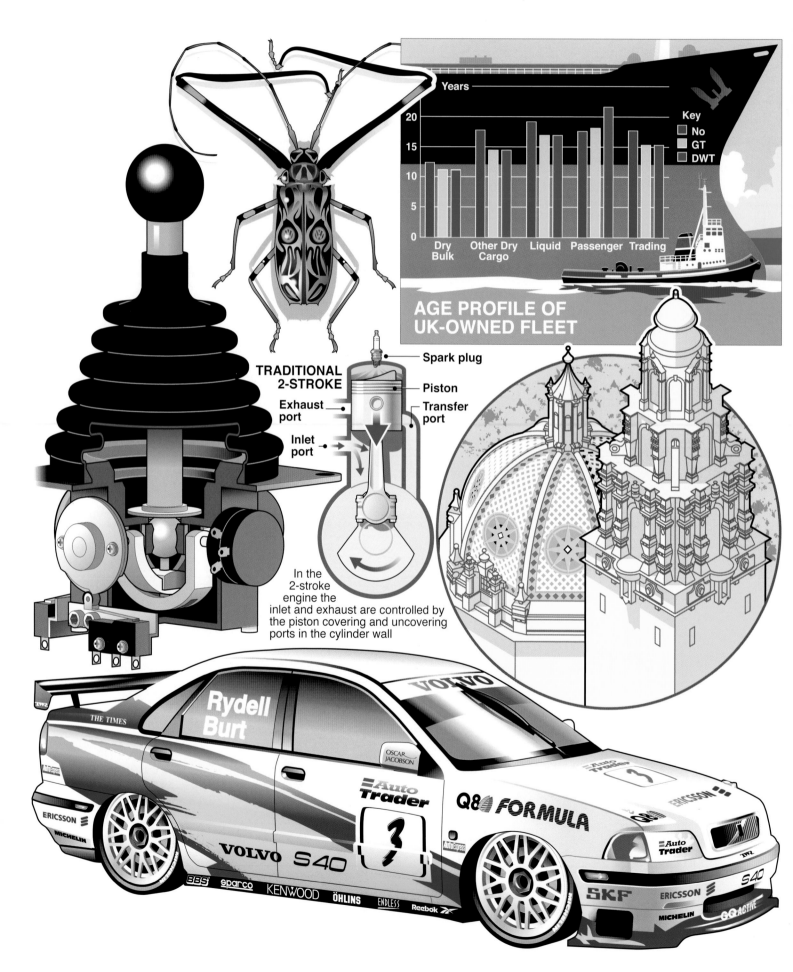

Years

Key
No
GT
DWT

Dry
Bulk
Other Dry
Cargo
Liquid
Passenger
Trading

**AGE PROFILE OF
UK-OWNED FLEET**

**TRADITIONAL
2-STROKE**

Spark plug

Piston

Exhaust
port

Transfer
port

Inlet
port

In the
2-stroke
engine the
inlet and exhaust are controlled by
the piston covering and uncovering
ports in the cylinder wall

Rydell
Burt

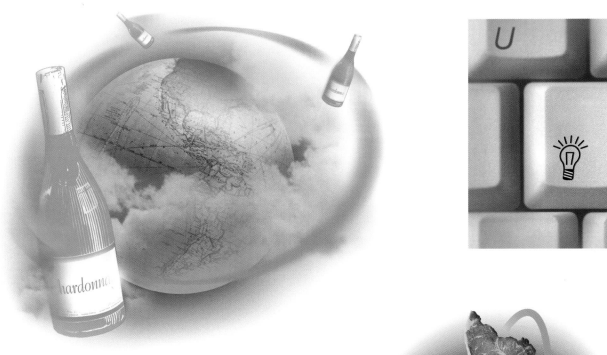

Mary Ann Smith design + illustration

phone: (212) 691-3570 | fax: (212) 989-2609 | email: masmith@panix.com

New York, NY

ALLAN M. BURCH
404 Red Maple
Kirbyville, MO 65679
TEL/FAX (417) 335-2410
e-mail: allanburch@inter-linc.net

Clientele includes: *The Boston Globe,
Bicycling, Harvard Business Review,*
Major League Baseball, *Science*
Magazine

**JASON BULLINGER
ILLUSTRATION**
TEL (605) 338-9836

Clients include:
BEC Records
Kingdom Records
KMTT 103.7 FM Seattle, WA
Artists & Graphic Designers Market
The Unknown Writer

See Directory of Illustration #16 for
additional work or call for portfolio.

Member of Graphic Artists Guild

JOHN HANLEY
ILLUSTRATION

815   459   1123
JHANLEY108@AOL.COM

• P A T R I C K   H A S L O W •

ILLUSTRATION 847.458.9488 www.patrickhaslow.com

403 La Fox River Drive Algonquin, IL 60102

427

LINO
31 Holton Street
Danvers, MA 01923
TEL (978) 750-4069
e-mail: linotopia@hotmail.com

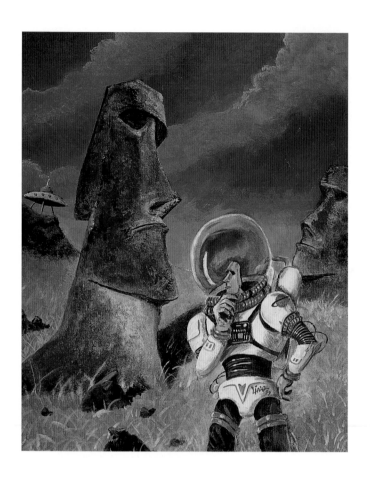

Lino
ILLUSTRATION

CHARLES HENRY JAMES

Toll-free 1-877-9-CREATE (1-877-927-3283) • www.chjames.com

ANTHONY REZENDES
13429 Moscow Trail
Austin, TX 78729
TEL (512) 416-1912
FAX (305) 723-5812
e-mail: rezendes@flash.net
http://www.flash.net/~rezendes/

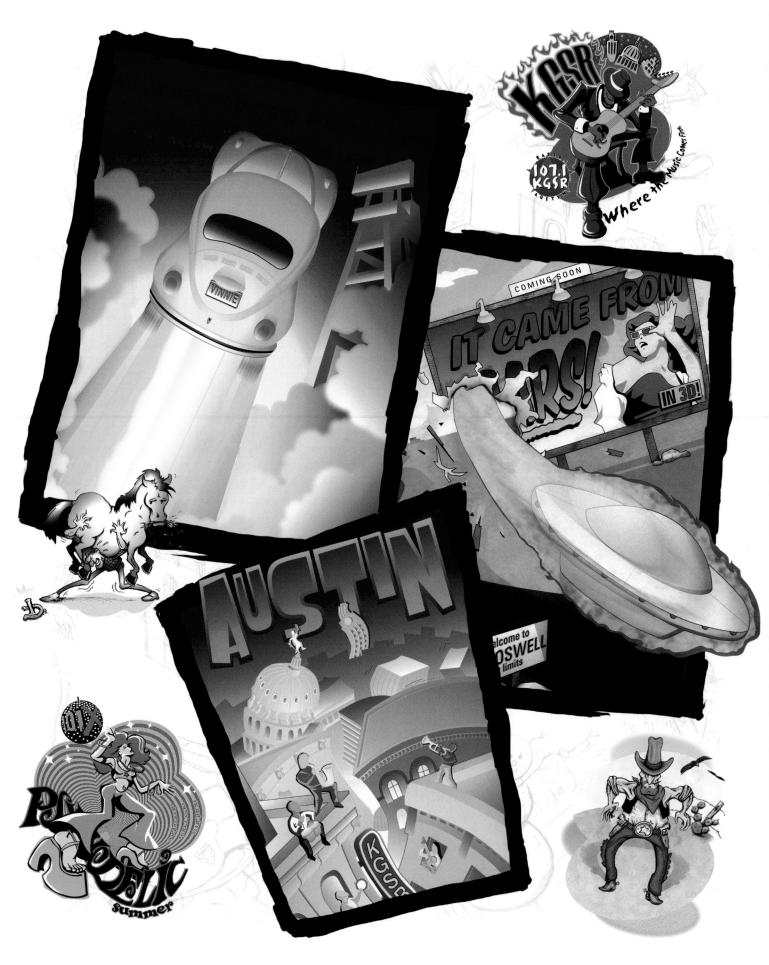

John Grigni

3104 Branchwood Drive
Greensboro, NC 27408
(336) 545-1495
jpgrigni@triad.rr.com

Special Forces
proposed cover

Ventiun
Story illustration

Magic Store
3-D Model & Painting

Little Pistol in Toyland
3-D Modeling

Attack Bot
3-D Modeling and Computer painting
Self promotion

Deluxe Illuminati
Card game illustrations - Steve Jackson Games

Junk Mail

Professional Sports

Alcohol & Tobacco

KGB

Cyberpunk genre piece

Neil Stewart / tel: (416) 516-3535 / fax: (416) 516-2418 / email: nsv@interlog.com

ART GLAZER
2 James Road
Mt. Kisco, NY 10549
TEL (914) 666-4554

GROWTH

**SUZANNE
CHERYL GARDNER**

Cezanne Productions
P.O. Box 11172
Bainbridge Island, WA 98110
TEL (206) 780-0230
e-mail:
suzanne@cezanneproductions.com

Please view my
complete and
always changing
portfolio at:
cezanneproductions.com

The *Tree Of Life* and *Dancing Bears*.
It is *The Fool* that trusts fully,
For the Angels That Watch Over Us.
Buffalo symbolizes abundance.
Ahhh…The Magic of Life!

434

Paul Weiner
Ph/Fx: 617•738•0446
PWeiner@world.std.com
Brookline, MA 02445

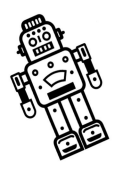

436

PAT MEYERS DESIGNS
139 Alala Road
Kailua, Hawaii 96734
TEL/FAX (808) 263-0258
e-mail: patmeyers@poi.net
pat_meyers@kailuahs.k12.hi.us

graphics, collage, watercolor
& computer illustration for
kids books, greeting cards,
home textiles & product design

art samples & client list on request

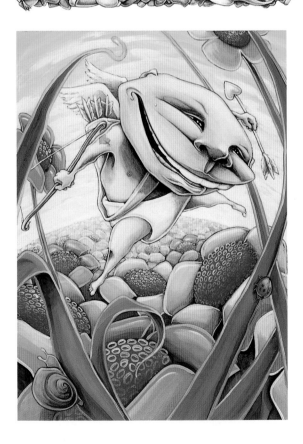

jAMeS fOrRESt
1-888-tiN-tuNA
846-8862

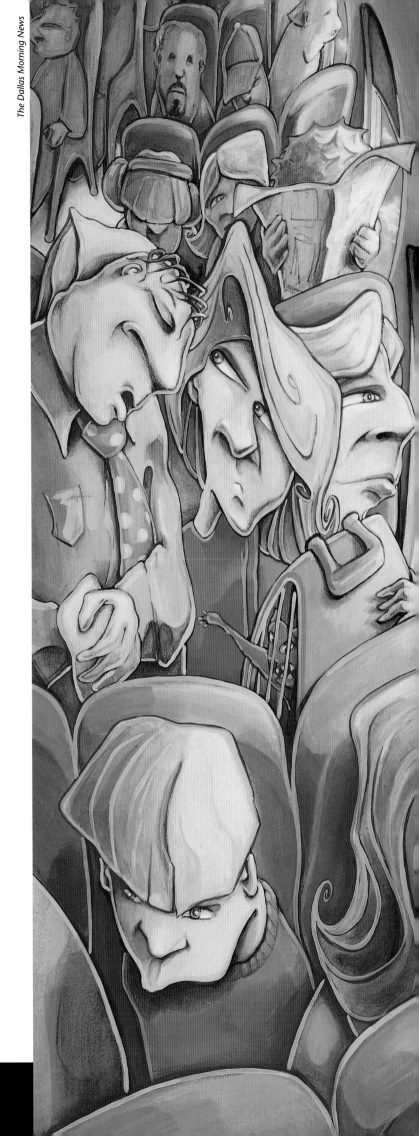

www.michaelinley.com
VOICE:614.486.2921
FAX:614.487.6020

angela martini

576 11th St. #3 b'klyn, ny 11215

718.499.3142

a@angelamartini.com
www.angelamartini.com

illustrator!

"Katbot & Eddie" ©2000 Funny Garbage, Inc.
for funny Garbage

for the wall street journal

for my own personal enjoyment

for empire magazine

for winex magazine

J O H N
H A R T
ILLUSTRATION

503.289.3477
fax 503.289.3542
hartosb@europa.com
www.johnhartart.com

ERIC PETERSON
(562) 438-2785

TOLL FREE:
(877) 435-0374
e-mail: etpet@aol.com

ERIC PETERSON
(562) 438-2785
TOLL FREE: (877) 435-0374
e-mail: etpet@aol.com

WILDLIFE ART LTD
Studio 16
25-27 Muspole Street
Norwich
NR3 1DJ
England

TEL 44 (01603) 617 868
FAX 44 (01603) 219 017
e-mail: info@wildlife-art.co.uk

Wildlife Art specialise in all areas of natural history illustration. Whatever the subject—birds, mammals, oceanic, even archeological and prehistory… chances are we'll have it covered!
Check out our web site:
www.wildlife-art.co.uk

Clients include: Readers Digest, HarperCollins, World Book Publishing, IMP Ltd, Editions Gallimard, Dorling Kindersley, Larousse, Macmillan, Weldon Owen etc.…

ROBIN BOUTTELL

MARC DANDO

PETER D. SCOTT

IAN JACKSON

PETER D. SCOTT

446

P.O. Box 575
26099 McCiver Circle
Conifer, CO 80433
scott@artimage.com
http://artimage.com

SCOTT ANNIS

TOLL FREE: 877·753·6588 or 303·674·1151   FAX: 303-838-8263   VIEW MORE AT: ARTIMAGE.COM

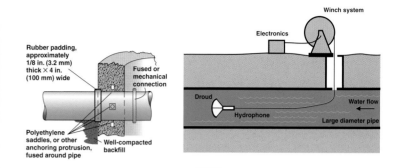

Rubber padding, approximately 1/8 in. (3.2 mm) thick × 4 in. (100 mm) wide

Fused or mechanical connection

Polyethylene saddles, or other anchoring protrusion, fused around pipe

Well-compacted backfill

Winch system

Electronics

Droud

Hydrophone

Water flow

Large diameter pipe

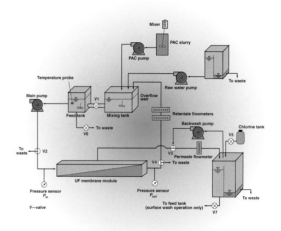

Mixer

PAC slurry

PAC pump

Temperature probe

Raw water pump

To waste

Main pump

V1

Overflow weir

Feed tank

Mixing tank

Retentate flowmeters

Backwash pump

Chlorine tank

To waste

V6

To waste

V2

V3

Permeate flowmeter

V5

V4

To waste

UF membrane module

Pressure sensor P_{in}

Pressure sensor P_{out}

To feed tank (surface wash operation only)

V7

V—valve

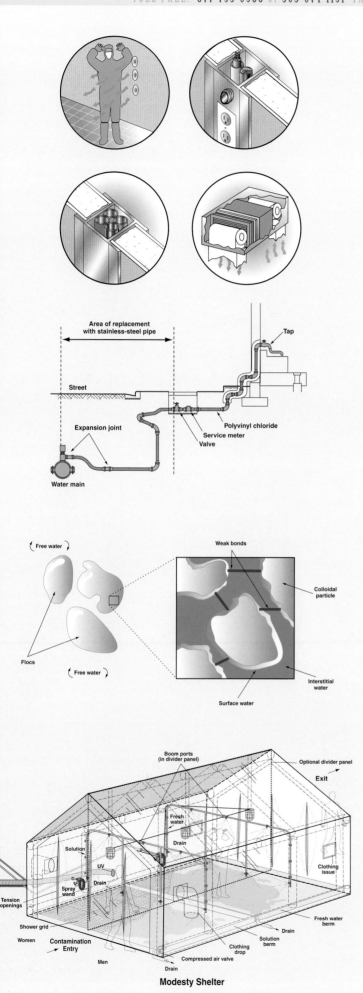

Area of replacement with stainless-steel pipe

Tap

Street

Expansion joint

Polyvinyl chloride

Service meter

Valve

Water main

Free water

Weak bonds

Colloidal particle

Flocs

Free water

Surface water

Interstitial water

Modesty Shelter

Boom ports (in divider panel)

Optional divider panel

Exit

Fresh water

Drain

Solution

UV

Clothing issue

Spray wand

Drain

Tension openings

Fresh water berm

Shower grid

Drain

Women

Contamination Entry

Solution berm

Men

Clothing drop

Compressed air valve

Drain

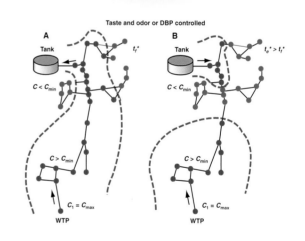

Taste and odor or DBP controlled

A

Tank

t_f^*

$C < C_{min}$

$C > C_{min}$

$C_1 = C_{max}$

WTP

B

Tank

$t_e^* > t_f^*$

$C < C_{min}$

$C > C_{min}$

$C_1 = C_{max}$

WTP

PAUL GAJ
Digital Illustration
108 West Main St.
Groton, MA 01450
TEL (978) 448-9689
FAX (978) 448-0179
e-mail: pgaj@tiac.net
www.pgajdesign.com

Clientele includes:
Analog Devices, Compaq Computer,
Harte-Hanks, IBM, IRIS Graphics,
Nortel Networks, PennWell
Publications, Sycamore Networks

©2000 Paul Gaj

RICHARD ELMER
504 East 11th Street
New York, NY 10009
TEL (212) 598-4024
FAX (212) 473-1655
e-mail: R2elmer@worldnet.att.net

PATTY O'FRIEL
1112 North Hoyne, Suite 2
Chicago, IL 60622
TEL/FAX (773) 384-3496
e-mail:patios@earthlink.net

When your written information needs a little color, go for a bit o' fun with some bold whimsical characters or spots! Done on the Mac, my work has jazzed up copy for McDonald's, Kraft, United Airlines, 7-11, DiscoverCard and Harcourt Brace, to name a few.

In addition to putting a smile on one's face, these illustrations are very web friendly!

To see more work, check out Black Books 1996 thru 2000 and American Showcase 24.

food   kids stuff   financial   people   gadgets   critters

BEEP...

come play at www.pattyo.com

212 • 775 • 1484

jody • wheeler

375 south end ave. • 12t • n.y. n.y. • 10280

clients: Scholastic   Delta Airlines   UNICEF   Colorbök
Marcel Schurman   Random House   Penguin Putnam   Harper Collins

See Directory of Illustration #9, 11, 12, 14, 15, 16 for additional work.

SCOTT BAKAL

1 888 234 4492
1 631 231 0148
website
www.scottbakal.com
email
info@scottbakal.com

website
ww.scottbakal.com

1 888 234 4492

time inc.

new york law journal

mutual funds magazine

cmp media

delta

email
info@scottbakal.com

1 631 231 0148

eBay

wizards of the coast

boating magazine

fleet financials

twa

SCOTT BAKAL

LORRAINE DEY
P.O. Box 142
Jackson, NJ 08527
TEL (732) 928-5510
FAX (732) 928-5232
e-mail: info@deystudio.com
www.deystudio.com

Client List:
Bristol-Myers Squibb
Somfy Systems, Inc.
W. Zinsser & Co.
Silver Burdett-Ginn
Delaire USA
Bank Investment Marketing
Rodale Press

Men's Health Magazine
Securities Data Publishing
Audio Magazine
Myron Mfg., Corp.
DiMark Group & more.

Humorous editorial & product
illustration created digitally and
delivered direct to your desktop via
e-mail, Zip disk, or CD Rom.
Visit us at: www.deystudio.com
Stock images also available.

Member: Graphic Artists Guild

lorraine dey studio

732.928.5510
spot editorials, icons, & products
delivered to your desktop!

NANCY WHITE CASSIDY

Beardsley Road
New Milford, CT 06776
TEL (860) 350-3423
e-mail: nanartist@erols.com
www.nancycassidy.com

Specialized illustration of: children, animals & wildlife, landscape, people, places and just things in general. Work created in pastel, oil, acrylic, pen & ink, or graphite.

Additional work may be seen in Directory of Illustration, volumes 15 & 16, or by requesting additional samples.

Past clients include:
Harcourt-Brace
Scott-Foresman
IBM Corporation
BJC Health Services
Farm Credit

JT YOST ILLUSTRATION
3208 Beanna St.
Austin, TX 78705
TEL (800) 745-7013
e-mail: yostt@hotmail.com

See Directory of Illustration #16 for
additional work or call for portfolio

Hannah Bonner
125 Palfrey Street
Watertown MA 02472
T. 617·924·2620

The Mediterranean islands produced many peculiar animals in the millions of years before humans arrived:

CORSICA, SARDINIA: LARGE PIKA, ODD DEER.

CYPRUS: A TINY-HIPPO

TILOS: WAIST-HIGH ELEPHANT

CRETE: BOTH GIANT AND DWARF DEER

MALTA: GIANT·TORTOISE GIANT SWAN

SICILY: PYGMY ELEPHANT GIANT DORMOUSE SMALL HIPPO

The Balearics had a giant dormouse, a large owl, and a knee-high relative of the goat called Myotragus balearicus.

Alas, poor fossil! I know it well. these forward-facing eyes and rodent-like teeth are a dead giveaway.

With no predators to flee from, Myotragus became stocky and slow, a little eating machine with teeth that could handle even the toughest plant matter.

MARGARET KASAHARA
1212 North Nevada Avenue
Colorado Springs, CO 80903
TEL/FAX (719) 520-1622

MICHAEL ANDERSON
22 Howard Drive
Belleville, IL 62223
TEL/FAX (618) 538-5622

Michael Anderson illustrates architectural subjects for architects, builders and interior designers in a variety of media including pen and ink, color pencil, airbrush, markers and watercolor.

See also:
*Architecture In Perspective
12, 13,14 &15
Directory of Illustration 16*
Member: American Society of Architectural Perspectivists

ROBERT ROTH

Roth's imaginative pictures
have a distinct charm. His
whimsical line, paired with
a strong sense of design,
create a visual treat.

-THE NEW YORK TIMES

Robert's work has appeared
in fortune 500 literature, national
advertising, major magazines,
and publishers. He has received
many distinguished honors
including 4 Awards from
the Society of Illustrators.

American Express

represented by

t 401.245.1426 **f** 401.245.1459   **e** robertroth@earthlink.net

dear friend

HarperCollins

mine's light... no sugar

Ms. Powell's unique whimsical style has graced the pages of books, magazines,and fortune 500 companies.

represented by

t 401.245.1426   **f** 401.245.1459   **e** robertroth@earthlink.net

Roth
& CO

SCOTT POLLACK
TEL (516) 921-1908
www.scottpollack.com

CARLOTTA A. TORMEY
The Illustration Station
819 Grosvenor Place
Oakland, CA 94610
TEL (510) 451-3423
FAX (510) 451-2133
e-mail: cis819@pacbell.net

Clients include: Prentice Hall Regents, McGraw Hill, Grolier Inc., and Pearson Education. Mattels Barbie, Storybook Heirloom and Global Friends Dolls. Age Wave, Mature Living and UCSF Magazines. E&J Gallo, Fetzer and Buena Vista Wineries. Lindt and

Sprungli Inc. and Joseph Schmidt fine chocolates. Marcel Schurman, Paper Magic Group and Portal Publications.

Member Graphic Artists Guild and San Francisco Society of Illustrators

Additional work can be seen in The Directory of Illustration #10, 13 and 14 and CA Image 95

ILLUSTRATION

Les Misérables

RICHARD ELMER
504 East 11th Street
New York, NY 10009
TEL (212) 598-4024
FAX (212) 473-1655
e-mail: R2elmer@worldnet.att.net

DONNA PERRONE
I L L U S T R A T I O N
53 Second Avenue #4A
New York, NY 10003
212 254 9453

See more of my Illustrations-
Directory of Illustration 16, 15, 14
Stock Illustration Source- Volume 7
Portfolio Website- www.dirill.com

SCOTT NELSON
TEL (508) 865-5045

Scott Nelson & Son   22 Rayburn Drive • Millbury, Massachusetts 01527 • 508/865-5045
E-mail: NelsonandSon@Juno.com • http://homestead.juno.com/nelsonandson/files/index.html

DICK BOBNICK

3412 Barbara Lane · Burnsville, Minnesota 55337 · 952·890·7833

Websites: www.theispot.com/artist/bobnick and www.bobnick.com

DEREK DENNETT

ph. 403.541.0877

fx. 403.541.0880

CLIENTS

Harcourt

McGraw-Hill

MTV's Nickelodeon

Oxford University Press

National Wildlife Federation

Save the Children

Scholastic, Inc.

Silver Burdett Ginn

Sony

ELISE MILLS
ILLUSTRATOR

•

FOUR
BLOOMER ROAD
NORTH SALEM,
NEW YORK
10560
PHONE / FAX
914-669-5948

LUDMILLA TOMOVA
623 West 170th Street, Apt. 3B
NYC, NY 10032
TEL (212) 740-5447
FAX (212) 928-9724
e-mail: TOMOVA@EROLS.COM
WWW.ARTOMOVA.COM

VINCE NATALE ART & ILLUSTRATION
P.O. Box 1353
Woodstock, NY 12498
TEL (914) 679-0354
FAX (914) 679-0257

Clients: Lots of different ones;
Lots of the same ones.

Awards: Not as many as clients,
but a few.

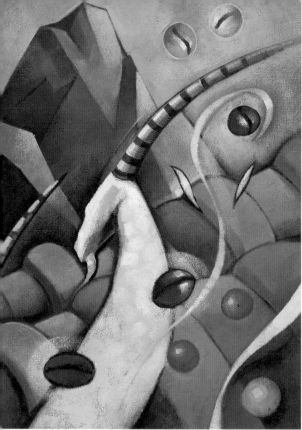

Renata Liwska

tel 403 209 5881

472

THOMAS OLBINSKI
187 East 4th Street, #5J
New York, NY 10009
TEL/FAX (212) 982-7582

CLIENTS INCLUDE:
The American Healthcare Association,
Bill Communications, Buick, Cahners
Publishing, Chicago Tribune, CMP
Publications, Inc., COOP Adriatica,
Coopers & Lybrant, Curant Communi-
cations, Dell, Fidelity Investments,
Met Life, Oxford University Press,

Shoe Carnival, The New York Times,
Time, University of Notre Dame,
The Wall Street Journal

MITCH RIDDER
RIDDER ILLUSTRATION
949 494 6457

P.O. BOX 4673 LAGUNA BEACH CA 92652

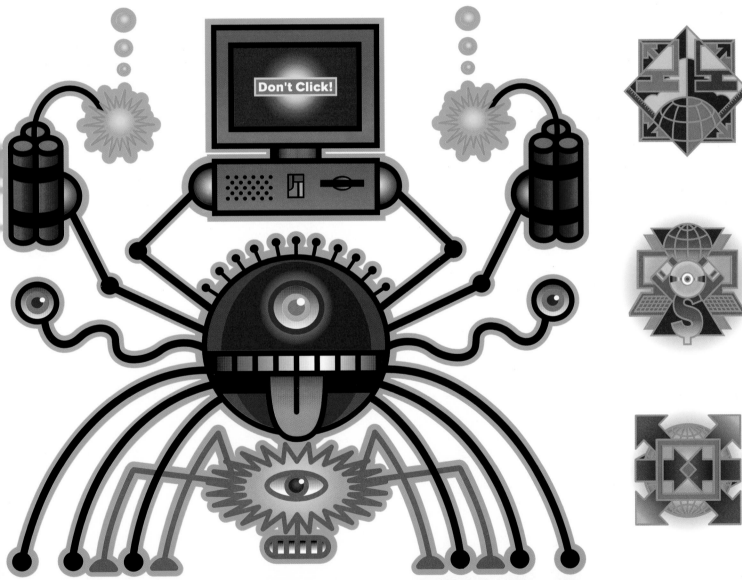

Don't Click!

JACK TOM DESIGN STUDIO ART · TO · GO

3 5
A Z Y
R O O K
L O A D

MONROE
CONNECTICUT
0 6 4 6 8

203

452-0889

e · Mail : art2go @ javanet . com

braszka@earthlink.net
www.altpick.com/brianraszka
www.brianraszka.com

BRIAN RASZKA

775.624.6145

stay healthy
first time teacher magazine/black fish design

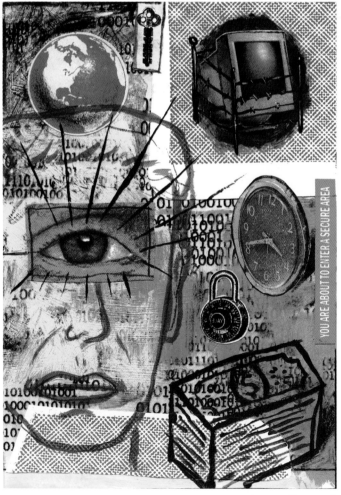

get security smart
information week magazine

the hired stomach
seattle magazine

braszka@earthlink.net
www.altpick.com/brianraszka
www.brianraszka.com

BRIAN RASZKA

775.624.6145

thepavement.com brochure
j walter thompson-agency

howard johnson's 75th anniversary brochure
christy macdougall mitchell-agency

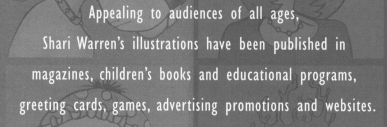

Joseph Kelter

JOSEPH KELTER ■ 4 VILLAGE ROW-LOGAN SQUARE ■ NEW HOPE ■ PA 18938
TEL 215.862.4860 ■ FAX 215.862.4861 ■ EMAIL:JOSEPH@KELTER.COM ■ WEB:WWW.KELTER.COM

☎ 773-264-1152

FAX 773-264-0916

480

Norm Lanting

36 Crosthwaite Avenue North
Hamilton Ontario
Canada L8H 4T9
905.549.1929
cfyi@icom.ca

Advertising,

Book and

Editorial

Illustration

May The Force Be With You!

DaRyLL CoLLiNS
HuMoRouS iLLuSTRaTioN

darylla1c@aol.com

PHoNe: 513-683-9335

FaX: 513-683-9345

FIONA KING

BOX 232722 ENCINITAS CA 92023
442 OR 760 942 1121 / 888 522 3745

Music CD Cover, **Rounder Records**

Trade Show Display, **Bright.net Internet**

Promotional comic book, **Bright.net Internet**

Training comic book, **Progressive Insurance**

Don Simpson, 1605 Harewood Square, Wexford PA 15090
Phone: 724 940-4175 • Cell: 724 312-6439
fiasco@MEGATONMAN.com • www.MEGATONMAN.com

**CHARLES BEYL
ILLUSTRATION**
TEL (717) 285-2905
FAX (717) 285-9572
e-mail: cbillus@redrose.net

Original, humorous illustrations for
editorial, publishing, advertising and
interactive media clients.

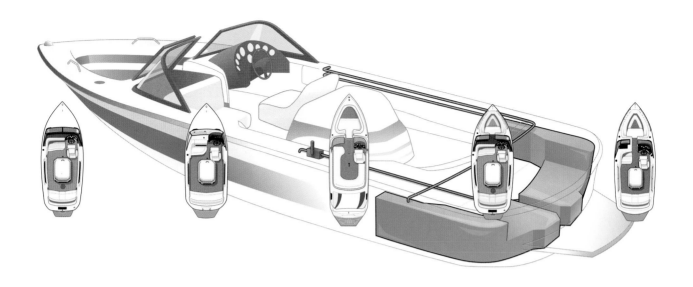

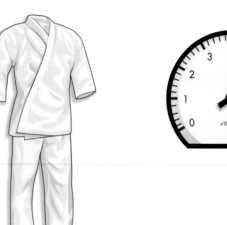

david
herrick

407~999~9955
davidherrick.com

Debbie Drechsler
ILLUSTRATION
605 Wright Street
Santa Rosa CA 95404
707.579.2548
debbie@debdrex.com

See my complete portfolio at www.debdrex.com

EDITH BINGHAM
Cut Paper Designs

831-636-8397

1999 E.Bingham

LAURIE A. CONLEY
6223 Bright Plume
Columbia, MD 21044
TEL (410) 730-8619
FAX (410) 730-8394
e-mail: lconley1@home.com

Thoughtful illustrations in conté, pastel and charcoal pencil.

See *Directory of Illustration #14, #15* and *CA Illustration Annual 1991* for additional work.

ANDREW SHIFF

tel: 508-435-3607

fax: 508-435-5625

azshiffnco@aol.com

153 Clinton Street
Hopkinton, MA 01748

ANDREW SHIFF

too, with a little help from my Mac

SOMETIMES YOU JUST GOTTA GET YOUR HANDS ON A FUNNY PICTURE OR TWO.

HAPPILY, THE SOLUTION IS JUST A PHONE CALL AWAY.

WHO KNOWS? YOU MIGHT EVEN WIN A FANCY AWARD!!

WHY NOT CALL UNCLE MIKE? HE'LL GET IN TOUCH WITH YOU AS SOON AS HE FINISHES HIS FREE LANCE.

BARBARA TRIFLETTI
P.O. Box 9614
South Lake Tahoe, CA 96158
TEL/FAX (530) 573-1964
e-mail: btrifletti@aol.com

Successful Art Director/Designer
for various manufacturers.
Includes: Universal Studios,
Gloria Vanderbilt, Cannon Mills.

Representation:
ArtVisions/Neil Miller
12117 SE 26th St., Suite 202
Bellevue, WA 98005-4118
TEL (425) 746-2201
FAX (877) 208-8719
e-mail: neilm@artvisions.com
Web: www.artvisions.com

Ken Stetz

"Across the Estuary" Highlights for Children magazine, January, 2000 - awarded *"Best of Issue"*

"First Men on the Moon" Cricket Magazine, July, 1999

Ken Stetz
Advertising, Editorial, & Book Illustration
Neptune, NJ • Studio Phone: **(732) 775-1915** • Studio Fax: **(732) 775-5284**

BILL FIRESTONE
4810 Bradford Drive
Annandale, Virginia 22003
TEL (703) 354-0247
FAX (703) 354-0346
e-mail: firestone@radix.net

Clients Include:
National Trust for Historic Preservation,
Freddie Mac, Recorded Books, Inc.,
American Horticultural Society, The
American Red Cross, Loyola College in
Maryland, *Chesapeake Magazine*, *Log
Home Living*, *Fine Woodworking*.

Additional work can be seen in:
Directory of Illustration #11, 13
Workbook 18
American Showcase 21

Award-winning illustrator. Call for
complete portfolio.

JAMES LINDQUIST
1435 1st Street
Port Townsend, WA 98368
TEL/FAX (360) 385-5327

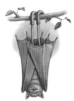

BARBARA SPURLL PHONE 1·800·989·3123 OR 416·594·6594

499

Showcase 19 - 24, Workbook 22 & 23, Society of Illustrators 40 - Call for fax, email, web site, portfolio, samples.

LEE CHRISTIANSEN
TEL (406) 446-2284

LEE CHRISTIANSEN
TEL (406) 446-2284

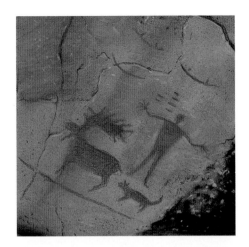

BRENDA SEXTON

the
DV
Guys

FOR ADDITIONAL ARTWORK:

DIRECTORY OF ILLUSTRATION 16
WWW.NEWSHOESDESIGN.COM

new Shoes
D E S I G N

5027 Greenbush Avenue
Sherman Oaks, CA 91423

☎ 818 995 8140
▤ 818 907 6795

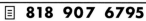

CELESTE JUNE HENRIQUEZ
310 NE 45th Street, Studio 6
Seattle, WA 98105
TEL (206) 547-8384
FAX (206) 547-8166
illustrations@celestehenriquez.com
www.celestehenriquez.com

Editorial, book, and educational
illustration.
Traditional drawing and
painting media.

See Directory of Illustration #16
for additional work.

Member: Graphic Artists Guild
Society of Children's Book
Writers and Illustrators

MILT CHUN
4946-4 Kilauea Avenue
Honolulu, HI 96816
TEL (808) 735-6436
FAX (808) 732-7405
e-mail: unclmilt@hula.net
miltchun@netscape.net

Illustration for print and the Web.

For additional work see the Directory of
Illustration #15, #16 and Milt's web
site at http://www.hula.net/~unclmilt

JENNY JAMES
P.O. Box 8383
San Jose, CA 95155-8383
TEL (408) 291-0509
FAX (408) 291-0595
www.jennyjames.com

KEVIN SPEAR
716 Imy Lane
Anderson, IN 46013
TEL (765) 640-8892
e-mail: Kevispear@aol.com
http://members.aol.com/kevispear

DICK PALULIAN

203 • 938 • 4831
VOICE & FAX

48A SIDE CUT ROAD   WEST REDDING, CT   06896

**CHAZ CHAPMAN
ILLUSTRATIONS INC.**
9929 SE Lincoln St.
Portland, OR 97216
TEL (503) 261-0871
FAX (503) 256-0027
e-mail: chaz@chazchapman.com

Clientele includes:
Sports Illustrated for Kids,
Saturday Evening Post,
Recycled Greeting Cards,
Medical Economics,
Infospace, Wegotcards.com,
Multnomah Publishing

For additional work and portfolio
Visit www.chazchapman.com

Chaz Chapman Illustrations Inc.
503-281-0871 email: chaz@chazchapman.com
portfolio: www.chazchapman.com

ADONIS, an accomplished young gentleman of undeniably good family, whose name, by the way, is Marble, and who, to avoid serious complications, is obliged during the action of the piece to assume disguises.

ALISON DeLANCEY
150 Browns Rd.
Williams, OR 97544
TEL (541) 955-5622

John Gerber

952.887.5169
john@mouseparty.com
www.mouseparty.com

Clients include:
Lawson Software
3M
Imation
Snap.com
Dow
Liberty Paper
Arctic Cat
Dairy Queen
Amport Foods
General Mills
Price Waterhouse Coopers
MTV

KRISTINE REAM
616 Dewalt Dr.
Pittsburgh, PA 15234-2430
TEL (412) 531-9487
e-mail: kream11@aol.com

Serving up bold, bright colorful illustrations for editorial, publishing or advertising clients.

Please see additional work in Directory of Illustration 16.

Clients include: Rodale Press, Weight Watchers, Macy's, Awards.com, Tyson Foods, Hudson Foods, Baker & Taylor Books, Sussex Publishers, Prevention Magazine, Jim Henson Productions, Runner's World Magazine, Vegetarian Times, Scholastic, Inc., Yoga Journal

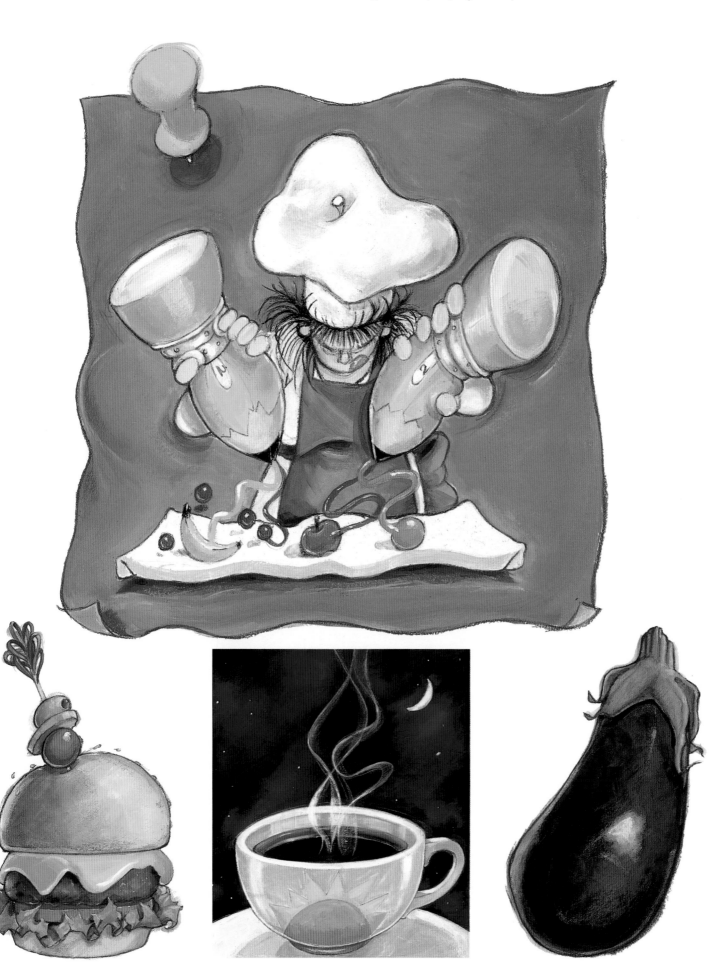

TAD HERR
STEPHAN AND HERR
141 West Market Street
Marietta, PA 17547
TEL (717) 426-2939
FAX (717) 426-3005
e-mail: stepherr@desupernet.net

See Directory of Illustration #16 for
additional work.

TERRY PACZKO
1836 Euclid Avenue
Cleveland Ohio 44115
TEL/FAX (216) 621-5840

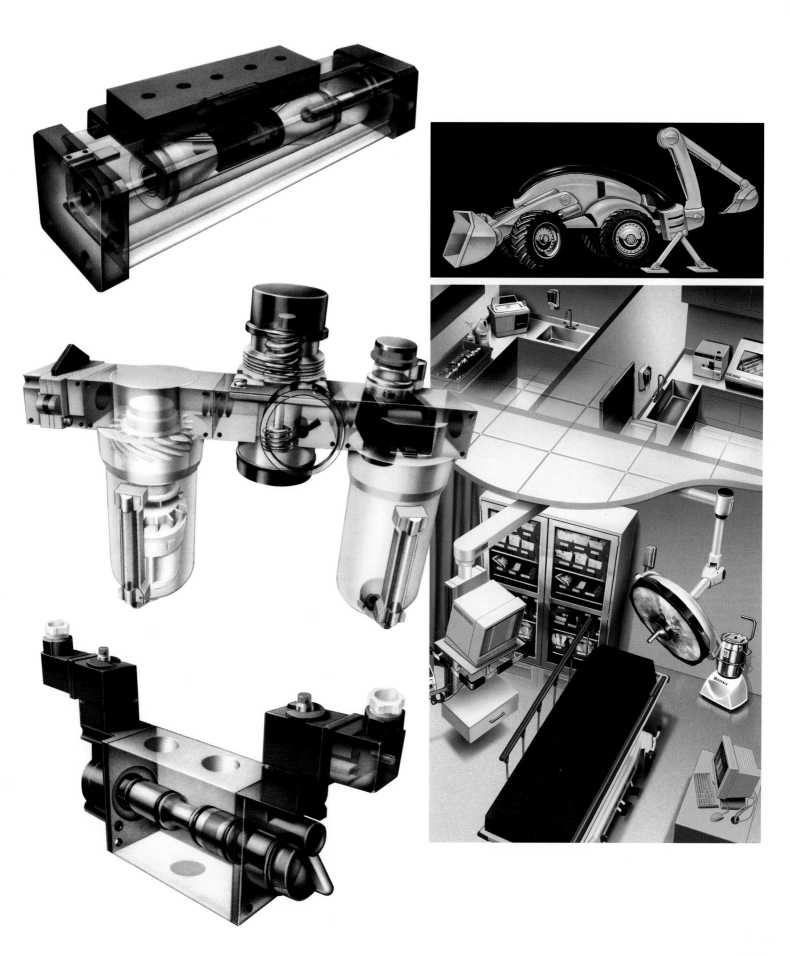

Sarah Hollander

1102 Tuckahoe Lane
Alexandria, Virginia 22302
T 703-548-0959   F 703-548-5506
E sarah-hollander@home.com
see Portfolio: www.dirill.com

Sarah Hollander

1102 Tuckahoe Lane
Alexandria, Virginia 22302
T 703-548-0959   F 703-548-5506
E sarah-hollander@home.com
see Portfolio: www.dirill.com

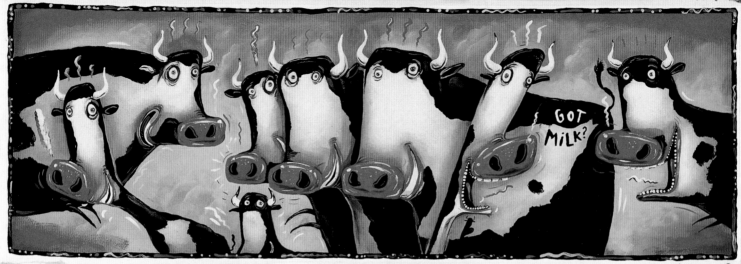

www.ricksealock.com

fax phone

FOR ← ILLUSTRATION

403 276 5428

"see the site"

"pack a lunch"

HOWDY

MAIL ME FOR MORE INFO OR PROMOS

NAOMI SHEA
35 Hyde Hill Rd.
Williamsburg, MA 01096
TEL (413) 268-3407
FAX (413) 268-3407
e-mail: naomi@naomishea.com
www.naomishea.com

SHANE HARR
633 Hawthorne #D
Houston, Texas 77006
TEL (713) 446-4478
FAX (713) 862-4827
e-mail: mail@shaneharr.com

Clientele includes:
Exxon, Shell, Toshiba, Igloo,
Houston Zoo, Specialized Bicycles,
Compaq Computer Corp., Lockheed,
Herman Hospital, Houston Lighting &
Power, Cameron, Foley's, Conoco

View portfolio at: www.shaneharr.com

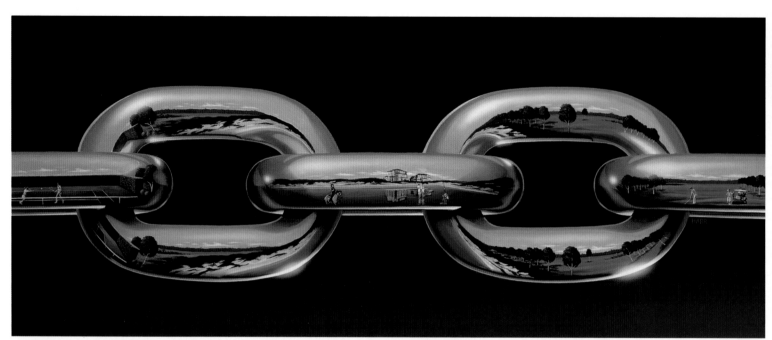

**LISA RAUCHWERGER
CUTTING EDGE
CREATIONS**
TEL Toll-Free: (877) 321-7925
Fax available
e-mail: Rauchie@aol.com

Specializing in bedazzled dragons, funky fish and other whimsical paper sculpture and cartoon illustration. More serious, symbolic papercut and calligraphic creations also available.

Member: Society of Children's Book Writers & Illustrators, American Guild of Judaic Art.

Author and illustrator of *Chocolate Chip Challah and Other Twists on the Jewish Holiday Table*. Please see Directory of Illustration 9 & 16 for more samples of my work.

Don Sullivan **720-851-1997** Fax 720-851-1998

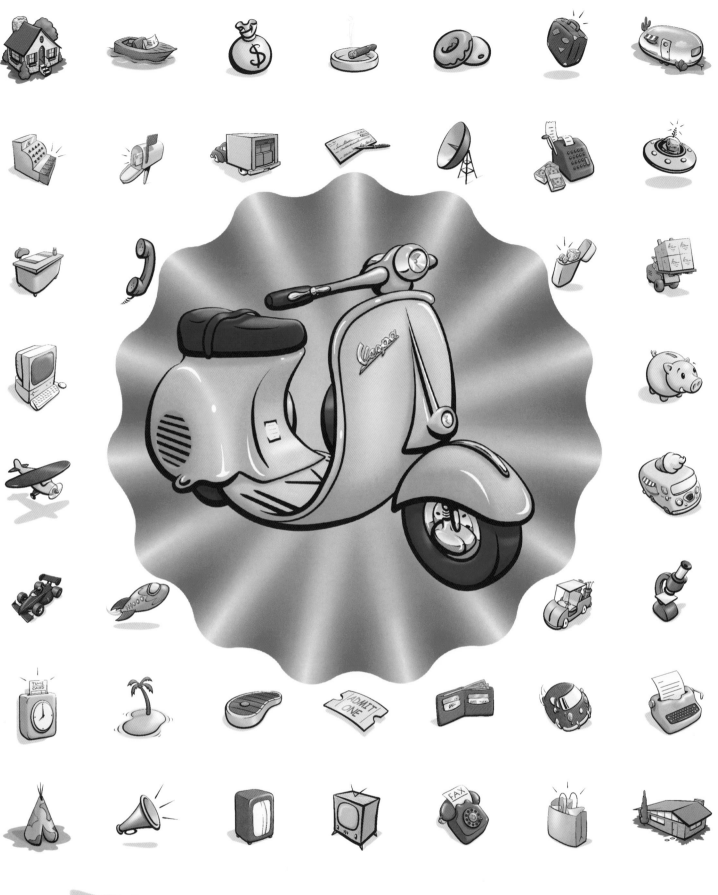

Robert L. Prince

972-491-6779
phone and fax

visit www.robertlprince.com

Robert Winn Pitt

tel: 877-407-8906

fax: 404-378-1021

pittwinn@mindspring.com

http://www.pittwinn.com

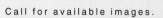
Call for available images.

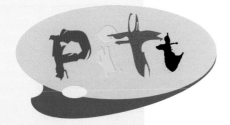

Bob Pitt

tel: 877-407-8906

fax: 404-378-1021

pittwinn@mindspring.com

http://:www.pittwinn.com

stock available.

**JEFF SADOWSKI
ILLUSTRATION**
TEL (650) 508-0873
FAX (650) 610-0643
e-mail: jsadowski2@aol.com
www.vabiz.com/jeffsadowski

527

KERSTI WELLS
W148 N7058 Terriwood Dr.
Menomonee Falls, WI 53051
TEL (262) 250-7623
FAX (262) 250-7635
www.kersti.net

Clients include:
Avon, Bronx Zoo, Doris Day Animal League, Great Train Stores, Henry Ford Museum & Edison Institute, Humane Society of the United States, Jackson & Perkins, Jefferson National Expansion Historical Assoc. (St. Louis Arch), Kennedy Space Center, Ronald McDonald House.

Lighthearted watercolor illustrations for textiles, stationery, paper products, apparel, gifts & books.

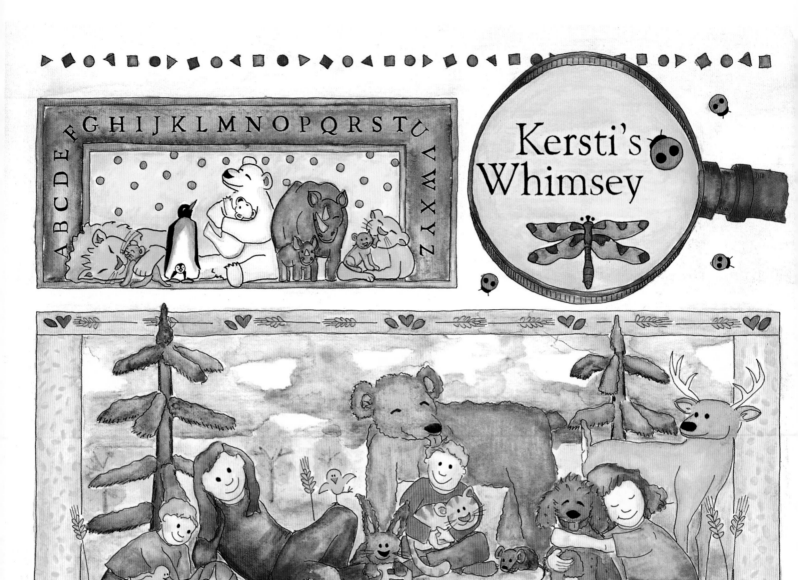

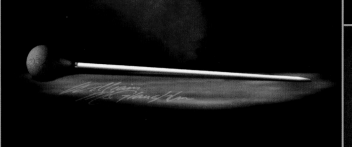

**HOLT ILLUSTRATION/
GRAPHICS**
207 51st Street
Western Springs, IL 60558
TEL (708) 784-9458
FAX (708) 784-9458
e-mail: sdholt@interaccess.com

autumnal equinox

TOM R. ICKERT
354 East 83rd Street
Suite #5-A
New York, NY 10028
TEL (212) 794-9723
E-mail: tickert@nyc.rr.com

Clients:
Xerox, Crayola, IBM, New York Life,
NBC, Amtrak, NYC Department of
Parks, Cambridge University Press,
Princeton University Press, Computer-
land, *Inside Sports*, *Scholastic* Maga-
zines, MacMillan, *Instructor*, Harcourt
Brace Jovanovich

Amy J. Price • 616-459-7595
amyjprice@aol.com • members.aol.com/amyjprice

matt manley . 616-459-7595 . fax 616-458-6255 . mattmanley@aol.com
oil paintings in a digital environment

BRENT WATKINSON
TEL/FAX (913) 677-0062
www.illustrate.com/brent

Clientele includes:
American Express
Avon Books
Cook's Illustrated
Federal Reserve Bank
Lipton Foods

NASA
MGM/United Artists
Putnam Publishing
Time-Warner
Sony Music

**MARK E. WALKER
ILLUSTRATION**
3840 Arroyo Rd.
Fort Worth, TX 76109
TEL (817) 920-9430
FAX (817) 924-8905
www.contact-me.net/MarkEvanWalker

For additional styles see
Directory of Illustration 14,16,
and Black Book 2000.

Clients Include: Dell Magazines, Pier 1
Imports, Half-Price Books, Shell-Tone
Publications, The Lord Group, Riccelli
Creative, *Gas Daily's NG, The Mystery
Review.*

Humorous and serious traditional
illustration for books, editorial, comics,
advertising, comps, and storyboards.

Member of the Dallas Society of
Illustrators

LAURIE LEOF
PMB 709, 300 Queen Anne Ave. N
Seattle, WA 98109
TEL (888) 782-6263
e-mail: thebestlaurie@hotmail.com

RICH NELSON

248-545-5242

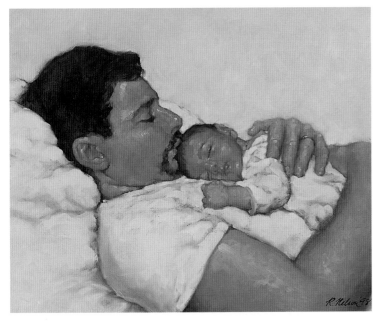

DAVID SCOTT MEIER ILLUSTRATION

17398 E. Dolphin Street
Sugarloaf, FL 33042
TEL/FAX (305) 745-8835

Pictured below: assorted collage elements of things Greek.
Client: Harcourt School Publishers.
Art Direction: Stephen Wirt.

Fast turn around time.
Meier's patterned work has pleased the art directors of numerous publications and has been used for gift wrap and stationery design; editorial and entertainment spot illustration; juvenile picture books and mural design. See previous numbers of this publication

for further examples of paint on paper.

Clientele includes: American Medical News; Atlantic Monthly; Big Blue Dot; Essence; Houghton Mifflin Co.; Ligature; McGraw-Hill: Marcel Schurman; Simon and Schuster

JOHN T. QUINN
20327 Cedar Creek Street
Canyon County, CA 91351
TEL/FAX (661) 298-2029

eric yang digital illustrations

phone: 714-969-5314   fax: 714-969-5304   e-mail: etyang@pacbell.net
http://www.eric-yang.com

eric yang digital illustrations

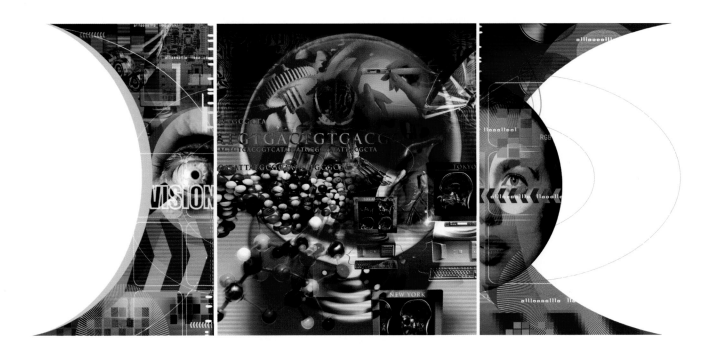

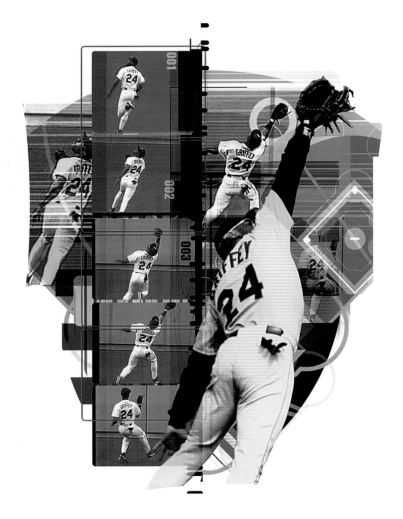

phone: 714-969-5314   fax: 714-969-5304   e-mail: etyang@pacbell.net
http://www.eric-yang.com

Eric James Spencer

860 429 8882

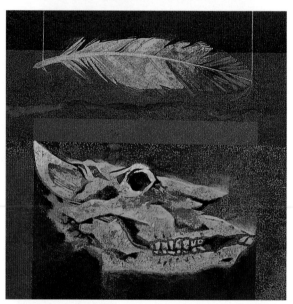

41 Atwoodville Road Mansfield Center Connecticut 06250

ANN STEPHENSON
RED FOX DESIGN
P.O. Box 142
Mecklenburg, New York 14863
TEL (607) 387-5209
FAX (607) 387-3122
e-mail: apsart@clarityconnect.com

Portfolio online:
www.apsart.clarityconnect.com

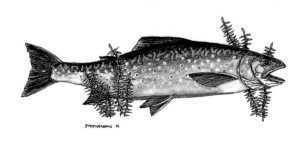

FOXGRAPES

543

**JOHN HAYS
ILLUSTRATION**
5510 Glenallen Street
Springfield, VA 22151
TEL/FAX: (703) 941-6961
e-mail: ajhays@pressroom.com

Clientele includes: Army Times,
Air Force Times, Navy Times,
Marine Times, Military Market

Member: Graphic Artists Guild

Specializing in: Electronic Illustration,
Pen & Ink, Charts & Maps, Editorial

See online portfolio at:
http://www.pressroom.com/jah-net/art

DAVe EMBER
BEND OREGON
541.383.2110
dember @ aol.com

DENNIS BALOGH
8183 Joyce Rd.
Broadview Hts., Ohio 44147
TEL (440) 546-9223
    (330) 996-3556

Clients include: Harcourt Brace
School Publishers, Medical Economics
Magazine, RN Magazine, Patient Care,
American Way Magazine, The Atlantic
Monthly, Guitar Player Magazine,
The Washington Times, RCI Premiere
Magazine, Arista Records

To view more of my work, see
Directory of Illustration 15 & 16
Portfolio on-line at www.dirill.com

SHARON LANE HOLM
6 North Forty Drive
New Fairfield, CT 06812
TEL/FAX (203) 746-3763

Client list includes:
Millbrook Press Inc.
School Zone Publishing
Playskool
Dutton
Houghton Mifflin
Macmillan Publishing
Harcourt Brace & Co.

Random House
Group Publishing
Grolier Publications
McClanahan Book Co.
Intervisual Books Inc.
Silver Burdett & Ginn
Family Life Magazine
Bon Appetit

Additional work:
Picture Book 1998, 1999, 2000

Member SCBWI

GEORGE MIDDLETON
P.O. Box 626
Carlisle, MA 01741
TEL/FAX (978) 371-1304

RICK LOVELL
2860 Lakewind Court
Alpharetta, GA 30005
TEL (770) 442-3943
FAX (770) 475-8321
e-mail: ricklovell@mindspring.com

To see more of my work, please visit
www.ricklovell.com

Represented in the New York area by
ArtWorks: (212) 627-1554

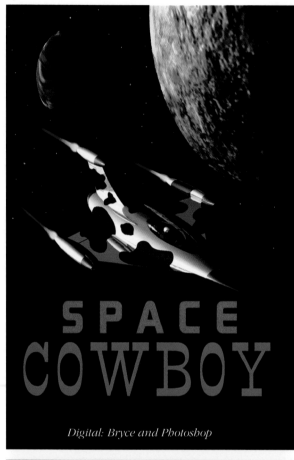

Digital: Bryce and Photoshop

Traditional Media

Digital: Painter and Photoshop

Digital: Painter and Photoshop

Traditional Media

Represented in New York by

Artists Representatives
212•627•1554
fax212•627•1719

Traditional Media

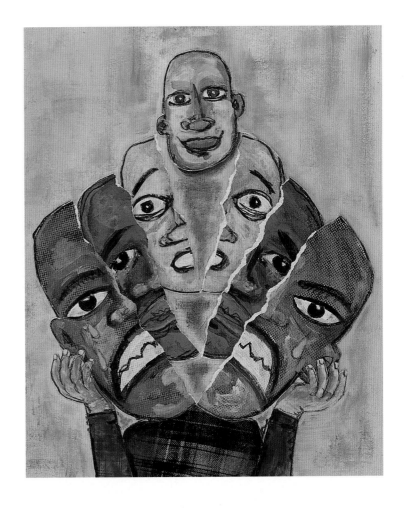

JAMES DONAHUE (718) 639-8867
STUDIOJFD@HOTMAIL.COM
WWW.MODERNANGEL.COM/DONAHUE

BOB SOULÉ
TEL (301) 598-8883
FAX (301) 598-5665
e-mail: bob@bobsoule.com
www.bobsoule.com

Twenty-two years of free-lance experience. Specializing in electronic illustration. Clients include: Giant Food, TIAA-CREF, AARP, US EPA, DOT, Dept. of Education, Council of Governments, IBG, Porter-Novelli, Hewlitt-Packard, Washington Opera Society, Arena Stage, *Washington Post*, World Bank, Peeking Duck, Modern Curriculum, and Harcourt-Brace.

Please visit my website for a complete portfolio and for stock sales: www.bobsoule.com. Illustration topics include animals, children, computers, corporate life, education, financial, and health for editorial, advertising, annual report, brochure, cd cover, chart, exhibit, and maps.

STEVEN LYONS STUDIO

stevenlyons.com

voice(415)459-7560   fax(415)453-8657

RON ZALME
Cartoonist/Illustrator
936 County Road 619
Newton, NJ 07860
TEL (973) 383-1392
FAX (973) 383-0821
e-mail: ronzalme@nac.net

CINDY YOST
60 Harborside Drive
Milford, CT 06460
TEL (203) 876-1577

JOSÉ PEÑA
TEL (408) 866-9456
e-mail: jrpena@pacbell.net

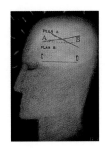

LAURENCE KNIGHTON

Digital
Illustration

larsky@cyberhighway.net
tel/fax: (208) 344-0335

**SCOTT W. PETTY/
BEE HIVE STUDIOS**
11991 Driftstone Drive
Fishers, IN 46038
TEL (317) 842-2412
e-mail: spetty@iei.net
www.scottpetty.com
Representation: Karen Lairamore

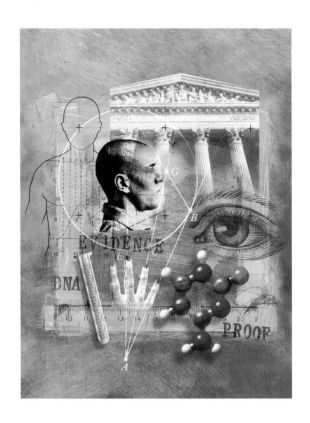

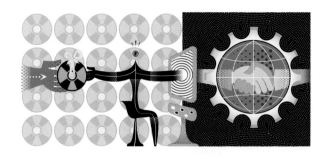

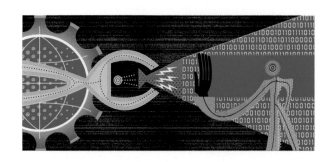

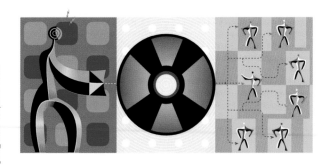

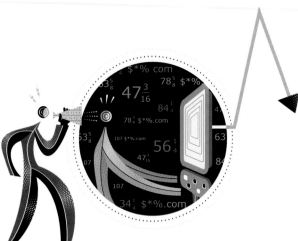

all images © 2000 Campbell Laird

212 219 3767

www.theispot.com/artist/claird

CARL WALKER
·····○ DIGITAL GRAPHIX ○·····
40 ELEVEN O'CLOCK ROAD · FAIRFIELD, CONNECTICUT 06430
TEL: 203·254-7989   FAX IN STUDIO

graze at the COW

MIKE TOFANELLI
9514 Village Tree Dr.
Elk Grove, CA 95758
TEL/FAX (916) 683-8224
e-mail: mtofanelli@jps.net

For additional work see:
Directory of Illustration 16
American Showcaase 20, 21, 22

564

M.E. Cohen's
SM**ART**ART

"Leave the thinking to us"

Heart surgery and its side affects. — **Forbes**

You call this easy living? Too little time. — **Newsday**

Putting the brakes on spending. — **American Management Association**

A PC picture that is better than HDTV. — **PC Magazine**

Phone
973-783-1171

Fax
973-783-2182

Mail
28 Aubrey Road
Upper Montclair, NJ 07043

E-mail
smartart@home.com

Web
www.theispot.com/
artist/mecohen

 Clients Pizza Hut, Time Warner, Walt Disney, AT&T, Andrews & McNeel, Ameritech, Gibson Greetings, Standard & Poors, Forbes, E.D.S., N.Y.Times, Nickelodeon, Barrons, Scholastic, Sesame Street, Wall Street Journal, U.S. News & World Report, Newsweek, Bell Atlantic, DDB Needham, Ogilvy & Mather, A.M.A., CNA Insurance, National Law Journal, Washington Post

DAVID BOND   ILLUSTRATOR   (1-800) 474-1964 acc.#02

AMY E. REICH
2658 Griffith Park Blvd., Ste. #424
Los Angeles, CA 90039
TEL/FAX (323) 664-1598
e-mail: ameow@earthlink.net
http://home.earthlink.net/~ameow

Specializing in children's art, textile design and editorial—especially travel, natural health and music as subjects. Also specializing in animation background color design. Clients include: Walt Disney Television Animation, Nickelodeon Animation, Cartoon Network, Universal Animation and Film Roman Inc. Gouache is my favorite medium. All paintings shown are painted with gouache.

Top: Book cover, back to front, for a book about children and homeopathic medicine.
Bottom/L–R: Spot for self-promo, illustration for a book, my personal web site illustration.

the
Lemon
DROP

Martini Bar

JUDGE COHEN
9402 Belfort Road
Richmond, VA 23229
TEL/FAX (804) 741-5061
e-mail: judcohen@erols.com
www.reuben.org/jcohen

See Directory of Illustration #16
for additional work

STEVE CARRANZA
1525 2nd Street
Manhattan Beach, CA 90266
TEL (310) 318-0194
FAX (310) 379-1954
e-mail: scarranza@earthlink.net

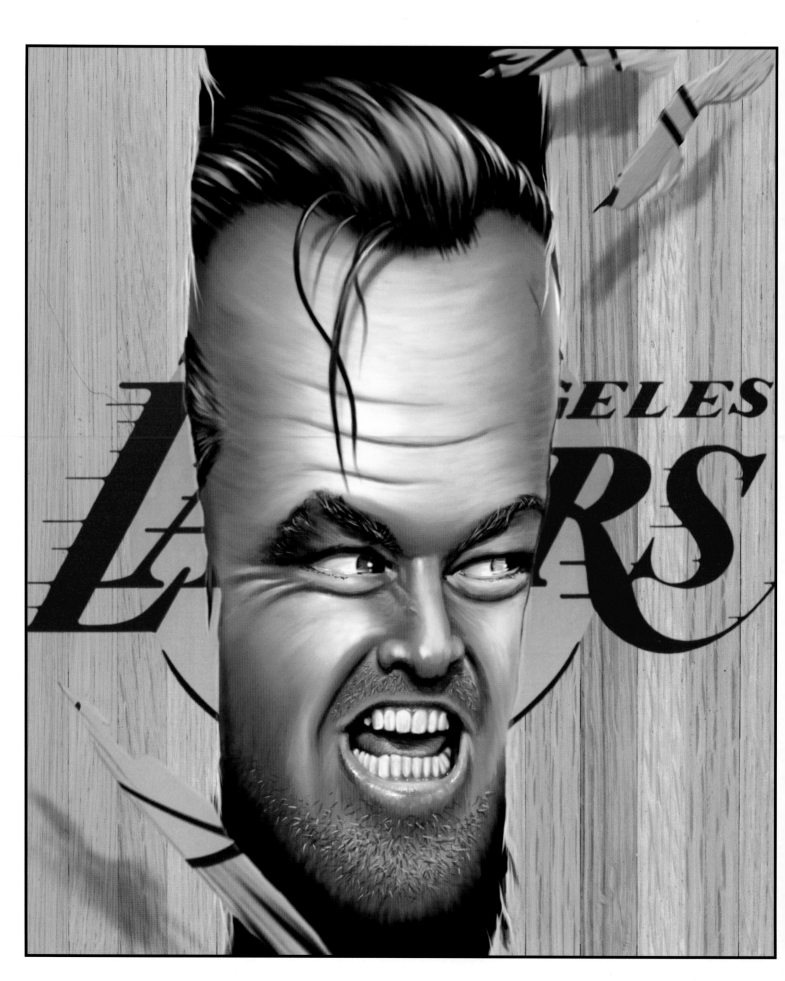

DOUG JONES
1408 Brenthaven Drive
Brentwood, TN 37027
TEL/FAX (615) 370-0212

KEN CONDON
126C Ashfield Mountain Road
Ashfield, MA 01330
TEL/FAX (413) 628-4042
e-mail: kenart@crocker.com
www.crocker.com/~kenart

KEN CONDON
126C Ashfield Mountain Road
Ashfield, MA 01330
TEL/FAX (413) 628-4042
e-mail: kenart@crocker.com
www.crocker.com/~kenart

**PETER BENNETT
ILLUSTRATION**
1340 El Prado Avenue #37
Torrance, CA 90501
TEL/FAX (310) 782-7801

Clients include: Sony Music Corp.,
Los Angeles Times, Forbes Global
Finance, American Airlines, Peterson
Publishing, Entrepreneur, Inc.,
Men's Health, Beyond Computing,
CMP Media, Mac World, Men's
Fitness, Shape, Atlantic Monthly,
Harcourt Brace Publishing,

Guitar Player, Publish, Windows NT,
Cio, Newsday

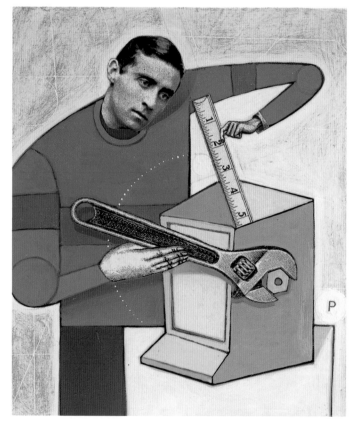

DAVID SCHULZ
409 Ridge Road
Middletown, CT 06457
TEL (860) 346-3541
FAX (860) 704-8341

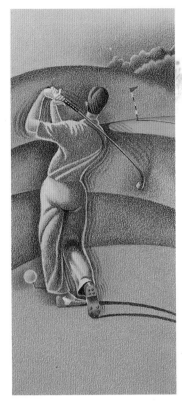

Project - Design 2-D and 3-D logos for an entertainment company.

Project -Illustrate a program cover for the New York City Centers "Great American Musicals" series .

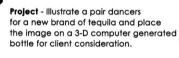

Project - Design a series of icons to be used on various surfaces for a company that makes tool belts and holders.

Project - Illustrate a series of employee portraits for a hi-tech company.

Project - Illustrate a pair dancers for a new brand of tequila and place the image on a 3-D computer generated bottle for client consideration.

Project - Replace the old "Rug Doctor" logo with a more modern, fresher one.

Project - Illustrate a series of "Funny Fruit" faces for a new brand of liqueur.

705
705 Pier Ave.
Hermosa Beach, CA

Project - Design a new, hip looking logo and neon sign for a nightclub.

BOB SCHUCHMAN

ILLUSTRATION and DESIGN

310-376-1448

ILLUSTRATION FOR THE FUTURE

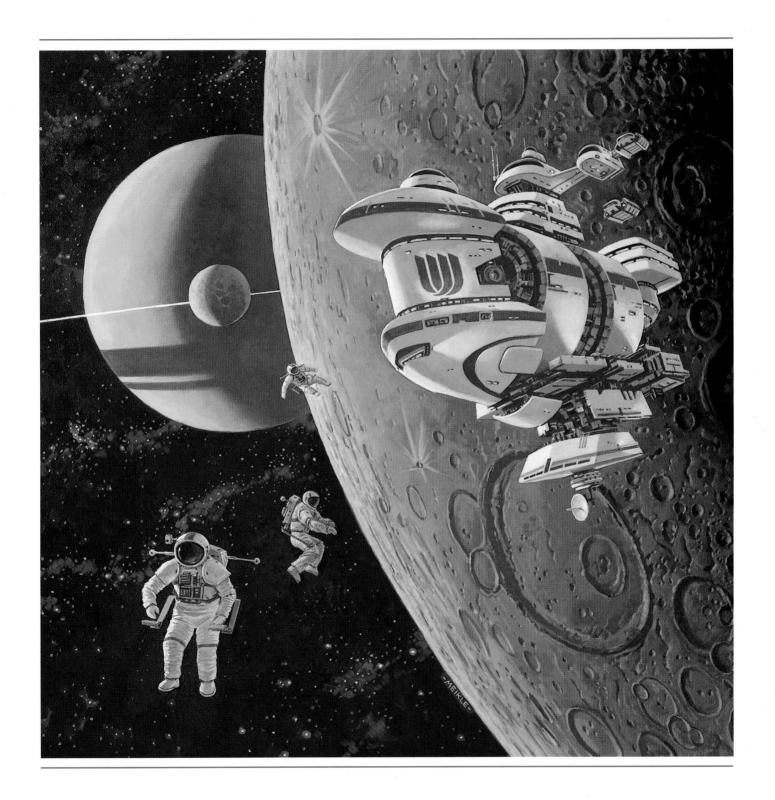

DAVID MEIKLE

STUDIO 801 585 6463 ▪ HOME 801 588 0713 ▪ FAX 801 585 6883

DEANN
RUBIN

45 Surrey Lane Sudbury MA
01776
978·579·5990 djstudio@flash.net

BEVERLY DOYLE
19547 Hill Drive
Morrison, CO 80465
TEL (303) 697-7936

JIM CONNELLY STUDIO
8964 Bosworth Dr.
Jenison, MI 49428
TEL (616) 457-1284
FAX (616) 667-1023
www.jimconnellystudio.com

JIM CONNELLY STUDIO
8964 Bosworth Dr.
Jenison, MI 49428
TEL (616) 457-1284
FAX (616) 667-1023
www.jimconnellystudio.com

CAROLzaLoom LINOCUT iLLUSTRATION
302 HIGH FALLS ROAD, SAUGERTIES, NEW YORK 12477 - 845-246-7441

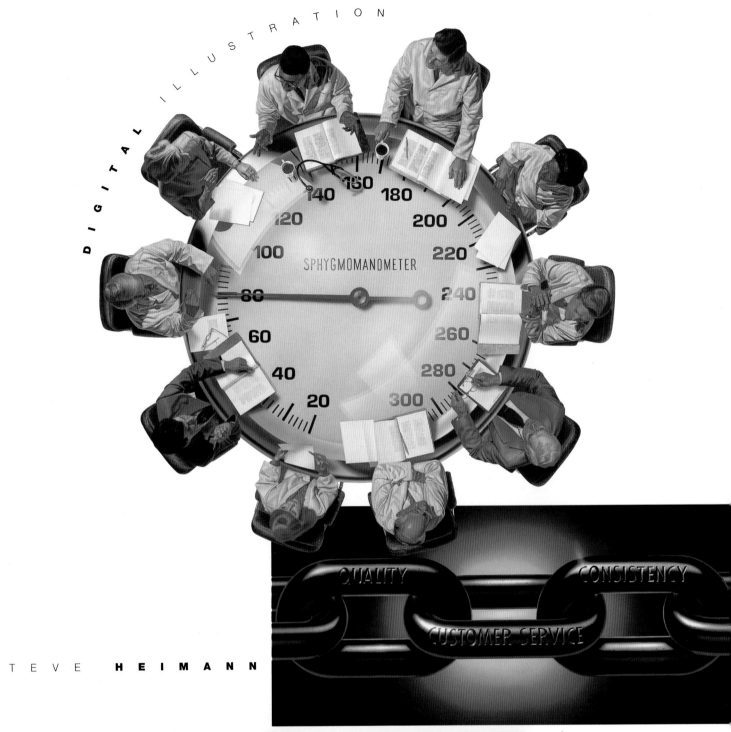

STEVE **HEIMANN**

201.797.5434

Melanie Hall
845·657·8242

www.dirill.com

HELEN E. ENDRES
2506 6th Street
Monroe, WI 53566
TEL (608) 328-4535
FAX (608) 328-4550
e-mail: endres7@utelco.tds.net

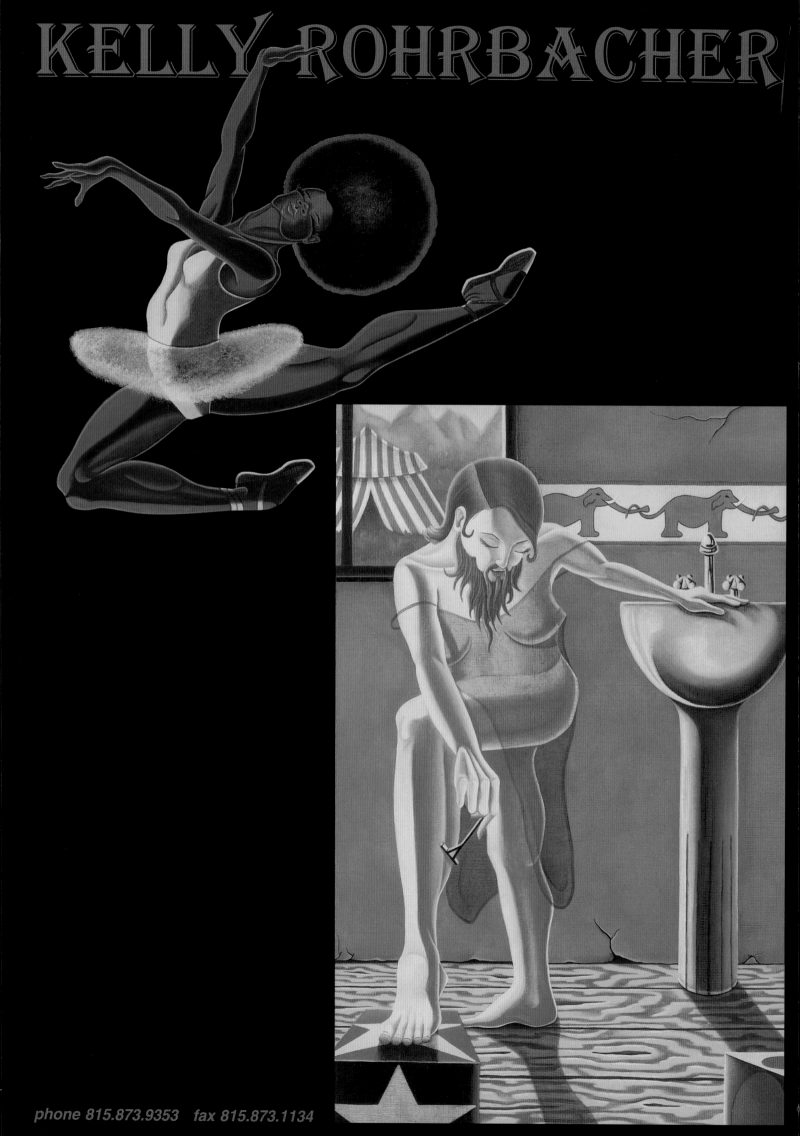

KELLY ROHRBACHER

phone 815.873.9353   fax 815.873.1134

BOT RODA
78 Victoria Lane
Lancaster, PA 17603
TEL (717) 393-1406
FAX (717) 393-4449
e-mail: botroda@redrose.net

ROD LITTLE • 712 10TH ST. N.E. WASHINGTON, D.C. 20002 • TEL•202•543•1180/FAX•202•547•5442

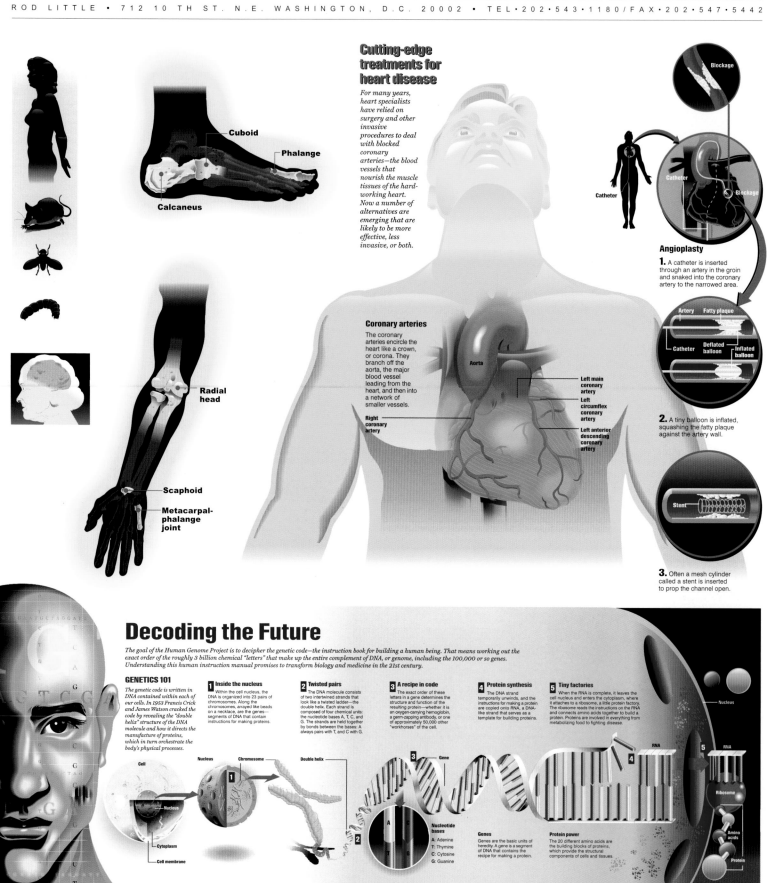

E-MAIL: info.ill@radix.net • COMPLETE PORTFOLIO AVAILABLE@WEBSITE:www.radix.net/~info.ill

ROD LITTLE • 712 10 TH ST. N.E. WASHINGTON, D.C. 20002 • TEL•202•543•1180/FAX•202•547•5442

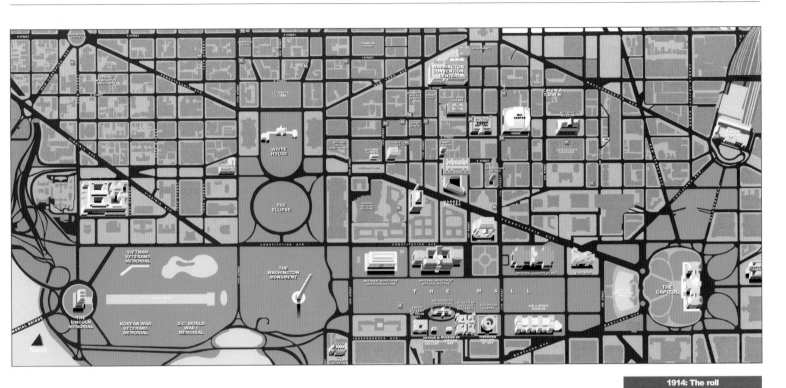

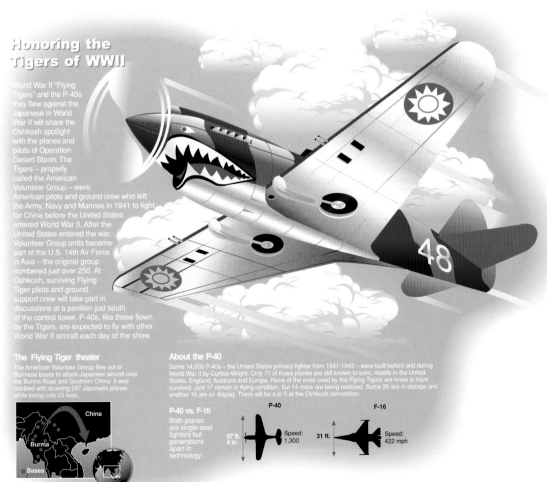

Honoring the Tigers of WWII

World War II "Flying Tigers" and the P-40s they flew against the Japanese in World War II will share the Oshkosh spotlight with the planes and pilots of Operation Desert Storm. The Tigers – properly called the American Volunteer Group – were American pilots and ground crew who left the Army, Navy and Marines in 1941 to fight for China before the United States entered World War II. After the United States entered the war, Volunteer Group units became part of the U.S. 14th Air Force in Asia – the original group numbered just over 250. At Oshkosh, surviving Flying Tiger pilots and ground support crew will take part in discussions at a pavilion just south of the control tower. P-40s, like those flown by the Tigers, are expected to fly with other World War II aircraft each day of the show.

The Flying Tiger theater

The American Volunteer Group flew out of Burmese bases to attack Japanese aircraft over the Burma Road and Southern China. It was credited with downing 297 Japanese planes while losing only 23 lives.

About the P-40

Some 14,000 P-40s – the United States primary fighter from 1941-1943 – were built before and during World War II by Curtiss-Wright. Only 71 of those planes are still known to exist, mostly in the United States, England, Australia and Europe. None of the ones used by the Flying Tigers are know to have survived. Just 17 remain in flying condition, but 14 more are being restored. Some 26 are in storage and another 16 are on display. There will be 4 or 5 at the Oshkosh convention.

P-40 vs. F-16

Both planes are single-seat fighters but generations apart in technology:

P-40
37 ft. 4 in.
Speed: 1,300

F-16
31 ft.
Speed: 422 mph

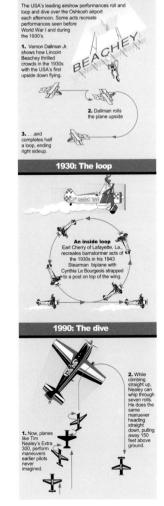

1914: The roll

The USA's leading airshow performances roll and loop and dive over the Oshkosh airport each afternoon. Some acts recreate performances seen before World War I and during the 1930's.

1. Vernon Dallman Jr. shows how Lincoln Beachey thrilled crowds in the 1930s with the USA's first upside down flying

2. Dallman rolls the plane upside

3. . . . and completes half a loop, ending right sideup.

1930: The loop

An inside loop
Earl Cherry of Lafayette, La., recreates barnstormer acts of the 1930s in his 1943 Stearman biplane with Cynthia Le Bourgeois strapped to a post on top of the wing.

1990: The dive

1. Now, planes like Tim Nealey's Extra 300, perform maneuvers earlier pilots never imagined.

2. While climbing straight up, Nealey can whip through seven rolls. He does the same manuever heading straight down, pulling away 150 feet above ground.

E-MAIL: info.ill@radix.net • COMPLETE PORTFOLIO AVAILABLE@WEBSITE:www.radix.net/~info.ill

N.C. ARNOLD
1610 Bridges Drive
High Point, NC 27262
TEL (336) 887-8383
FAX (336) 889-8585
e-mail: Nicole@cncartwork.com
www.cncartwork.com

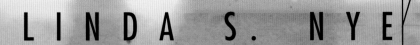

Seid Ramazan

718-261-7243

COREY PANDOLPH ILLUSTRATION

207-773-1003

WWW.CPANTOON.COM

GREGORY T. NELSON
1525 Parkway Street
Dubuque, IA 52001
TEL (319) 582-1573
FAX (419) 828-3206
e-mail: gtn-illustration@excite.com

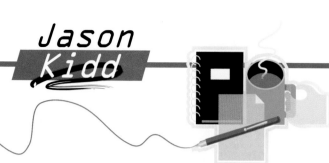

Jason Kidd

1-800-466-4060   Fax:(650) 355-8051   www.j2morrow.com

Tom Morrow

JT Morrow

1-800-466-4060   Fax:(650) 355-8051   www.j2morrow.com

Jesse Sparks

Shakespeare in Hollywood

SCENE 1   TAKE 2

DAVID FeBLAND
670 West End Avenue Suite 11-B
New York, NY 10025
TEL: (212) 580-9299
FAX: (212) 580-3030
e-mail: dfebland@aol.com

CHARLES PEALE

Telephone: 804-293-3394

Fax: 804-293-9406

MARILYN JANOVITZ
41 Union Square West #920
New York, NY 10003
TEL (212) 727-8330
FAX (212) 627-2524
e-mail: mjanovitz@aol.com

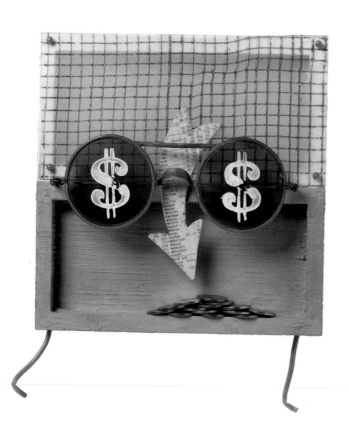

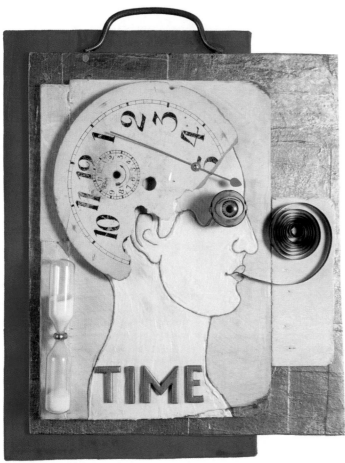

JERRY GONZALEZ

PHONE/FAX
(718) 204-8762

DIGITAL ILLUSTRATION

GPL ILLUSTRATION
39 Fraser Drive
Salem, NH 03079
TEL (781) 608-0664
FAX (603) 894-5190
e-mail: orr4Fan@aol.com

STEVE MCAFEE

770-925-2481 ■ WWW.STEVEMCAFEE.COM ■ 1-800-484-8329 EXT:1276

STEVE MCAFEE

770-925-2481 ■ WWW.STEVEMCAFEE.COM ■ 1-800-484-8329 EXT:1276

KATE McKEON
1516 Deerhaven Drive
Crystal Lake, IL 60014
TEL/FAX (815) 477-8518
e-mail: mkmckeon@mc.net

CHUCK MACKEY
167 Fells Ave.
Medford, MA 02155
TEL (781) 395-8693
e-mail: cwmackey@mindspring.com
http://cwmackey.home.mindspring.
  com/chuckmackey.html

Clients include:
Reebok
Inc. Magazine
Cahners

See Directory of Illustration #16
for additional work
Stock images available or
call for portfolio

KIM FRALEY Illustration

PRODUCTS

EDITORIAL

PEOPLE
(and other animals on the planet)

To see more samples, please
see Directory of Illustration
Volumes 14, 15, & 16

KIM FRALEY

(760) 735-8818
Voice and Fax

Kim Fraley 9107 Mt. Israel Road, Escondido, CA 92029

MARY O'KEEFE YOUNG
62 Midchester Avenue
White Plains, NY 10606
TEL (914) 949-0147
FAX (914) 949-3781
email: mokyoung@aol.corn

Clients include:
Abbott Labs, Atheneum Books, American Way Magazine, Better Homes and Gardens, Carolrhoda Books, Contemporary Pediatrics, C.R. Gibson, Charlesbridge Publishers, Estee Lauder, Harcourt Brace Jovanovich, Health Communications, Ideals Publications, Jewishlights, Marshall Cavendish, Mature Living Magazine, The New York Times, Random House, Reader's Digest, Scholastic, Silver Burdett & Ginn, Simon & Schuster, Sovereign Media, Treasure Bay, Upside Magazine.

For additional work see:

American Showcase #19, 20
Directory of Illustration #14–17
Picturebook 97, 98, 99

Online Portfolio updated monthly
www.maryokeefeyoung.com

609

Carl Wiens

613-476-2500

Illustrations that Work

carlwiens.com

D A V I D

G R O F F

740 · 363 · 2131

e· GROFFILINC@aol.com   w· illustrator's.org

BUCK JONES
HUMOROUS ILLUSTRATOR
4313 65th Street
Des Moines, IA 50322
TEL/FAX (515) 278-0379
e-mail: buckyjones@earthlink.net
www.reuben.org/buckjones

See Picturebook 2K page 282
for additional work or call for
further samples.

Humorous Illustrator
515-278-0379 phone & fax
buckyjones@earthlink.net

Polly M. Law
Thrums End Art Studio
845-247-9026
pmlaw@ulster.net
online portfolio@:
www.thrumsend.co
m/GALLERY.HTML

KERI LEE MARINO
illustration
212.779.3541
kerimarino@aol.com

DRAWS CHARACTER

TODD PEARL CHARACTER & ANIMATION DESIGN • (248)203-9880 • FAX (248)203-9881 • **Toll-free (888)820-3175**

www.toddpearl.com

GHEE ILLUSTRATIONS
TEL/FAX (404) 688-2161
e-mail: ghee@bellsouth.net
www.gheeillustrations.com

**STEFANIE YOUNG
ILLUSTRATION**

2427 Bay Street
San Francisco, CA 94123
TEL/FAX (415) 776-1218
www.illustrera.net

Additional work can be seen in:
American Showcase 22 (page 1439)
American Showcase 21 (page 1438)

View www.illustrera.net for latest work

Member:
Graphic Artists Guild
Society of Illustrators, S.F.

JIM COHEN
107 Miller Road
Hawthorn Woods, IL 60047
TEL (847) 726-8979
FAX (847) 726-8988

JACKIE URBANOVIC
TEL (301) 495-9481
e-mail: jurbanovic@yahoo.com

NEUBECKER.COM 212-333-2551

ROBERT NEUBECKER   212-333-2551

HOWARD FINE

908 875 4251

Additional work can be seen at **Dirill.com** Portfolio On-line

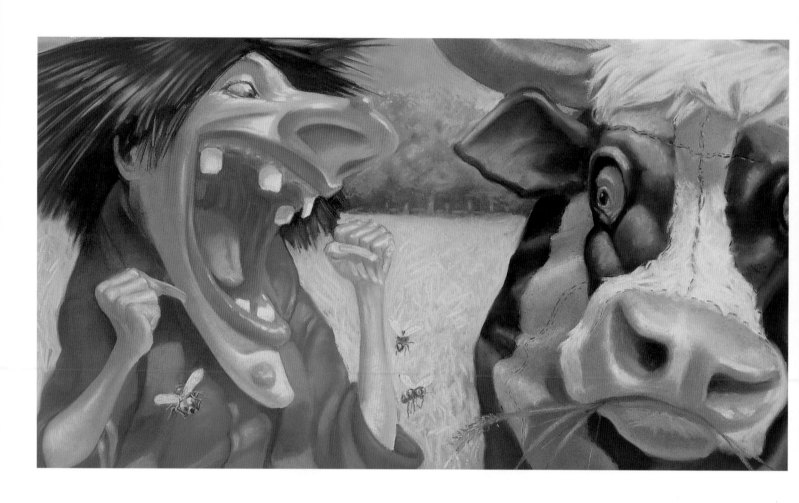

CAROL TABER
33 Wareland Road
Wellesley, MA 02481
TEL (781) 431-7267
FAX (781) 235-0203

LINDA HANLY
P.O. Box 1325
Solvang, CA 93464
TEL (805) 686-0808
e-mail: hanly13@aol.com

SUSAN HUNT YULE
I L L U S T R A T I O N
www.susanhuntyule.com
(212) 226-0439

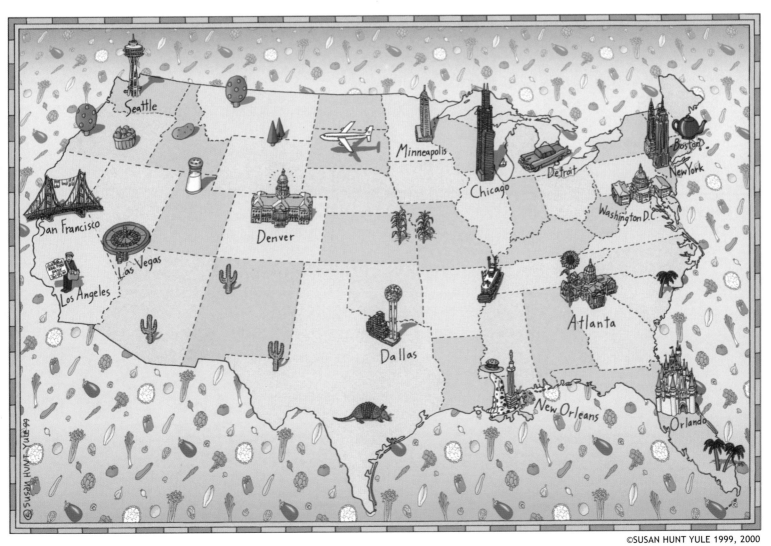

FRED BELL
212 North 77th Street
Milwaukee, WI 53213
TEL (414) 771-0472
e-mail: fred@bellart.com
http://www.bellart.com

See also:
Black Book '97, '98, '99, '00

Clients include:
Gymboree Stores
Hal-Leonard Music Publishing
Long Beach Aquarium

Dave Cutler • 941 472 1538 or 203 938 7067 • Member, Society of Illustrators & Graphic Artists Guild • see more in SOI Annuals, American Showcase, Blackbook, Workbook.com, theispot.com/artist/cutler • stock illustrations available

THOMAS DANNENBERG
407 Mill Street
Richmond Hill, Ontario
TEL (905) 884-9166
FAX (905) 884-8322

Clients include: American Express, Bank of Montreal, BF Goodrich, British Airways, Cadbury Limited, Canadian Airlines, Casino Berlin, City of Berlin, Coca-Cola Limited, Colliers Macauley Nichols, Cosmopolitan, Daimler-Benz AG, Financial Post, Financial Times, Fortune Magazine, Globe and Mail, IBM, Kraft General Foods, Merrill Lynch, Nestlé Enterprises, Price Waterhouse, The Robb Report, Royal Bank, Schering AG, TD Visa, Toronto Star, Toronto Life, Universal Studios, Walt Disney Attractions Inc.

My images have been published on every continent except Antarctica (a tough market to crack).

BEA WEIDNER
3410 West Penn St.
Philadelphia, PA 19129
TEL (215) 842-0495
e-mail: bea@cookiefriends.com

Spring Craft Show

April 13th and 14th at St. Davids Center Atrium

Shuttle Service is available on Thursday from the 145 Building and Great Valley to St. Davids Atrium from 11:30 a.m. to 1:30 p.m.

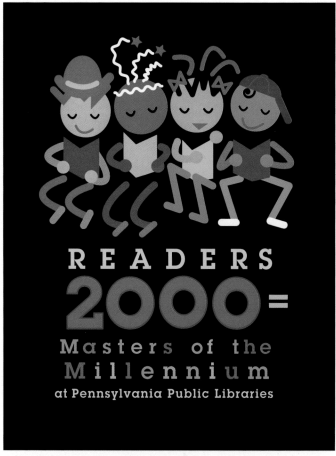

READERS
2000=
Masters of the
Millennium
at Pennsylvania Public Libraries

Take Our Children to Work Day
Reaching Into the Future
April 27, 2000

KATE ENDLE
ILLUSTRATION
206·632·9684

J.F. MAHONEY

illustrating products and the built environment and presenting design ideas in an audience-appropriate fashion
clients include: Warner Brothers, GAP, Gruner & Jahr, Williams-Sonoma, Addwater, Landor, Port of San Francisco

1640 San Pablo Avenue, Suite C, Berkeley CA 94702 tel: 510-524-9773 fax: 510-524-9776

BARBARA RHODES ILLUSTRATION

7114 Columbine Drive
Carlsbad, CA 92009
TEL (760) 929-1049
FAX (760) 602-1253

Clients include: American Red Cross, CBS, Cleo/Gibson Greeting Cards, Inc., Culbertson Winery, *Dance Aerobics* Magazine, "*FIRST*" Magazine, Golden Door Spa, Harcourt Brace Jovanovich, Inc., J. C. Penney, La Valencia Hotel, Macmillan/ McGraw-Hill, New American Library, *New York/Newsday* Newspaper, Petite Sophisticate, Inc., Scripps Memorial Hospital, "*Woman's World*" Magazine, Cook Communications Greetings.

See also: Graphic Artists Guild's Directory of Illustration Vol. 7, 8, 9 & 10.

Member: Society of Illustrators, San Diego

Thomas Harper
Illustration

vox **714.530.5215**

pāg **949.721.4732**
fax **714.530.5327**

xpharaoh@earthlink.net

METRO

Ron Blalock

RON BLALOCK ILLUSTRATION
703-764-2071 / RONB@PATRIOT.NET

HOLLEY FLAGG
FLAGG DESIGN
103 East 84th Street
New York, NY 10028
TEL (212) 734-5790
FAX (212) 472-6635
www.holleyflagg.com

See also Directory of Illustration:
#14, p. 562, #15, p.565,
#16, p.802 and www.holleyflagg.com

HOLLEY FLAGG
FLAGG DESIGN
103 East 84th Street
New York, NY 10028
TEL (212) 734-5790
FAX (212) 472-6635
www.holleyflagg.com

Robert W. Schmitt

brushwork

simple

elegant

powerful

Giving Voice to Hope 2000

event identity

The Art & Science of Feng Shui

風水

THE ANCIENT CHINESE TRADITION OF SHAPING FATE

Henry B. Lin

book cover

Building Bridges
PRACTICAL OUTLOOKS ON PASARR

collateral

logos

Theater
MU

**ergodyne
corporation**

PARK PLACE CLINIC

Robert W. Schmitt

612 333-1881

visit
www.winternet.com/~designrs
or
www.dirill.com

60 South 15 th. Street, Pittsburgh Pennsylvania, 15203

412-381-1030   jjblumen@aol.com

Laine
Roundy

98 QUASSUK ROAD, WOODBURY, CT 06798   203-263-7531   FAX 203-263-7478

DON PETERSEN
7004 Via Quito
Pleasanton, CA 94566
TEL/FAX (925) 484-0342

Humorous art for any habitat

Clients include: Addison-Wesley,
Advanced Micro Devices, Apple
Computer, ASPCA, Burger King,
Harcourt Brace, Hero Arts,
Hewlett-Packard, KGO-TV (ABC),
KQED (PBS), Memorex, National

Wildlife Federation, Oracle, Oxford
American, Pearson Learning,
Pentagram Design, Portal Publications,
Safeway Stores, SQL Server, United
States Postal Service

Member: San Francisco Society of
Illustrators

For additional work please see
Directory of Illustration #13–16 or
portfolio online at www.dirill.com

"It started with a spark and ended with a mark."

expedited

MARK BURNS | TYPE DESIGN

DALLAS TEXAS
[TELEPHONE] 214 319 9903
www.burnsite.com

AARON GRBICH

2 2 0   C A L D E C O T T   L N   2 1 3   O A K L A N D   C A   9 4 6 1 8

PHONE 510 649 8017   FAX 510 649 1510   E-MAIL GRBICHA@AOL.COM

Christophe Vorlet

804 · 296-6502

www.vorlet.com
christophe@vorlet.com

LINDA S. WINGERTER
784 Savin Avenue
West Haven, CT 06516
TEL (203) 933-7519
FAX (203) 931-1786
e-mail: i@lindawingerter.com

Clients include: Wall Street Journal Classroom Edition, Global Investment, National Gardening Magazine, Houghton Mifflin, McGraw Hill, William Morrow, Cricket, Ladybug, American School Board Journal, Aqua Magazine, Kirchoff/Wohlberg, Little Brown, Mindscape,

Scholastic Press, Samuel Weiser, Northwestern University Press, Williamson Publishing, Boston Lyric Opera

See also Directory of Illustration #16, page 406

Seattle, WA 98115
TEL (206) 526-8927
FAX (206) 523-2429

Douglas Schneider

(858) 695-6796

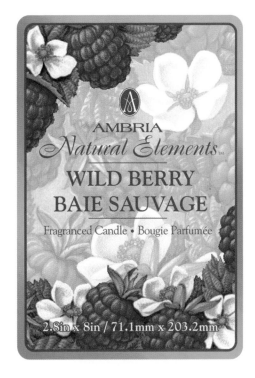

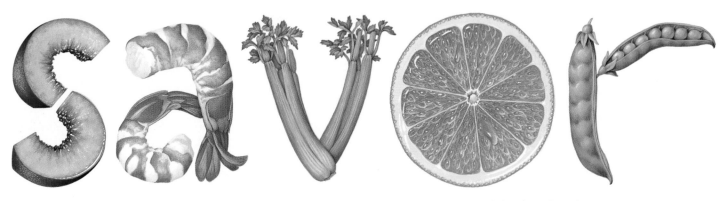

To view additional work, please see Workbook 15-21, Showcase 19-21 and douglasschneider.com

EXTRAORDINAIR ART INC.
815-678-0038
Gary Fasen
E-mail gary@air-art.com gary@rsg.org

Additional work can be seen in Directory of Illustration number 13, 14 and 16. Visit my website at air-art.com

tfitz

theresa fitzgerald
design/illustration
tel. 718.965.2248
fax. 718.965.2337
tfitzstudio@earthlink.net
394 eighth street 2L
brooklyn, ny 11215

call

Clients: Nickelodeon, Scholastic, Golden Books, King Features, Learning Pathways, British Airways, Scott Adams Foods, Inc., Museum of Natural History, Mattel

He loves me not

He loves me

**JO LYNN ALCORN
PAPER ART**
92 LeMay Street
West Hartford, CT 06107
TEL/FAX (860) 561-4202

Clientele includes:
CT Audubon Society, Unisource,
4Walls.com, Ranger Rick, Scholastic,
Sesame Street

MICHAEL McPARLANE
TEL (412) 247-5288

Innovative Systems Inc.
Northern Telecom (Cda)
NTT Data (Japan)
Molson (Cda)
Yamaha Piano (Japan)
YWCA
Chicago Tribune
Kiplingers

Las Vegas Life
LA Times Magazine
Newsday
Showbiz
tele.com
US News & World Report
Washington Times
Canadian Business(Cda)

Globe & Mail (Cda)
National Post (Cda)
Tatler (UK)
For additional samples, see
Directory of Illustration #16,
Page 513, or log on to
www.dirill.com

Lyman Dally (973) 763-6910
Fax (973) 763-6510
E-mail Epidemic@ix.netcom.com

Have worked extensively in (but not limited to) the Health and Fitness industries.
Partial Client list includes: MAXIM Magazine   FLEX Magazine   TWINLAB
WARNER LAMBERT   SCHWARZENEGGER/LORIMER PRODUCTIONS
MUSCULAR DEVELOPMENT Magazine   JOHNSON & JOHNSON
CONDÉ NAST   TCI DIGITAL CABLE   U.S. ARMY

Kevin Williams

Digital Photo Retouching
Digital Product Illustration
Corporate Trademarks

800 933-9361 toll-free
323 299-9912 voice
323 299-9412 fax

1.

2.

3.

1. **Intergraph**
2. **Maxum Rumpus**
3. **Maxum TagBuilder**
4. **Neutrogena Cosmetics**
5. **Oil of Olay Cosmetics**
6. **Loreal and Revlon Cosmetics**
7. **California Anesthesia Associates**
8. **American 3D Corporation**
9. **Griffin Three Springs***
10. **FDR Interactive Technologies**
11. **MindLeader.com****
12. **Aportis Technologies**
13. **Perfect Fit**

* Designed in cooperation with Linda Hulford
** Pending approval at press time
Also see Directory of Illustration 11

4.

5.

6.

7.

8.

9.

10.

11.

12.

13.

12 SOUTH MAIN STREET

PO BOX 356

STEWARTSTOWN, PA 17363

JIM STARR
ILLUSTRATION

STUDIO: 717 993 6598

FAX: 717 993 9537

E-MAIL: jim@jimstarr.com

WEBSITE: www.jimstarr.com

For additional samples check out my website: www.jimstarr.com

Jim's stock portfolio available @
www.stockart.com
800 297 7658

12 SOUTH MAIN STREET

PO BOX 356

STEWARTSTOWN, PA 17363

STUDIO: 717 993 6598

FAX: 717 993 9537

E-MAIL: jim@jimstarr.com

WEBSITE: www.jimstarr.com

JIM STARR
ILLUSTRATION

For additional samples check out my website: www.jimstarr.com

BOB LYNCH
1829 Prindle Drive
Bel Air, MD 21015
TEL (410) 893-9175
e-mail: blynch@clark.net
www.clark.net/pub/blynch

VISIT OUR WEBSITE

18

Number of Pets

CityMarket

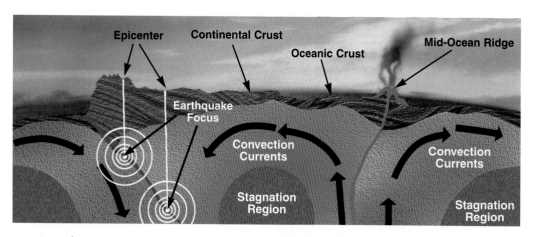

Epicenter   Continental Crust   Oceanic Crust   Mid-Ocean Ridge

Earthquake Focus

Convection Currents   Convection Currents

Stagnation Region   Stagnation Region

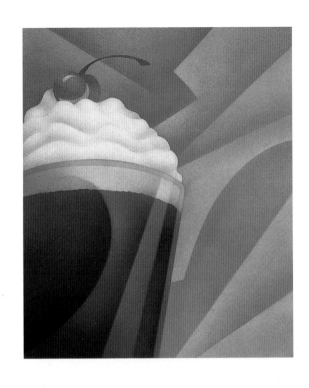

WEAVER

W

MICHAEL

MICHAEL WEAVER ILLUSTRATION
913.432.5078

JOANNE CHARBONNEAU
8967 Lajeunesse
Montreal PQ Canada
H2M 1S1

www.jocha.com
joanne@jocha.com
TEL (514) 381-2466
FAX (514) 381-2237

jocha
illustrator

Chris Cocozza Illustration
203-266-5517

artist@javanet.com

STEPHEN SCHILDBACH
1521 15th Ave., Apt. R
Seattle, WA 98122
e-mail: schildbach@hotmail.com
www.speakeasy.org/~bach
1-888-422-0320 ext. 1521
TEL/FAX (206) 720-6486

STEPHEN SCHILDBACH
1521 15th Ave., Apt. R
Seattle, WA 98122
e-mail: schildbach@hotmail.com
www.speakeasy.org/~bach
1-888-422-0320 ext. 1521
TEL/FAX (206) 720-6486

JEFF CLINE
50 Springholm Drive
Berkeley Heights, NJ 07922
TEL/FAX (800) 770-4089
e-mail: jcillos@aol.com

Visit www.jeffcline.com
for additional samples.

Magazine cover, *Investment Dealers' Digest*

Caribiner International for Xerox, *Comdex '99*

Caribiner International
for Xerox, *Comdex '99*

COMIC

Illustration &
Graphic Design
Editorial
&
Advertising
Traditional &
Digital Media

art

WHY NOT
GIVE A CALL
TODAY!

Henry Holt & Company; Random House Audio Books
Blue Avenger Cracks The Code

WILLIAM SHAKSPEARE

EDWARD DE VERE

Cover Illustration for Expert Gamer

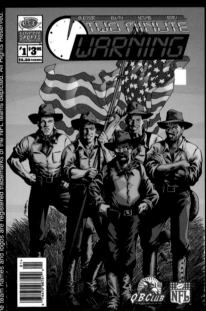

Cover Illustration for Official U.S. Playstation Magazine

TUSK

Tusk Story for Heavy Metal

NFL Custom Comic Book for Ultimate Sports

On-Line Comic Strip & Character Design for Electronic Arts Street Sk8er 2 website. (www.streetsk8erz.com)

IDEA+DESIGN WORKS, LL

Ted Adams

2168 BALBOA AVE, SUITE 4
SAN DIEGO, CA. 92109

858-270-1315 phone
858-270-1308 fax

on-line portfolio @
www.ideaanddesignworks.com

robots live @
www.robotmegastore.com

Robert Crawford

www.rcrawford.com/art.htm

123 Minortown Rd., Woodbury, CT 06798   P&F-203-266-0059 email - robert@rcrawford.com

SUSIE DUCKWORTH
2912 Kings Chapel Rd., No. 7
Falls Church, VA 22042
TEL (703) 698-8987
TOLL-FREE: 1-877-815-4248
FAX (703) 849-9164
e-mail: DuneDuck@aol.com

Clientele includes:
Humane Society of the United States,
American Red Cross, Neighborhood
Reinvestment Corporation, FEMA, EPA,
The Washington Post, National Wildlife
Federation, Project WILD, North Ameri-
can Association for Environmental
Education, Gallaudet University.

See Directory of Illustration #17
Portfolio On-Line at www.dirill.com
for additional work.

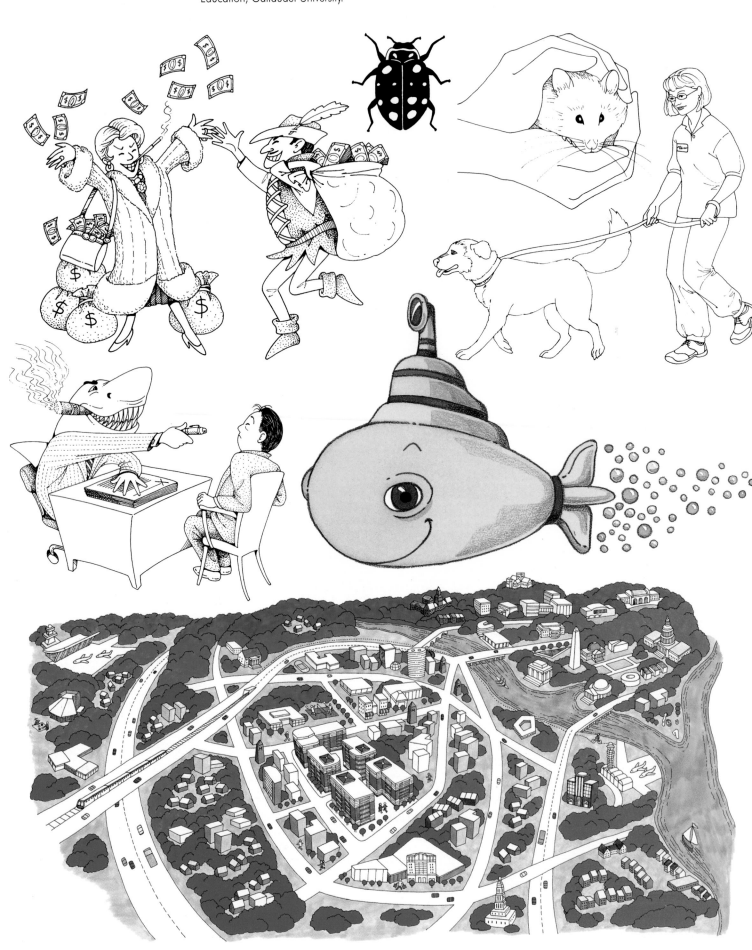

674

SCOTT G. BROOKS
www.SGBrooks.com
e-mail: Brooksini@aol.com
TEL (703) 812-9281

CHARLIE POWELL
1228 Martin Road
Santa Cruz, CA 95060
TEL (831) 457-9470
FAX (831) 457-0226
e-mail: cpowell@cruzio.com

CHARLIE POWELL
1228 Martin Road
Santa Cruz, CA 95060
TEL (831) 457-9470
FAX (831) 457-0226
e-mail: cpowell@cruzio.com

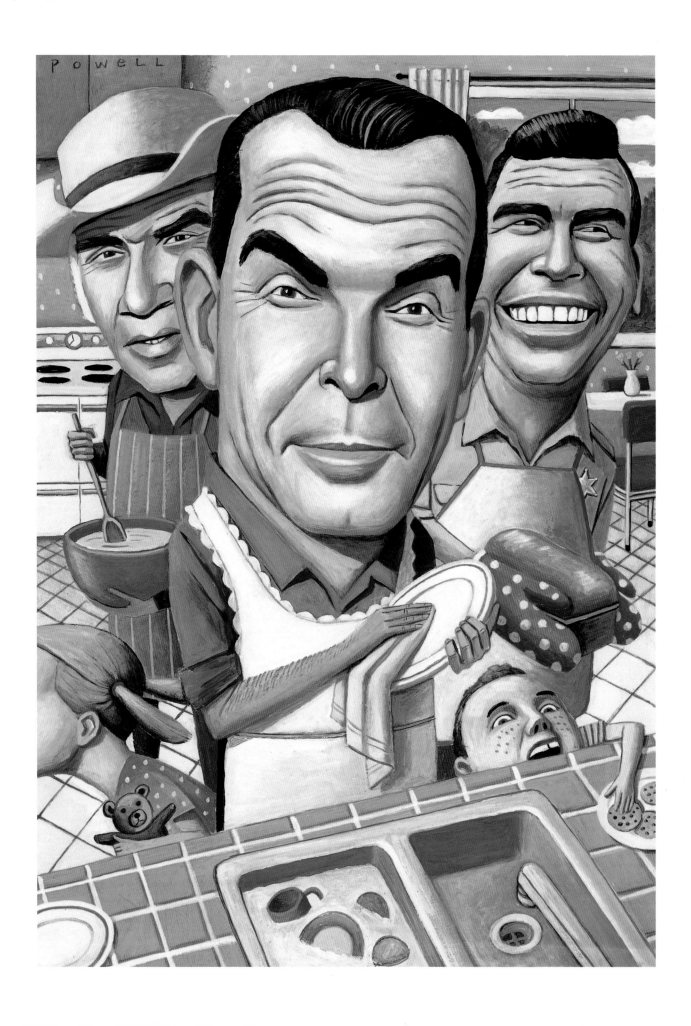

MELISSA GRIMES
ILLUSTRATION
Collage/pen & ink
901 Cumberland Road
Austin, TX 78704
TEL (512) 445-2398
e-mail: melissagrimes@mindspring.com

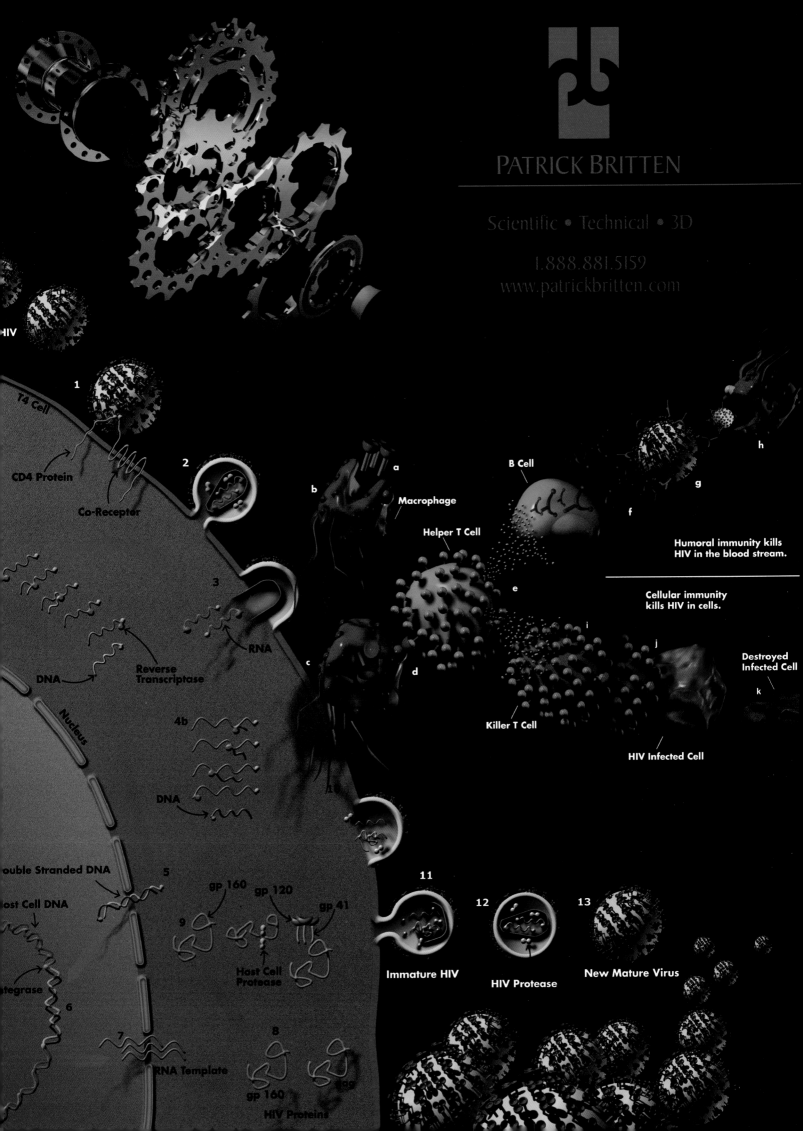

deb hoeffner
illustration
973-838-5490
deb@smokerise.net

Online portfolio and stock illustrations at
www.theispot.com/artist/dhoeffner

Partial client list:
The New York Times, Deutsche Bank, Simon & Schuster,
AT&T, Rocky Mountain Elk Foundation, PC Magazine,
Medical Economics, US News and World Report

MAGUÉ
TEL (415) 664-9541
www.mague.net/~mague

Magué
415 664 9541   www.mague.net/~mague

Almaden Wineries/HKA Design

Meredith Integrated Marketing

Oracle Corporation

FIESTA

tamales

JUVENAL MARTINEZ
203 N. Wabash, Ste. 1302
Chicago, IL 60601
TEL (312) 782-3290
FAX (312) 782-3291

HEATHER RAMSEY
Oceanside, CA
TEL (760) or (442) 967-5977

Clientele includes: American Council on Exercise, AIGA, UTNE Reader, San Diego Home & Garden, Petersons Youth Group Publications, The LA Weekly, Writers Guild of America.

See Directory of Illustration 16 for additional work.

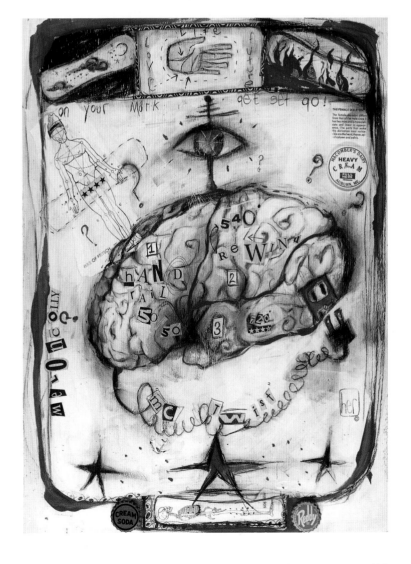

MELANIE MARDER PARKS
5 Broadview Lane
Red Hook, NY 12571
TEL/FAX (845) 758-0656
e-mail: parks@ulster.net

See portfolio at www.dirill.com,
Directory of Illustration #13–16,
CA Annual 41.

India in 1939.
Paul Scott's fictional
places are in red.

MELANIE MARDER PARKS
5 Broadview Lane
Red Hook, NY 12571
TEL/FAX (845) 758-0656
e-mail: parks@ulster.net

See portfolio at www.dirill.com,
Directory of Illustration #13–16,
CA Annual 41.

GINNY JOYNER
504 B. Dalton Drive
Colchester, VT 05446
TEL/FAX (802) 655-0899
e-mail: joynerart@aol.com

KATHRYN BORN
P.O. Box 200663
Arlington, TX 76006
TEL (817) 640-7052
FAX (817) 633-5625
e-mail: kbmi@worldnet.att.net

Clients include:
IDG Books Worldwide, Rodale Press,
World Wildlife Fund, *Wall Street
Journal, Contemporary Pediatrics*
Magazine, Dura Pharmaceuticals,
American Heart Association.

See on-line portfolio at
www.dirill.com.

SCOTT W. LUKE
1657 N. California Blvd., Suite 207
Walnut Creek, CA 94596
TEL (925) 930-7576
FAX (925) 930-7925
e-mail: scott@lukedesign1.com

See Directory of Illustration #10, 11,
12, 16 for additional work or call for
portfolio.

John **Bolesky**
503-241-7324

John Bolesky
431 NW Flanders #202
Portland, Oregon 97209
Phone 503-241-7324
Fax 503-242-0522

SCOTT MATTHEWS
7530 Ethel Ave.
St. Louis, MO 63117
TEL (314) 647-9899
FAX (314) 647-9985
e-mail: mramoeba@aol.com
Representation: Braun Art International

www.mramoeba.com

JEFFREY ALLON
304 Ashbourne Road
Elkins Park, PA 19027
TEL/FAX (215) 635-1984
e-mail: homeallon@juno.com

Clients include: McGraw-Hill,
Cricket Magazine, Spider Magazine,
Pitspopany Press, Addison-Wesley,
UAHC Press

Picture Book 98, p. 155
RSVP #23, p. 206

CLAUDIA MCGEHEE
ILLUSTRATION

ILLUSTRATION FOR ALL SEASONS

174 SHRADER ROAD IOWA CITY, IA 52245

TEL 319/ 351 5640   FAX 319/ 351 8770   E-MAIL cmcgehee@inav.net

ROBERT LANE
6711 East Avenue
Chevy Chase, MD 20815
TEL (301) 215-7974
FAX (301) 652-8780
e-mail: studiol@icnt.net

Creative Services
A digital illustration,
retouching and special
effects resource for
print and multimedia.

Hothouse Designs, Inc.
2 Ellis Place
Ossining, NY 10562
P > 914.941.1738
F > 914.941.1809
E > art@hothousedesigns.com

www.HothouseDesigns.com

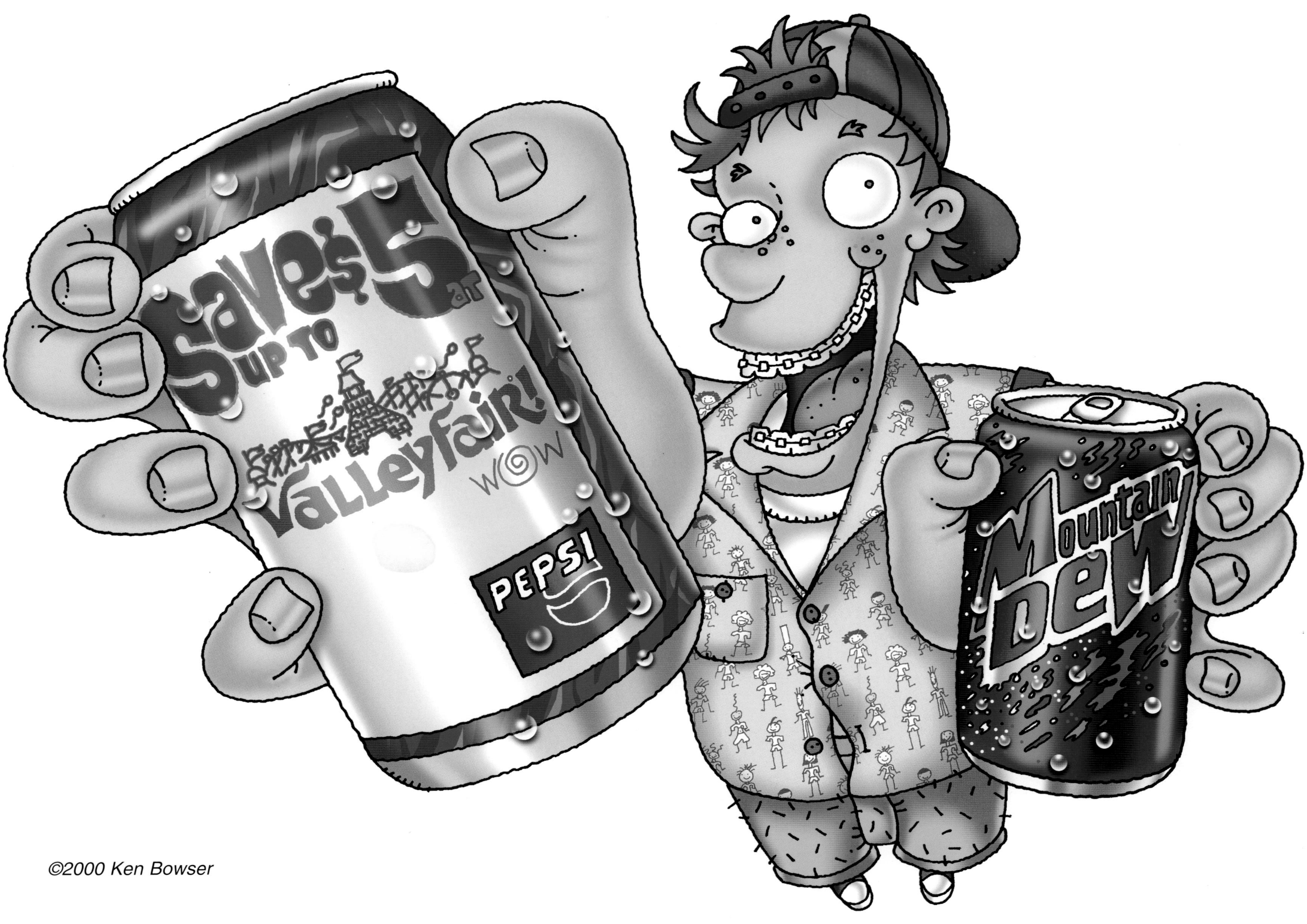
Save $5 at
UP TO
Valleyfair!
WOW
PEPSI
Mountain Dew

CRAIG McKAY
15 Parkway Avenue
Cincinnati, OH 45216
TEL/FAX (513) 821-8052
e-mail: monkeywithcrayon@fuse.net
Representation: AIR Studio, Inc.

Clients Include:
Disney
Kenner/Hasbro
Procter & Gamble
Nerf
Tonka

Sunoco
Henson Productions
Kroger
Girl Scouts of America
Six Flags
Warner Bros.

LINOCUTS

Hugh Armstrong III P.O.Box 4621 Milton,FL.32572 850-983-1340 email:hughha3@earthlink.net   web:home.earthlink.net/~hughha3

THOM MONTANARI
51 Lambertville-Hopewell Road
Hopewell, NJ 08525
TEL (609) 466-7753
FAX (609) 466-7939
www.avantimotorsports.com

Clients include: Audi, BMW, Chrysler,
Saab, Ford, Volkswagen, Kodak, Sony,
Duracell, Bausch & Lomb, James River,
STP, Quaker State, Pirelli, Miller Beer,
Universal Studios

CJ enterprises

C.J.Enterprises
Connie Kolupa
Voice 310.641.8468
Fax 310.641.2565
c.j.ent.@ix.netcom.com

TAIA MORLEY
3034 47th Avenue South
Minneapolis, MN 55406
TEL (612) 724-2339
FAX (612) 724-3273
e-mail: tm@redracerstudio.com

For more samples:
www. redracerstudio.com
DI #16

Clients include: General Mills,
Mayo Clinic, Fisher-Price Toys, Hasbro,
Mattel, Carter's Augsburg Fortress
Publishers, Redleaf Press

MICHAEL SURLES
300 Stony Point Road, #191
Santa Rosa, CA 95401
TEL (707) 579-1229
FAX (707) 575-5649
e-mail: mitts@sonic.net

Clients include:
Aegis Group, Chevron, Chevrolet,
Expo '88 Australia, General Motors,
OCI International, OCLI, Ortho,
Beringer, Chateau De Baun,
Chateau St. Jean, Dry Creek Vineyard,

Gallo, Kendall-Jackson,
Robert Mondavi, Mumm Napa Valley,
Suntory USA/Japan

**SCOTT WATKINS
ILLUSTRATION**
4340 Yorkshire Ct.
Loganville, GA 30052
TEL/FAX (770) 466-6510
e-mail: Scottiart@aol.com

COLLEEN DORAN

12643 DAYBREAK CIRCLE • NEWPORT NEWS, VA 23602 • PHONE • FAX 757.874.5247

E-MAIL • CBDORAN@BELLATLANTIC.NET   WEBSITE • WWW.COLLEENDORAN.COM

Specializing In:

Children's Book Illustrations

Graphic Novels/Comic Books • Story Boarding

Character Design • Game Illustrations

Anime/Manga

Clients:

Lucasfilm Ltd. • The Walt Disney Company
Parker Brothers • DC Comics • Imagine Entertainment
Marvel Comics • Joshua Morris • Archie Comics
Byron Preiss Entertainment • Image Comics, Inc.
Big Blue Dot • Harris Publications • Topps Incorporated
The Cahners Group

Member:

Graphic Artists Guild

Association of Science Fiction
and Fantasy Artists

National Cartoonists Society

Sean Parkes
HUMOROUS ILLUSTRATOR

STUDIO • 905-666-2145   FAX • 905-666-7832
E-Mail • sean@seanparkes.com

www.seanparkes.com

JANE RAMSEY
Illustration-Traditional and Digital
133 S. Church Street, Macungie, PA 18062
Phone 610.965.9480   Fax 610.966.2394
ramsey@enter.net
Additional samples at janeramsey.com

SUNNY KOCH
555 Martin Road
Santa Cruz, CA 95060
TEL (831) 425-7422
FAX (831) 457-8914

MARYJO KOCH
555 Martin Road
Santa Cruz, CA 95060
TEL (831) 425-7422
FAX (831) 457-8914
e-mail: birdnest2000@aol.com

Clients include:
Audubon Magazine
Ghurka
Stewart Tabori and Chang
Harper Collins
Rizzoli International

Schurman Fine Papers
Portal
Traveling Bear Press
Wallquest
Smith Mark

In view of the fact that none of the camels had name-tags, we decided to call ours "Amelia," after Amelia Peabody, the heroine in Susan's favorite mystery novels. Amelia walked single file

Camel Colors
Burnt Sienna   Yellow Ochre   Van Dyke Brown   Ivory Black

behind two other camels as we made our slow, easy approach to the pyramids. Like all Dromedaries, Amelia had a wide, upturned mouth that made her look like she was always smiling. Every so often she turned her inquisitive eyes back toward us, as if making sure we hadn't fallen off.

Before roads and motorized vehicles Dromedaries were used extensively to transport goods over vast distances. This earned the sturdy creature its nickname, the "Ship of the Desert." Their long eyelashes, closeable nostrils, and ear-fur keep blowing sand out. Their broad, flat hooves are designed not to sink in loose sand

Monday, February 19

One gets on a camel in:
The sitting position   it then kneels   pushing up its back legs   and then its front legs

David Peters

corporate

Miss America
AIR RACING TEAM

RENO

1969
1999

30 years a champion

advertising

digital illustration
photo collage
orchestrated chaos

tel-310-390-3528 fax-310-397-5383
email-dpetersart@aol.com

editorial

JEFF SUNTALA
20206 Bradgate Lane
Cleveland, OH 44149
TEL (440) 238-5909
FAX (440) 846-6155
e-mail: www.suntala.com

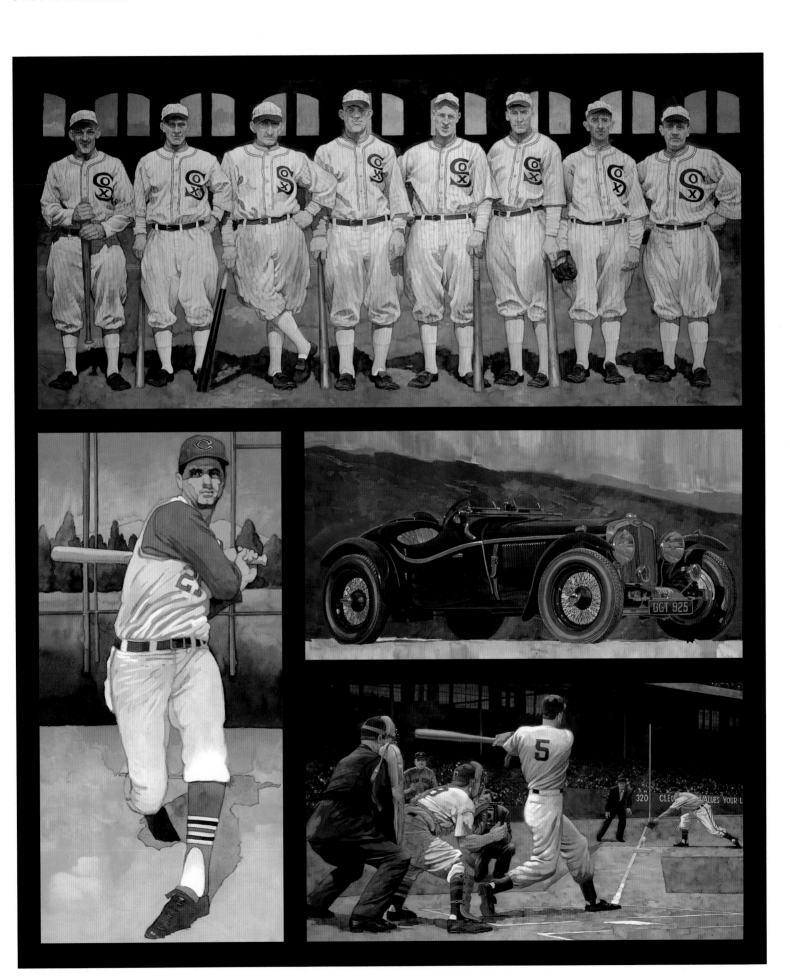

SHARON COUGHRAN-RAYDEN
1049 Via Cielito
Ventura, CA 93003
TEL (805) 644-2455
FAX (805) 477-0123
e-mail: Sharon@cielhaus.com

Clientele:
Glencoe/McGraw-Hill
Holms & Meier Publishers
Kinkos

Sharon Coughran-Rayden

C I E L H A U S

KRISTIN MOUNT
5214 N. LaCrosse Avenue
Chicago, IL 60630
TEL (800) 455-9717
e-mail: kristin@gm-studio.com

MARTY VOELKER
TEL (630) 653-3070
e-mail: nvoelker@flash.net

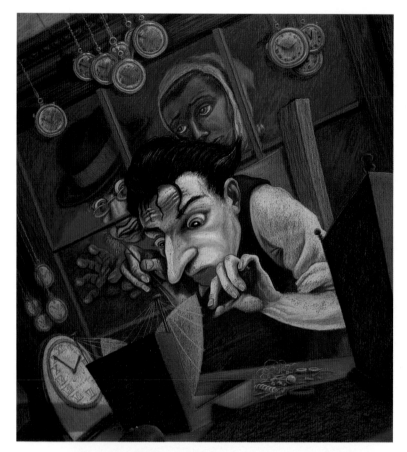

MELODY J. SARECKY
4420 Ridge Street
Chevy Chase, MD 20815
TEL (301) 941-0475
FAX (301) 941-0476
e-mail: msarecky@bellatlantic.net

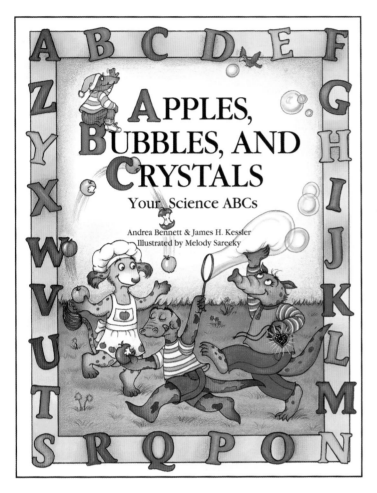

Meet Archie of the orchard,
An apple kind of guy.
He picks a batch, then cooks them
For apple sauce and pie.

When Archie cuts up apples,
The slices all turn brown.
They don't look very yummy,
Which makes his buddies frown.

But Archie is a good cook
Who knows a special way
To stop the color changing
At any time of day!

Ernesto is an egg cook.
He cooks them everyday.
He scrambles some and boils some,
Then puts the rest away.

He stores the eggs together,
The boiled ones with the raw.
Mixing up his egg supply–
A breaking of EGG LAW.

With all the eggs together,
Ernesto now must guess
Which eggs are the boiled ones,
Or risk a scrambled mess!

EGG-STRA EGG-CITEMENT

What You'll Need:
- hard-boiled egg
- raw egg
- 2 cereal bowls

1. Have partner place an egg in each bowl. Don't watch!

2. Spin each egg. Which one do you think spins faster?

3. Stop the spin with your finger, then quickly take your finger off. What happens?

4. Do you think you know which egg is which? Crack one open and see!

**JOSEPH WALDEN
HUMOROUS
ILLUSTRATION**

36 Studio Hill Road, Suite #1B
Briarcliff Manor, NY 10510
TEL (914) 762-6736
FAX (914) 923-5833
e-mail: joseph.art@att.net

Clients include:
EPlay.com, Ideals Children's Books,
Christopher Radko, Junior Trails,
Action Tracks, Good Advice Press,
The Irish News

Published Children's Books:
Grandpa's Smile
The Peanut Butter and Jelly Game

Website:
www.josephwalden.com

SCBWI Member

picture books & humorous illustrations...

www.josephwalden.com
(914) 762-6736

JIM NUTTLE
14904 Wellwood Road
Silver Spring, MD 20905
TEL (301) 989-0942
FAX (301) 989-1342
e-mail: mail@jimnuttle.com

Scratchboard and digital illustrations
for corporate, editorial, advertising,
and publishing. On-line portfolio at
www.jimnuttle.com. See my ads in
Directory of Illustration #16 and
Picturebook 2001.

MICHAEL SPRONG
1301 Tanager Lane
Garland, TX 75042
TEL (877) 471-1521
FAX (972) 276-6958
e-mail: sprongdesign.com

ALAN STUDT
ILLUSTRATION

8575 Broadview Road
Broadview Heights, OH 44147
TEL (440) 546-1374
e-mail: scribble@juno.com
www.alanstudt.com

Clientele includes:
The Upper Deck Company
Cleveland Cavaliers
Cleveland Indians
Beckett Publications

DARCIE PARK

1-888-465-4ART
(1-888-465-4278)

To see more work call for the actual portfolio or
visit my on line portfolio at: www.dirill.com

**BARBARA SWANSON
SHERMAN**
380 West 12th Street, #5B
New York, NY 10014
TEL (212) 924-0559
FAX (212) 255-7006
e-mail: vividbarb@compuserve.com

Adam Garlinger
ILLUSTRATION

291 Greenfield Rd • Bridgewater, New Jersey 08807
Phone 908.707.0625 • Fax 908.203.0334

MATT JARAMILLO
ILLUSTRATION
4611 W. 38th Ave.
Denver, CO 80212
TEL (303) 455-8013

Gary **Hallgren** **art**
all-purpose comic
and **illustration**
(631) 399-5531 hallgren@i-2000.com

www.dirill.com   www.theispot.com   www.theispot.com/stock   www.designersgroup.com

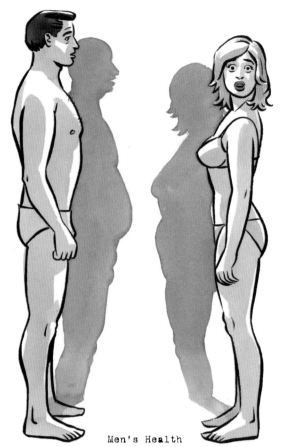

Men's Health

Business Week

Disney Adventures

Disney Adventures

Men's Health

Disney Adventures

Business Week

The Wall Street Journal

Business Week

Business Week

**CHRIS LUNDY
RUNAWAY POOCH
STUDIOS**
126 Brook Road
Plymouth, MA 02360
TEL/FAX (508) 224-7944

PIERRE GOSSELIN
Toll-Free
1-877-743-7734
(1-877-PIERRE-G)

More of my work may be
seen on p. 442 of the Directory of
Illustration #16.

Dana's
Espresso Bar
PURVEYOR'S OF FINE COFFEES AND TEAS

Good eats for Goodwill

ARTS & SCIENCE

DISCOVERY CENTER

CSDA
25
THE CONCRETE SAWING
& DRILLING ASSOCIATION
25th ANNIVERSARY
CONVENTION • MAUI

DELAWARE AREA
CHAMBER OF COMMERCE

LYNNE FOSTER

309 WEST 100 STREET NEW YORK NEW YORK 10025 EMAIL lagoulue@worldnet.att.net

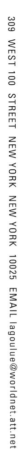

INTELLIGENT ART WITH A MESSAGE

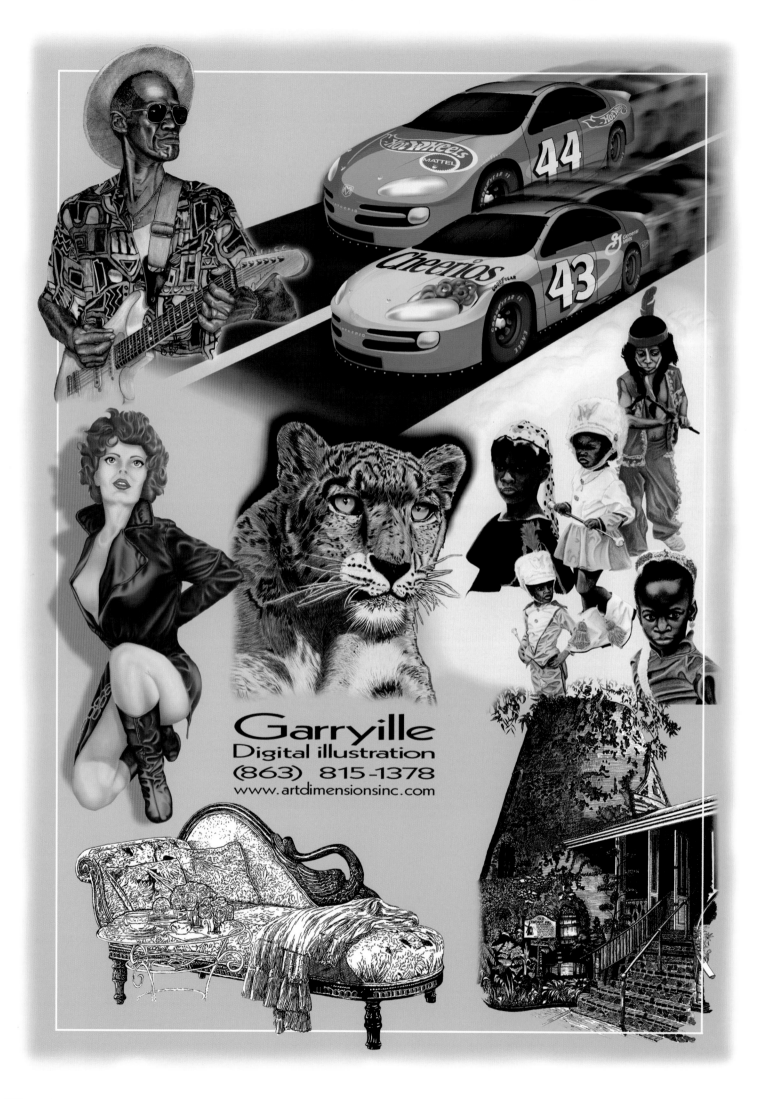

Garryille
Digital illustration
(863) 815-1378
www.artdimensionsinc.com

BRIAN
LIES

Phone: (781) 319-0456
E-mail: blies@acunet.net
www.brianlies.com

Hoddley, Poddley
A Mother Goose Rhyme • Art by Brian Lies

Hoddley, poddley, puddles and fogs,
Cats will play with the terrier dogs;
Cats in blue jackets and dogs in red hats,
What will become of the mice and
the rats?

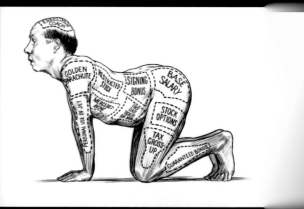

t collins / illustrator • 203 762 8871 • www.theispot.com/artist/m col

STACEY SCHUETT
7805 Anthony Street
Sebastopol, CA 95472
TEL/FAX (707) 824-2869
e-mail: schuett@sonic.net

733

MICHAEL E. THOMAS
P.O. Box 11061
Savannah, GA 31412
TEL (912) 201-0105

STEVE FIRCHOW
DAYDREAMS AND NIGHTMARES
ILLUSTRATED

1410 WELLESLEY AVENUE, #107 LOS ANGELES, CALIFORNIA 90025

310-826-9858

Clients include: Cactus Games, Frontline Music Group, Ace Books, Image Comics,
Mattel Toys, The Beeline Group, Goldberg Moser, O'Neill Advertising, TSR Inc.,
Hanna Barbera Inc., Video Games Magazine, Sega Genesis,
DC Comics and Wizards of the Coast.

GINA ZORNOW
4547 Croton Drive
New Port Richey, FL 34652
TEL (727) 815-3991
e-mail: gmzornow@iname.com

ROMAN DUNETS
10279 Holly Hill Road
Glen Allen, VA 23059
TEL/FAX (804) 550-3859

See Directory of Illustration #14, #15,
and #16 for additional work.

Lester Coloma

BRAD WALKER
I L L U S T R A T I O N

TEL. 509-738-4440   FAX 509-738-4777   BWALKER@TRIAX.COM

Illustration / Design
Telephone: 415.389.0332
Facsimile: 415.389.0632

E-Mail: wrieser@R2design.com
Website: www.R2design.com
www.dirill.com / www.theispot.com

Represented in San Francisco by Corey Graham: 415.956.4750 / www.coreygrahamreps.com

Illustration / Design
Telephone: 415.389.0332
Facsimile: 415.389.0632

E-Mail: wrieser@R2design.com
Website: www.R2design.com
www.dirill.com / www.theispot.com

William Rieser

**ADAM ROGERS
ILLUSTRATION, INC.**
402 West Pender Street, Suite 504
Vancouver, British Columbia
Canada V6B 1T6
TEL/FAX (604) 687-3729
e-mail: a_rogers@telus.net

WENDY WAX
322 East 55th Street, 3C
New York, NY 10022
TEL/FAX (212) 371-6156
e-mail: wwaxx@earthlink.net

Collage Illustration

Clients include:
American Express
Bloomberg
Business 2.0
Children's Television Workshop
Child
Family Life
Food Arts

Good Housekeeping
HBO
Individual Investor
Medical Economics
New York Daily News
New York Law Journal
NYNEX Mobile Communications
Philips Magnavox

Small Business Computing
Sports Illustrated for Kids
Swing
UTNE Reader
The Washington Post
Viacom Interactive Media
See Directory of Illustration, #12–16
for additional work or call for portfolio.

JAY JOHNSON

214-762-8915

P.O. Box 850832 • Richardson, Tx 75085-0832 • jayj1@airmail.net

744

Jay Johnson

214-762-8915

P.O. Box 850832 • Richardson, Tx 75085-0832 • jayj1@airmail.net

Lockport, IL 60441
TEL (708) 645-1199
CELL (708) 602-8112
FAX (708) 645-1198
e-mail: WhatIsArt4@aol.com

Chicago Zoological Society, Paterno
Imports and Wineries.

Please call for portfolio showing.

FLASH ANIMATION
ILLUSTRATION & DESIGN

AfroPuff Design
phone: 310.358.3319
www.highpimpstress.com
email: adah@highpimpstress.com

Cheryl Phelps
76 Irving Pl. 5B
N.Y. N.Y. 10003
212·533·8236

Cheryl Phelps
76 Irving Pl. 5B
N.Y.N.Y. 10003
212·533·8236

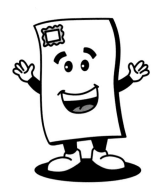

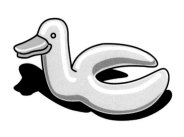

PAGE of CUPS

QUEEN of SWORDS

KNIGHT of SWORDS

D.STEVENS

CRISIS SOFTWARE

©2000 Daryl Stevens

DARYL STEVENS

digital illustration   212-741-1610   www.studio202.com

750

James Theodore

5 West Main Street   Westerville, Ohio 43081

614/898.5316   Fax 614/898.5217

JOCK MACRAE
(416) 690-0401

Rick Wheeler Illustration & Design • P.O. Box 673 • Moab, Utah 84532
email: rickarts@lasal.net • www.theispot.com/artist/rwheeler • please also see Directory of Illustration 16
phone: 435.259.3012 • fax: 435.259.1572

from a series of illustrations for a children's alphabet book on southwest Native American art & culture
Client: KC Publications

unpublished

HOLLY STONE-BAKER
244 Friar Tuck Drive
Baton Rouge, LA 70815
TEL (225) 273-0257
e-mail: whdesign@aol.com
http://www.whdesign.addr.com

Medium:
Collage

Member of:
• SCBWI
• Graphic Artists Guild

Also See:
• Direstory of Illustration
  Vol. 15, 16
• RSVP
  Vol. 22, 23

MARINA THOMPSON

digital illustration   www.marinathompson.com   fax 781 581 5808   voice 781 581 1725

VAN SEVEREN STUDIO
826 S. Quincy Street
Green Bay, WI 54301
TEL (920) 435-6313
FAX (920) 435-6346

**DICK GAGE
ILLUSTRATION/GRAPHICS**
1032 North Montana Street
Arlington, VA 22205
TEL/FAX (703) 241-7042
e-mail: rgage@cypressvisions.com

Clientele includes:
National Wildlife Federation
U.S. News & World Report
Defenders of Wildlife
Chamber of Commerce,
Washington, D.C.
Washington Post, Filnet, Inc.
Washington Stock Photo, Inc.

Specializing In:
Illustration
Information Graphics
Web page design
Editorial art

For additional work see:
Directory of Illustration #15–16
California Image '99
http://www.cypressvisions.com
http://www.wildspeculation.com
Art Crowd Magazine's International
Fall 2000 juried competition issue
Member: Graphic Artists Guild

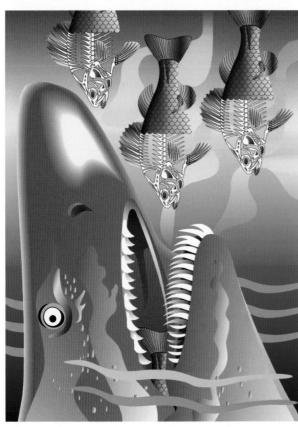

DICK GAGE

I L L U S T R A T I O N · G R A P H I C S

GREG VOTH
336 West 23rd Street/4th Floor
New York, NY 10011-2201
TEL/FAX (212) 243-2949
e-mail: greg@gregvoth.com

Clients include:
Coors Brewing Co., Inc.
General Foods, Inc.
Integer Group
Lexis-Nexis, Inc.
Polygram

See *Directory of Illustration #15*
(and other source books) and my
website for additional work. Call for
portfolio and samples. Electronic
portfolio available. Cable modem.

Jan Benham, whimsical illustrator
colorful characters cheerfully created
and delivered ON TIME

FUN-1 Illustration and Design Studio
4419 Reed Road
Columbus, Ohio 43220

614-326-3861

Linda Montgomery

705·435·3022

www.theispot.com/artist/lmontgomery

stock: www.images.com

email: lmontgom@idirect.com

GARY AAGAARD
335 Clinton Street, #3
Brooklyn, NY 11231
TEL (718) 694-0458
FAX (718) 923-1350
e-mail: aags@dellnet.com

Clients include: The Village Voice, Houghton Mifflin, Eisnor Interactive, The Oxford American, Rizzoli Publishing, The New York Times, The Los Angeles Times, Reader's Digest Books, Barnes and Noble, Good Housekeeping, Harcourt Brace, Emergency Medicine

For additional work see Illustrators 40, 41, and 42, Society of Publication Designers 35, Illustration West 35, online Illustration West annuals 36, 37, and 38 at www.SI-LA.org, and Portfolio On-Line at www.dirill.com

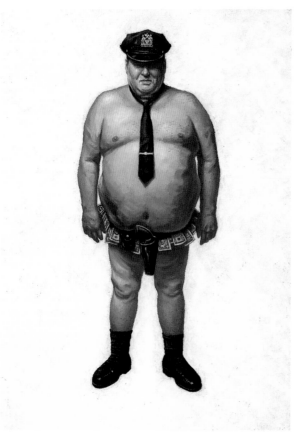

COPS AND RUBBERS   The Village Voice (cover)

THE HILLARY CLINTON CHEAT SHEET   The Village Voice

CLOTHES MAKE THE SUSPECT   The Village Voice (cover)

UNWANTED ADVANCES ARE A TURN-OFF   Message Media

Character Development

- Corporate
- Advertising
- Editorial

- Humorous Illustration

Co-Creator of the nationally syndicated comic strip BALDO.

BALDO

JIM CARLSON
ILLUSTRATOR
233 1/2 South Main Street
Galena, IL 61036
TEL (815) 777-3250
FAX (815) 777-3296
Member Graphic Artists Guild
© 2000 James Carlson, Inc.

Habitual Addy winner for large and small clients alike. This illustration is part of a permanent display featured at the Smithsonian's Washington Zoo. The exhibit illustrates the relentless growth habit of prairie grasses.

CLIENTS
AMT (IMTS Show)
Big City Reds (Hot Dogs)
Chicago Tribune Magazine
Kimberly-Clark
Kodak
South Bend Sporting Goods

S.C. Johnson & Son
Speed Queen

See Directory of Illustration #11 and #12 for additional work or call for portfolio.

BETSY EVERITT
Pink House Studio
582 Santa Rosa Avenue
Berkeley, CA 94707
TEL (510) 527-3239
FAX (510) 527-0276
e-mail: betsye@pinkhousestudio.com

Clients Include:
Baby Gap, Carole Hochman,
City of New York, Esprit, Estee Lauder,
General Foods, Harcourt, Inc.,
Hewlett Packard, Marcel Schurman,
Ms. Magazine, New Woman, Random
House, San Francisco Symphony,
Target, Workman Publishing.

JIM EDMON
133 Walton Ave.
Lexington, KY 40508
TEL (800) 530-5678
FAX (859) 381-8883
e-mail: edmondesign@mindspring.com

LOUISE MAX
P.O. Box 272
Jamaica, VT 05343
TEL (802) 297-2976
FAX (802) 297-0090

Clientele includes:
Gibbs-Smith Publishers, Spiegel,
Scholastic, Scott Foresman, Panasonic.

See Directory of Illustration #13–16
for additional samples.

MARTIN CÔTÉ
Representation: Lise Madore
TEL 1-888-440-8663
e-mail: madore@mlink.net

STEPHEN BURDICK
DESIGN

264 Beacon Street
Boston, MA 02116
TEL (617) 266-0655
FAX (617) 262-8389

Toll-free: (877) 723-4278 (SBD-4-ART)
e-mail: sbdesign@shore.net
Web: stephenburdickdesign.com

Clients include:
BI-Deaconess Medical Center
Boston Parks Department
HBM Inc.
Museum of Science, Boston
Physicians for Social Responsibility
Scitex Corporation
Sustworks.com
Wainwright Bank

Specializing in hand-drawn and
computer-enhanced illustration for
a variety of clients. Providing fast
and accurate creative services with
a flair for the new technology.
Estimates cheerfully provided.

Antonia Walker Illustrator

141 E 3rd Street #2E, New York, NY 10009 ✳ tel 212.677.9529 ✳ e-mail antonia007@rcn.com

Who ate my Nike?

Was it Sam?

Was it Bubba?

Was it Pepe?

Was it Giovanni?

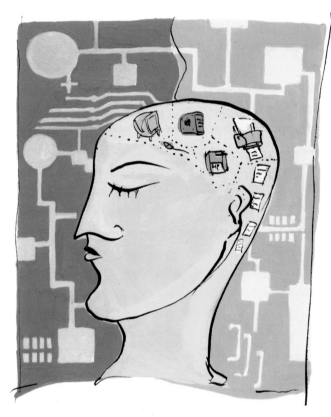

Shirt by Momino

sofa by EM Mobili

atomic
wedgie

final standings/long jump competition

Darren Mckee Humorous Illustration
162 Classen, Dallas, Tx 75218
Phone:(214) 343-8766

Gustaf Fjelstrøm | 408 253 6680 (studio) | 408 253 2907 (fax) | gustaf@botched.com | www.botched.com

Jim Durk

Durk Illustration

25108 Wolf Road

Bay Village, Ohio 44140

440-871-5835

fax:440-871-5836

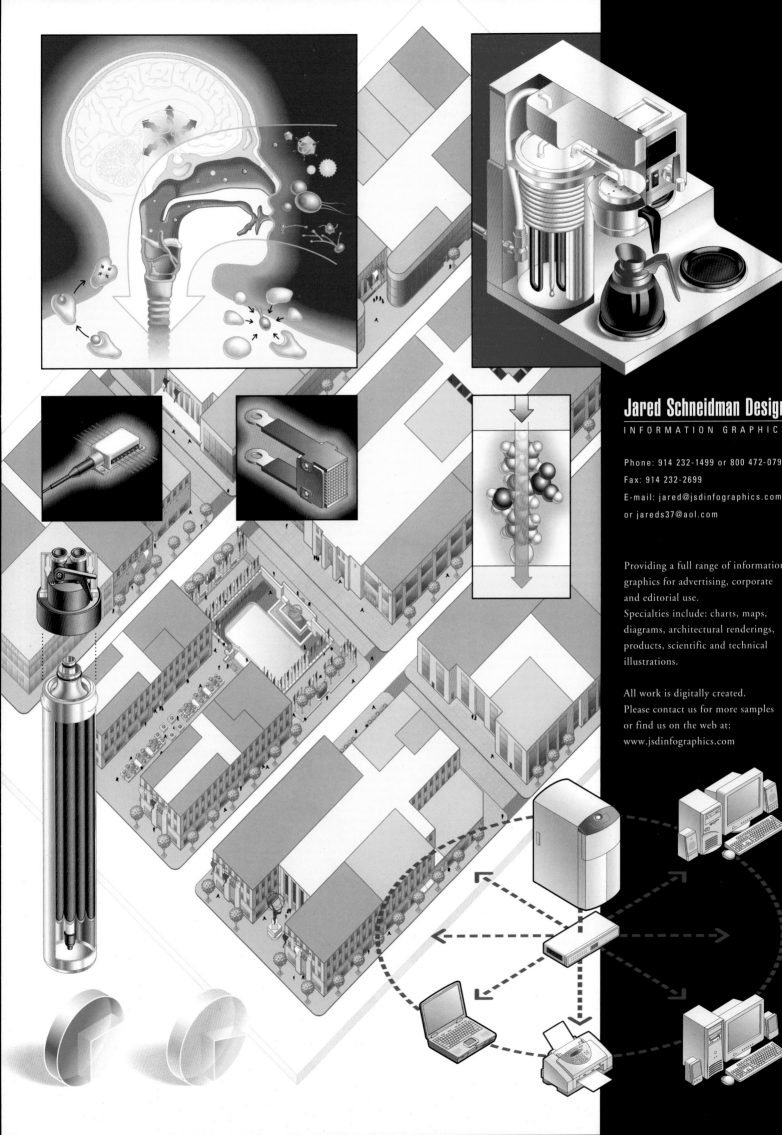

Jared Schneidman Design
INFORMATION GRAPHICS

Phone: 914 232-1499 or 800 472-079
Fax: 914 232-2699
E-mail: jared@jsdinfographics.com
or jareds37@aol.com

Providing a full range of information
graphics for advertising, corporate
and editorial use.
Specialties include: charts, maps,
diagrams, architectural renderings,
products, scientific and technical
illustrations.

All work is digitally created.
Please contact us for more samples
or find us on the web at:
www.jsdinfographics.com

DKH§illustrations.designs

deborah kay haines   traditional & computer   web & instructional

865¦300 3879 cel
865¦573 1832 ph
dkh_illusdesign@yahoo.com

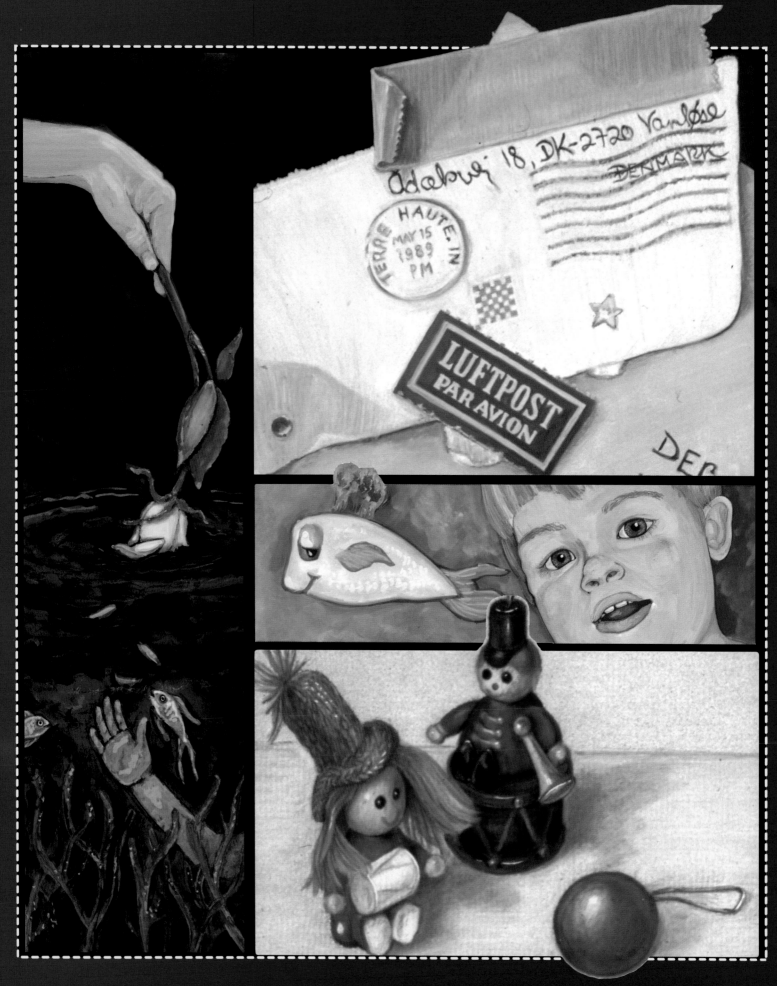

ROSANNE KALOUSTIAN

208-19 53rd Avenue
Bayside, NY 11364
TEL (718) 428-4670

Clients:
American Airlines
Golf Journal
Reader's Digest
Houghton Mifflin
Publications International
The Hartford Courant
McDougal Littel

Vantage Press
Modern Curriculum
Simon & Schuster
Woman's Day
Redbook Magazine
Interim Health Care
UPS
Mature Living Magazine

LL Bean
General Foods

Member Graphic Artists Guild

See Directory of Illustration #10, 11, 14, 16 for additional work.

ROSANNE KALOUSTIAN

Canton, GA 30114
TEL (770) 345-9576
FAX (770) 432-6872
e-mail: brb-wyr@mindspring.com

WATER FERTILITY

the aquatic food chain.

e term "trout stream,"
and most people think of flowing
water that is cold, clear and unpol-
luted. This stereotype is accurate,
but there are other requirements as
well. The quantity and size of trout
a stream produce depend on the
following

LETICIA PLATE

212-807 9728 www.theispot.com

Fall Sports

Burt Bacharach and Elvis Costello
at the Chicago Theater

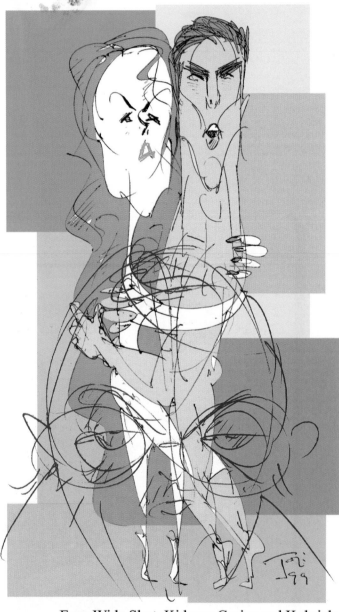

Eyes Wide Shut, Kidman Cruise and Kubrick

Madonna and Child

Call for Animation Reel!

JOE FOURNIER 708.848.2756

E-mail: joedraw@mcs.net   Web address: www.mcs.net/~joedraw

JOHN LYTLE
Post Office Box 5155
Sonora, CA 95370
TEL/FAX (209) 928-4849
e-mail: jlytle@mlode.com

Delivery: 17301 Fitch Ranch Road
Sonora, CA 95370

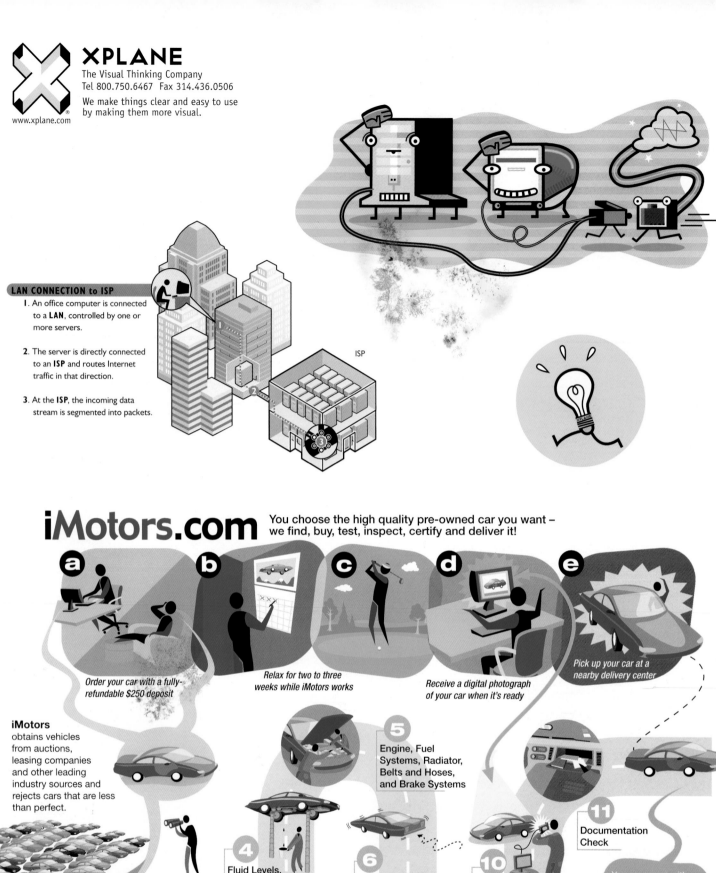

XPLANE
The Visual Thinking Company
Tel 800.750.6467 Fax 314.436.0506

We make things clear and easy to use by making them more visual.

www.xplane.com

LAN CONNECTION to ISP

1. An office computer is connected to a **LAN**, controlled by one or more servers.

2. The server is directly connected to an **ISP** and routes Internet traffic in that direction.

3. At the **ISP**, the incoming data stream is segmented into packets.

ISP

iMotors.com
You choose the high quality pre-owned car you want – we find, buy, test, inspect, certify and deliver it!

a Order your car with a fully-refundable $250 deposit

b Relax for two to three weeks while iMotors works

c

d Receive a digital photograph of your car when it's ready

e Pick up your car at a nearby delivery center

iMotors obtains vehicles from auctions, leasing companies and other leading industry sources and rejects cars that are less than perfect.

Your car then goes to the **Vehicle Certification Center** where it undergoes a 129 point inspection by certified mechanics and technicians to insure it's in outstanding condition.

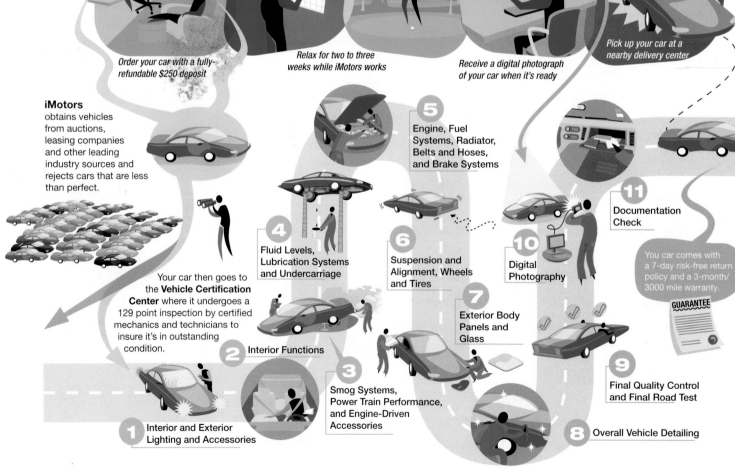

1. Interior and Exterior Lighting and Accessories

2. Interior Functions

3. Smog Systems, Power Train Performance, and Engine-Driven Accessories

4. Fluid Levels, Lubrication Systems and Undercarriage

5. Engine, Fuel Systems, Radiator, Belts and Hoses, and Brake Systems

6. Suspension and Alignment, Wheels and Tires

7. Exterior Body Panels and Glass

8. Overall Vehicle Detailing

9. Final Quality Control and Final Road Test

10. Digital Photography

11. Documentation Check

You car comes with a 7-day risk-free return policy and a 3-month/ 3000 mile warranty.

GUARANTEE

XPLANE
The Visual Thinking Company
Tel 800.750.6467 Fax 314.436.0506
We make things clear and easy to use
by making them more visual.
www.xplane.com

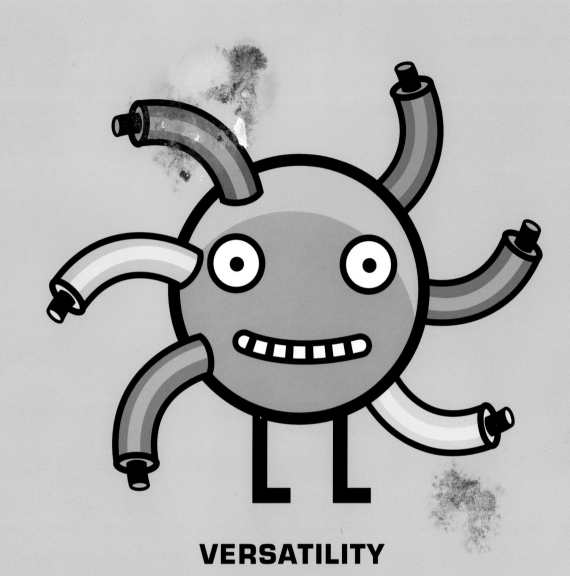

VERSATILITY

POWER

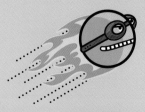

SPEED

CONTROL

PAUL MIROCHA
425 East 17th Street
Tucson, AZ 85701
TEL/FAX (520) 623-1515
e-mail: pmirocha@flash.net

Imagination and Illustration.
Design and Detail.
Traditional and Digital Media.

Also see Directory of Illustration
Vol. 14 p. 578, Vol. 15 p. 643, &
Vol. 16 p. 866.

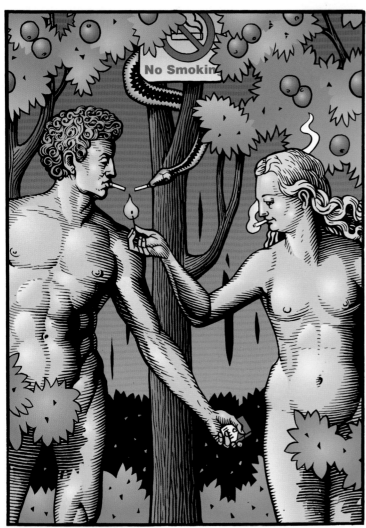

tudio 010 Illustration • Kevin Payne • Phone: 303•464•9222

lients include: Keyboard Magazine • Graphic Arts Monthly Magazine • Hal Leonard Corporation

bruna@WinkingEye.com

Phone: (510) 547-8141
Fax : (510) 547-5469

1245 Stanford Avenue
Emeryville, CA 94608

Illustration
Web Design & Consulting
Graphic Design

www.WinkingEye.com

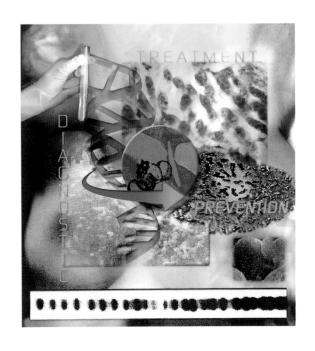

THINK "SILLY"

PLANET BOB

LITTLE BOY BOO

THINK THOMPSON BROS.

331 WEST STONE AVENUE
GREENVILLE, SC 29609
864/241-0810
864/241-0811 FAX

FOR LICENSING:
S.I. INTERNATIONAL
43 EAST 19TH STREET
2ND FLOOR
NEW YORK, NY 10003
212/254-4996
212/995-0911 FAX

IN THE SOUTHEAST:
WILL SUMPTER & ASSOCIATES
179 MASSENGALE ROAD
BROOKS, GA 30205
770/460-8438
770/460-8943 FAX

FUDDRUCKERS

THINK "SERIOUS"

PIEDMONT NATURAL GAS

YOUNG ADVENTURE

OMNIVORE

THINK THOMPSON BROS.

331 WEST STONE AVENUE
GREENVILLE, SC 29609
864/241-0810
864/241-0811 FAX

FOR LICENSING:
S.I. INTERNATIONAL
43 EAST 19TH STREET
2ND FLOOR
NEW YORK, NY 10003
212/254-4996
212/995-0911 FAX

IN THE SOUTHEAST:
WILL SUMPTER & ASSOCIATES
179 MASSENGALE ROAD
BROOKS, GA 30205
770/460-8438
770/460-8943 FAX

©2000 THOMPSON BROS.

Left; Alderac Entertainment Group
Above right; Atlas Games

SKAIRCROW GRAPHICS
THE ARTWORK OF JEFF A. MENGES

631~262~0633 • WWW.SKAIRCROW.COM
FANTASY • HISTORY • HORROR • ADVENTURE
TRADITIONAL ILLUSTRATION • DIGITAL DELIVERY

P.O. BOX 593 • NORTHPORT, NEW YORK • 11768~0593

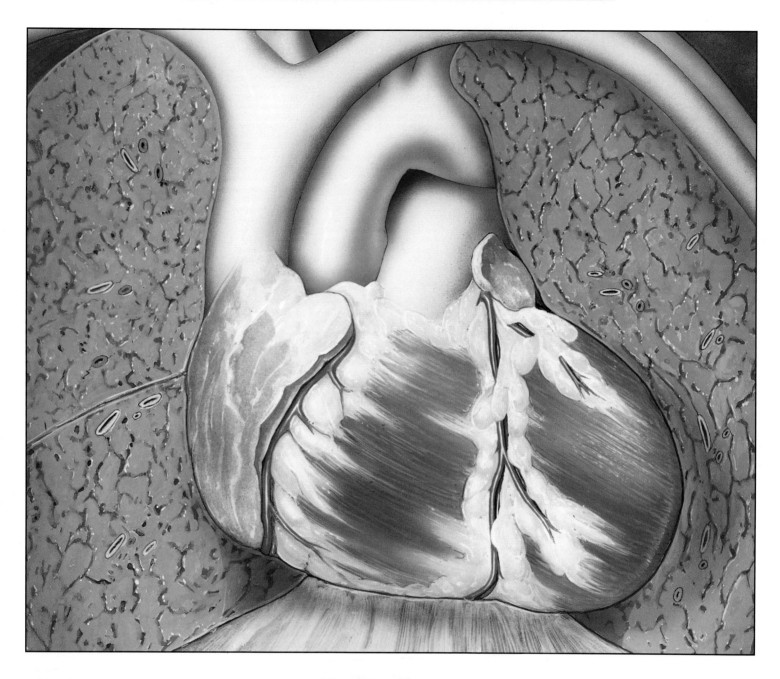
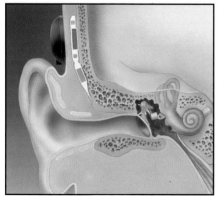
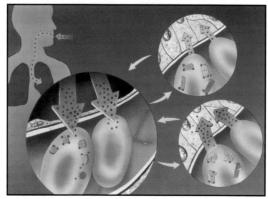
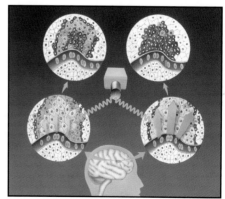

8fish

WWW.8FISH.COM/Illustration INFO@8FISH.COM 1.877.568.FISH

HOW YOU WANT IT. WHEN YOU WANT IT.

8fish

WE DO IT FOR MONEY.

We are commercial artists that work for pay. We do not illustrate for art-sake. Advertising is a business. Don't waste your time or money with finicky illustrators or lazy artists. Get it right, on time, every time, with 8Fish. We are versatile, talented and most of all, committed. Just ask our clients: Intel, 3Com, Iomega, Franklin Covey, Merrill Scott & Associates, Novell, and Maverik Country Stores.

Ask for Ernie Harker
WWW.8FISH.COM/Illustration
INFO@8FISH.COM
1(877) 568.FISH

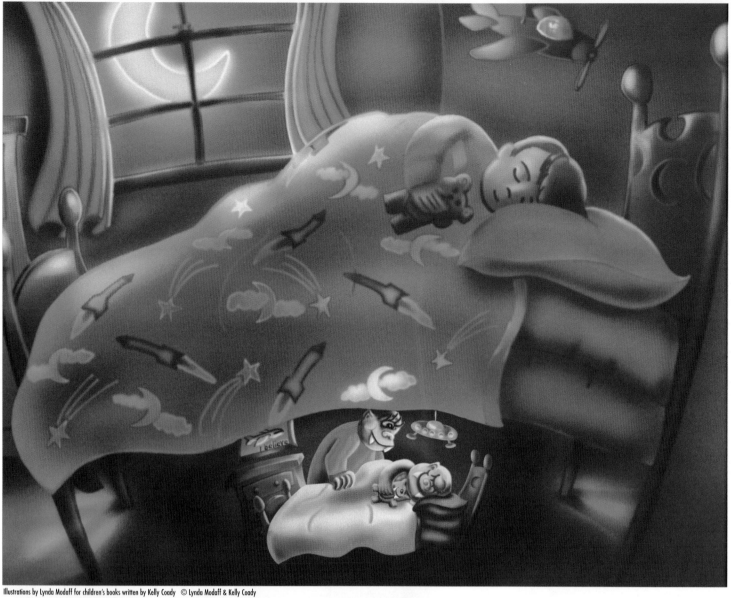

Illustrations by Lynda Modaff for children's books written by Kelly Coady   © Lynda Modaff & Kelly Coady

Illustration by Lynda Modaff

see more illustrations at **www.directoryofillustration.com**

tel & fax 310-641-6916, e-mail: **psychicdog@aol.com**

Clients have included: Dreamworks, Baskin Robbins, CareAmerica, TRW, DIRECTV, Warner Bros., Disney, Borax, OPI

PSYCHIC DOG
ILLUSTRATION

TODD LEONARDO
19110 Almond Road
Castro Valley, CA 94546
TEL (510) 728-1076
FAX in Studio

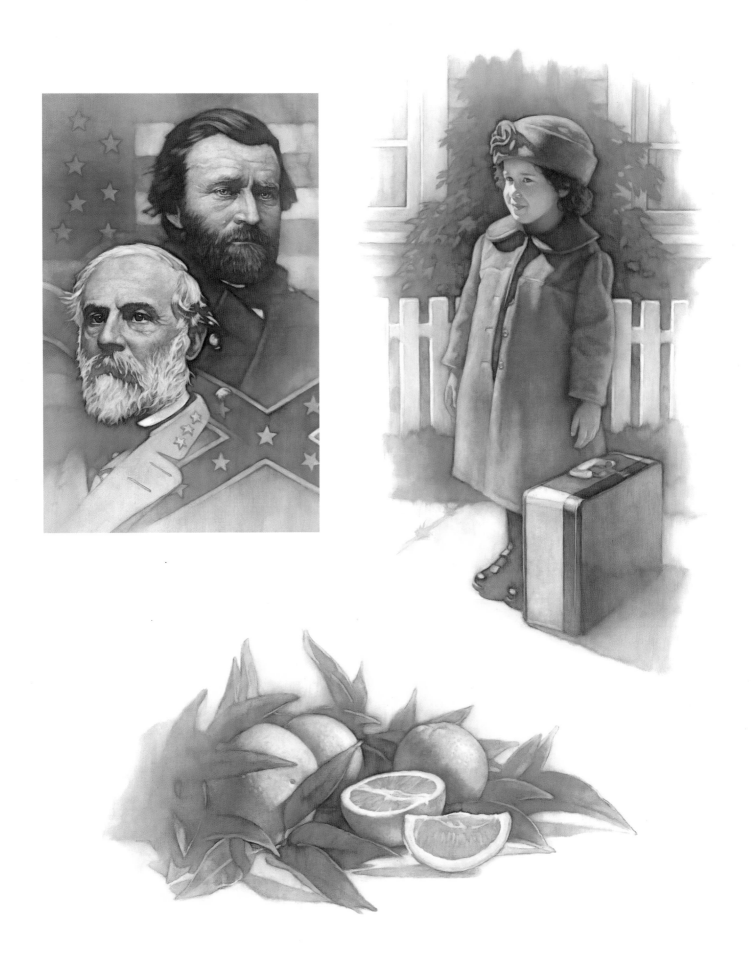

PAUL DOLAN ILLUSTRATION   773.528.8159
Digital Illustration, Graphic and Web Design.

GARY FIELDS
studios

30 Allen Drive • Wayne, NJ 07470
Phone 973 633-8060 • Fax 973 633-9917

dave@ward1.com

DAVID **DS** IEKS

tel: 800.929.2350

David Sieks Illustration
www.ward1.com/artist

PAUL JENSEN
4145 Minnehaha Avenue
Minneapolis, MN 55406
TEL (612) 729-7453
FAX (612) 729-7024

See Directory of Illustration #16
Be sure to visit:
www.pauljensen.com

NICOLE IN DEN BOSCH
in den Bosch illustration
& design
3304 Shore Drive
Annapolis, MD 21403
TEL (410) 280-5411
FAX (410) 280-6690

e-mail:
indenboschillustration@yahoo.com
web site:
www.indenboschillustration.com
www.portfolios.com/indenbosch

See Picturebook 2000 or
www.indenboschillustration.com
for additional work or call for portfolio.

1-888-730-7080 nadiarichie@hotmail.com

NADIA RICHIE

anamelaraillustrator.com
NYC 212.262.6273

LADIES

JARED PHILLIPS
FACE IT! STUDIOS

700-76 Broadway PMB #192
Westwood, NJ 07675
TEL (201) 635-1898
e-mail: faceitstudios@hotmail.com

See Directory of Illustration #16 for
additional work or call for portfolio

Jessica Wolk-Stanley

201-798-2273

www.olk-stanley.com

Steve Björkman
Studio 949.261.1411   Fax 949.261.7528
WWW.stevebjorkman.com

MICHAEL MCGURL

14 Garbosa Rd.
Santa Fe, NM 87505
Tel: (505) 466-6889
Fax: (505) 466-8253
e-mail: mrmike1@mac.com

STEPHANIE CARTER

TIM E • OGLINE • ILLUSTRATOR

Drawing on the Right Brain for the Left Brain.

tel: 877-907-5251 e-mail: contact@timogline.com
web-site: http://www.timogline.com

STEVEN R. CUSANO
80 Talbot Ct.
Media, PA 19063-5527
TEL/FAX (610) 565-8829
e-mail: cusanoart@aol.com

Maj. Gen. George E. PICKETT

ANNA VELTFORT
16 West 86th Street, #B
New York, NY 10024
TEL (212) 877-0430
FAX (212) 877-0584
e-mail: aveltfort@aol.com
www.annaillustration.com

Clients include: Post Cereals,
Hyperspace Cowgirls, Children's
Television Workshop, Simon &
Schuster, Houghton Mifflin, and
Oxford University Press.

Gregory Benton

clients include

Nickelodeon

Disney

Entertainment Weekly

TIME

Tower Records' PULSE!

Watson-Guptill

New York Times

TAXI

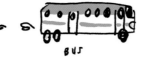
SIDE   FRONT

BUS

front.loading
dump truck.

Shelly Meridith

55 mercer street Floor 4 nyc 10013

212 • 941 • 1905   Fax 212 • 226 • 3227

ShellyM@Shellyadventures.com

www.Shellyadventures.com

Kitty

Glenda Rogers
I L L U S T R A T I O N
3 1 5 / 4 5 1 - 3 2 2 0

Specializing in conceptual illustration for corporate, editorial, and advertising use.

Clients include: AT&T, Carrier Corp, Pitney Bowes, Southern Electric, LILCO, Northeast Utilities, United Technologies, US Marine Corp, Miller Brewery, Niagara Mohawk, Veja-Editora Abril, Psychology Today

Call for samples. Also see Directory of Illustration 16

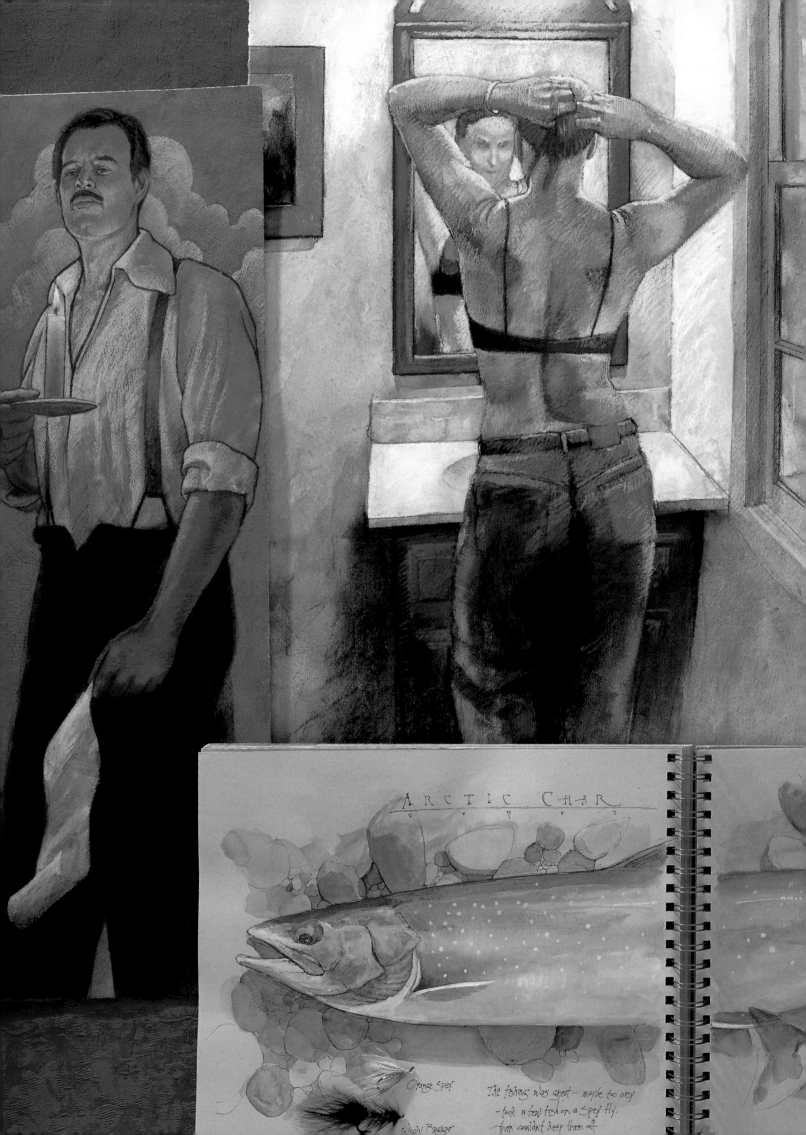

ARCTIC CHAR

Orange Spey

Wooly Bugger

The fishing was great - maybe too easy
- took a few fish on a Spey fly,
then couldn't keep them off

ker is determined when the bottom board is attached to the strongback (more rocker, more maneuverable/less rocker, better tracking).

spilling batten

batten maintains rib spacing

Mohawk

Adirondack

The planking bench is unique to Adirondack Guideboat building.

GRAYLING

RICHARD C. HARRINGTON
716 - 346 - 0772
www.rcharrington.com

DINO JUAREZ
1225 W. Lexington
Chicago, IL 60607
TEL (312) 243-5173
FAX (312) 432-9110

KEN CALL
1933 Kiest Avenue
Northbrook, IL 60062
TEL (847) 714-9523
FAX (847) 714-9524
Representation: East Coast—Sid Buck

PAUL VISMARA
1-888-VISMARA
1-888-847-6272
e-mail: pvismara@aol.com

Clientele Includes:
The Wall Street Journal, Nations Bank,
Reader's Digest, McGraw-Hill,
Ernst & Young, Forbes

See Directory of Illustration #13–16
for additional work or call for portfolio.

PAUL VISMARA
1-888-VISMARA
1-888-847-6272
e-mail: pvismara@aol.com

Clientele Includes:
The Wall Street Journal, Nations Bank,
Reader's Digest, McGraw-Hill,
Ernst & Young, Forbes

See Directory of Illustration #13–16
for additional work or call for portfolio.

845

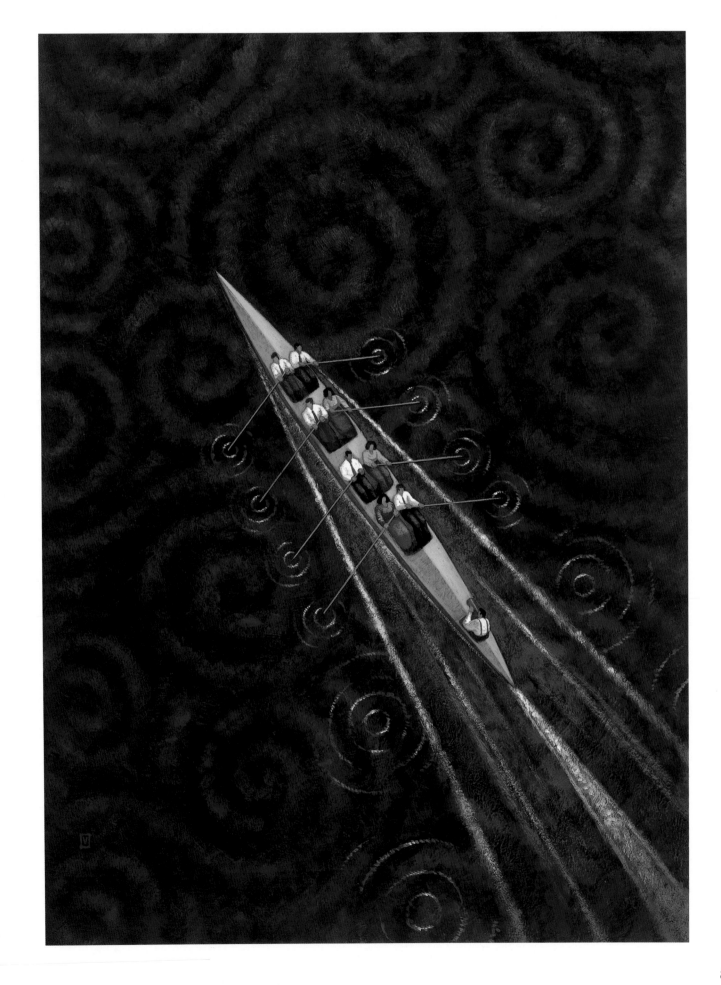

CAROL WAY WOOD
LUCKY BUNNY GRAPHICS
569 Barney's Joy Road
South Dartmouth, MA, 02748
TEL (508) 636-6699
FAX upon request

Clients include:
Clove Publications
D.C. Health
Houghton-Mifflin
New England Clam Jams
P.F. Collier/Macmillan-MacGraw-Hill
Scholastic Magazine

Scott Foresman/Harper Collins
Wells, Rich, Greene, Inc./IBM
White Heat, Inc./Harper Festival
Kodak Creative

**JOHN C. WARD
NIGHTLANCER
ILLUSTRATION**

125 Maryland Avenue
Freeport, NY 11520
TEL (516) 546-2906
e-mail: jwdoesart@aol.com

847

bw-illustration@mindspring.com

Brian Woodlief   423-902-2980

www.bw-illustration.com

PATRICK GIROUARD
7043 Wicker Avenue
Hammond, IN 46323
TEL (219) 844-3938
e-mail: art@pgirouard.com
www.pgirouard.com

Represented by
Portfolio Solutions
Janet DeCarlo
TEL (914) 226-8401
FAX (914) 226-8937

Howard Perlin

Illustration, Storyboards, Comps & Animatics
88-11 63rd Drive, Rego Park N.Y. 11374
Phone: 917-838-1068 Fax 718-803-2338
Visit me on the web at www.perlinstudio.com

**DAVID CHEN
ILLUSTRATION**
2211 Newton Drive
Rockville, MD 20850
TEL (301) 460-6575
FAX (301) 460-5351
e-mail: dchenart@erols.com

**DAVID CHEN
ILLUSTRATION**
2211 Newton Drive
Rockville, MD 20850
TEL (301) 460-6575
FAX (301) 460-5351
e-mail: dchenart@erols.com

**JAY KOELZER
ILLUSTRATION**
5322 Gallatin Place
Boulder, CO 80303
TEL (720) 353-9751
e-mail: jaybirdk@aol.com

Portfolio @ www.koelzer-vision.com

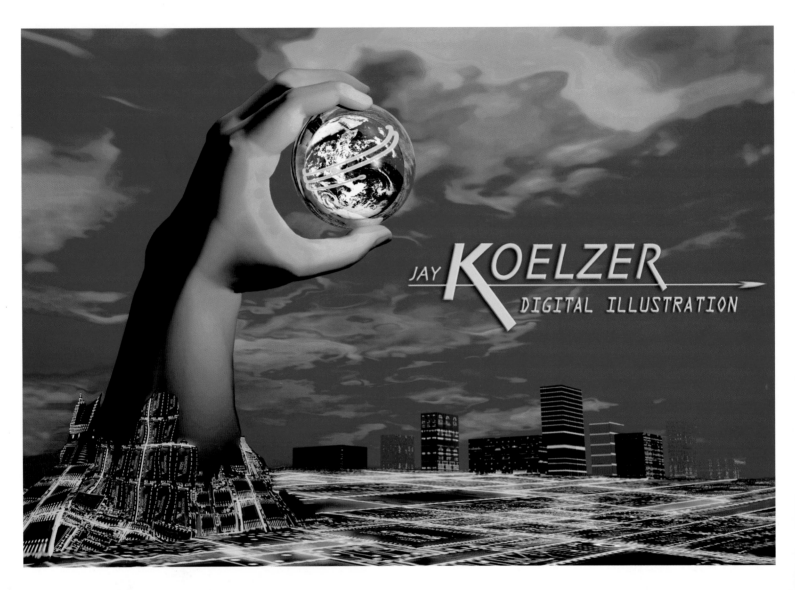

CONCEPTUAL ILLUSTRATION
FOR EDITORIAL, ADVERTISING & CORPORATE CLIENTS

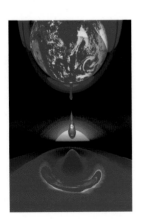

PORTFOLIO @ WWW.KOELZER-VISION.COM

JAMES
HUNGASKI
i l l u s t r a t i o n

(800) 818-6471
hungaskiillustration.com

RICHMOND ILLUSTRATION INC.

CARTOONS
CARICATURE
HUMOROUS ILLUSTRATION

Tom Richmond
3421 East Burnsville Parkway
Burnsville, MN 55337
952-882-9133 voice 952-882-2910 fax

www.tomrichmond.com

See more work in Directory of Illustration 12-16

EMAIL: brucie@albany.net
WEB PORTFOLIO: www.albany.net/~brucie

518.581.0288
or 518.587.8940

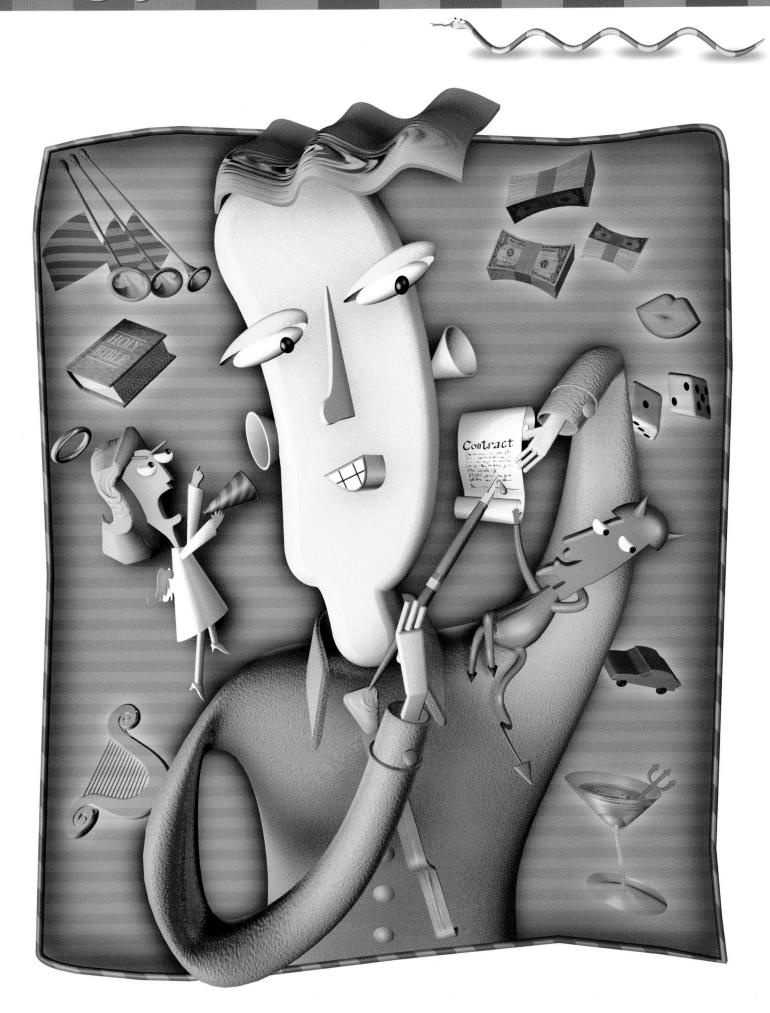

P·905·529·3429 F·905·529·8774 E·LPENG@HOME·COM

거봐!

Leave
it
to
BEELZEBUB

LEIF...

PENG!

CARTOON

ART

Clients:
Simon & Schuster
MAD Magazine
Washington Post
American Express
Children's TV Workshop
Time Warner
Netscape
MTV/Nickelodeon
Walt Disney Co.
Cartoon Network

DEAN
ILLUSTRATION

PHONE: 713/527-0295
FAX: 713/526-2456

BANNER ILLUSTRATION

212.971.1938
518.583.7982

718-398-9039
w w w . a r n o m a t i o n . c o m

KAROL KAMINSKI
908 Edgar Lane
Brunswick, OH 44212
TEL (330) 225-8195
FAX (330) 220-7695

See D #14–15–16 for additional
samples or call for portfolio.

tom white.images • *phone* 212.866.7841 • *e-mail* tom@twimages.com • *website* http://www.twimages.com

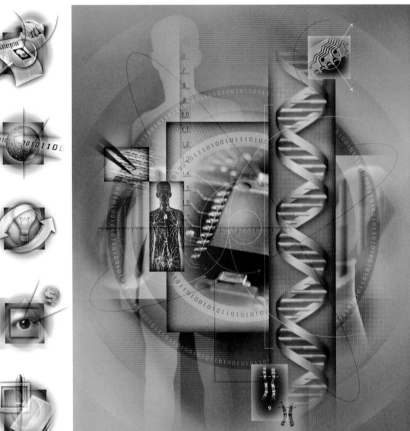

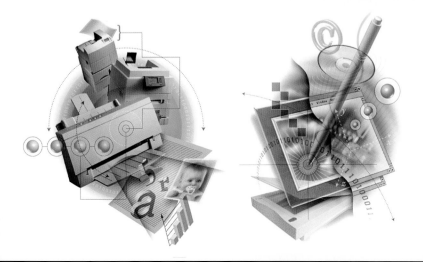

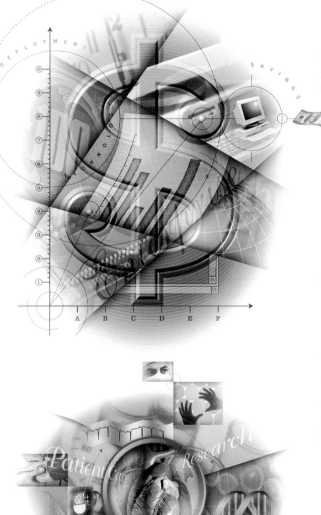

N. PEACH ARCHITECTURAL ILLUSTRATOR

3 Flemings Court
Sausalito, CA 94965
TEL (800) 905-7295
    (415) 331-3613
Fax (415) 331-1203
e-mail: n.peach@aol.com

N. Peach can dramatically change the way your clients view the project. Offering you solutions to your rendering needs from architecture to murals to children's books. Fast turnaround, flexible with changes & meets deadlines and budgets.

Education: Art Center College of Design, Pasadena, CA.

Member of the American Society of Architectural Illustrators

Published in Architecture in Perspective #13 & #14
See additional work in Directory #16
See additional work:
www.npeach-archillustrator.com
Also: www.design4thepassionate.com
(go to boxes #1, #2, #3, to see renderings & paintings)

Kathy Rusynyk

2309 Twp. Rd. 257 • Jeromesville, Ohio 44840
419/368-3664

RAT UNDER PAPER

❶

❷

❸

❶ **PUBLICATION:** OUT ❷ **PUBLICATION:** PLAYBOY ❸ **PUBLICATION:** MARKETING. *DON'T WALK AWAY RENÉE.*

Ric Borum Illustration & Design
502-B Stevehawkins Pkwy.
Marble Falls, Tx. 78654
Phone: (830) 798-0816
E Mail: borum@281.com

JAMBALAYA JUBILEE

MARQUIS
OIL & GAS INC.

REJOICE
AT THE WELL

THE Beaches OF TEXAS

SURFERS HEALING

JOHN HECK DESIGN

StepInside
.com

HERSHEY
WILDCATS

SACRED HEARTS
SCHOOL

76 HOWARD ST. DUMONT, NJ 07628.3123
PATRICK TOMASULO
TEL. 201.384.6225 WWW.LOGOINK.COM

Strictly ROSES
FLORIST & FLOWERS

SUPER BOWL XLV

©MM PATRICK TOMASULO

FOREVER

MEREDITH JOHNSON • 5228 PALM DRIVE • LA CAÑADA, CA 91011 • 818-790-8060 • FAX: 818-790-1709

meredithdraws@earthlink.net

**CATHERINE SPOSATO
ILLUSTRATION/DESIGN**
Brooklyn, NY 11228
TEL/FAX (718) 373-9080

Member:
Graphic Artists Guild of New York
See also
Graphic Artist Guild Directory #16

GLASGOW

Glasgow Media

a creative
communications
company

Voice
540-286-2539

Fax
540-286-0316

448 Hartwood Road
Fredericksburg. Va
22406

info@glasgowmedia.com

infoban@aol.com

www.glasgowmedia.com

TO VIEW MORE WORK:

- Creative Illustration
  Book, 1991-2001

- American Showcase,
  1992-2001

- New Media
  Showcase, 1993-1995

- Creative Sourcebook,
  1992-1998

- Mid Atlantic Creative
  index, 1999-2001

- Workbook, 1995-2001

- Diagraphics, Vol. 2,
  JCA, 1995

- Information
  Illustration, 1994

- Home Page,
  www.glasgowmedia.com

- Stock sales, SIS,
  Laughing Stock,
  www.glasgowmedia.com

see our
flashdemo:

www.glasgowmedia.com

Compaq: Connectivity

Manugistics: Human
interaction in a digital
world

3Com: Home Connect Cable modem

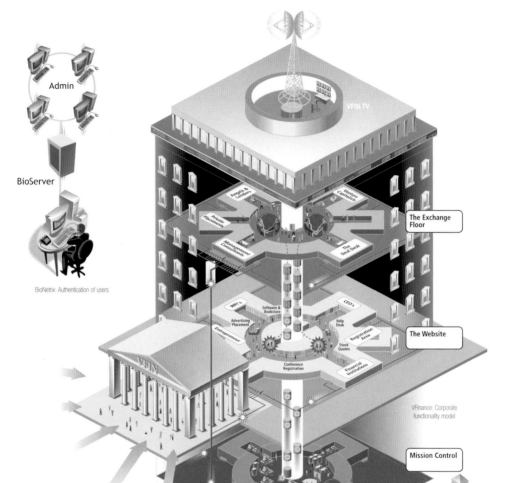

Admin

BioServer

BioNetrix: Authentication of users

VFinance: Corporate
functionality model

CUSTOMER
MANAGEMENT
SOLUTIONS

Mi8: Access to files at an
application service provider

Capital R&M: Putting enough
away in your nest egg?

Acquisitions

Bell Atlantic:
Working from home

Virtual Accountant:
System overview

Packeteer: Equal distribution
of bandwidth

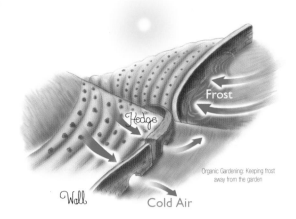

Frost

Hedge

Wall

Cold Air

Organic Gardening: Keeping frost
away from the garden

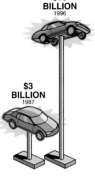

Republican National Committee: Telephone
solicitation still brings in cash

Should evolution
be removed from
public schools?

Christianity Today: Evolution in dispute

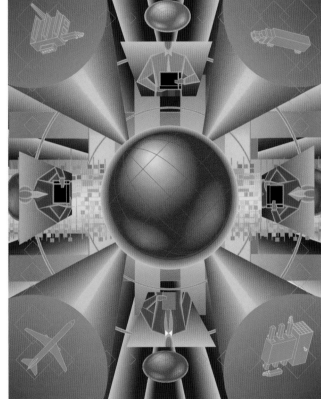

Impulse: The reality of the supply chain on the Internet

Software

Resellers

Distributors

Telesales

Retail
Outlets

Downloads   Internet

Customers

Mail
Order

Business Software Alliance: Software usability chain

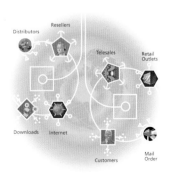

NAA: The whirlwind of technology

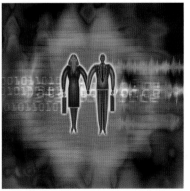

Bell Atlantic: The marriage of voice and data—Broadband

Biore Skin Care: Reducing
swelling of pores

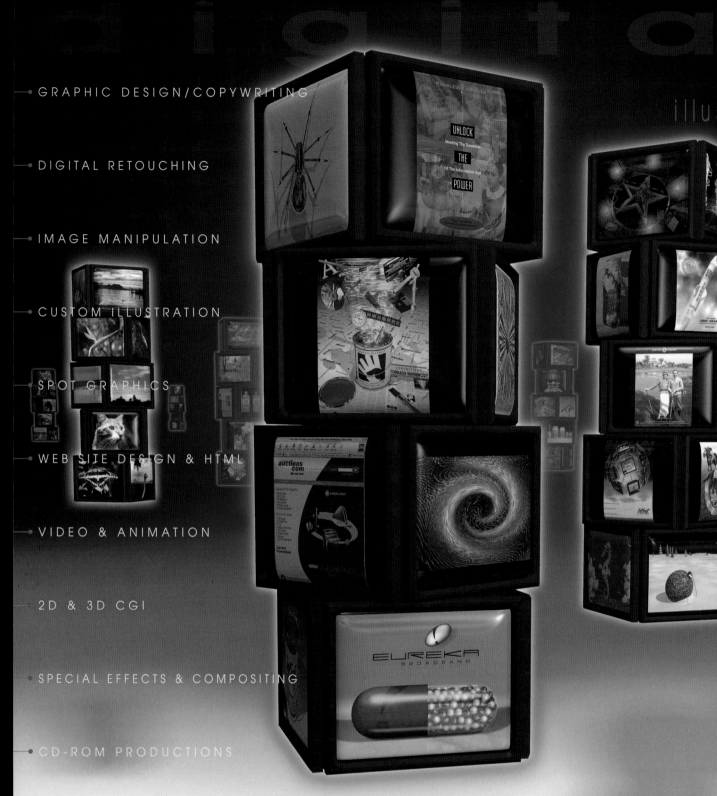

GRAPHIC DESIGN/COPYWRITING

DIGITAL RETOUCHING

IMAGE MANIPULATION

CUSTOM ILLUSTRATION

SPOT GRAPHICS

WEB SITE DESIGN & HTML

VIDEO & ANIMATION

2D & 3D CGI

SPECIAL EFFECTS & COMPOSITING

CD-ROM PRODUCTIONS

Michael D. Colanero

A VIRTUAL STUDIO IN ACTION

mdc@inkspotdesigns.com

954 946-2693 voice

954 946-2667 fax/data

MATTHEW ARCHAMBAULT
27 Garfield Ave.
East Islip, NY 11730
TEL/FAX (631) 277-4722
e-mail: marchambault@earthlink.net

Clients include:
Arte Publico Press, Augsburg Fortress Pub., Avon Books, Bantam Doubleday Dell, Ballantine Books, Barton Cotton Inc., Barbour Pub., Chariot Victor Pub., Christian Research Journal, Concordia Pub., Crossway Books, Daniel Weiss Assoc., Focus on the Family, Harcourt Brace, Harlequin, Harper, Herald Press, Krames Communications, Major League Baseball, Michaelis Carpelis Designs, New Hope Pub., Oxford University Press, Pages Pub., Parachute Press, Random House, Scholastic, Silvermoon Press, Steck Vaughn, TOR, Troll, Tyndale

What Do Royalty-Free Images Cost You?

Maybe a lot more than you think. When you sell your work for royalty-free use, you're not only giving up the rights to profit further from that image, you're helping to build a body of work that could cut you off from jobs in the future.

Think carefully before you do royalty-free work. We want you to have a hand in doing great creative work for many years to come.

Illustration by Steve Brodner © 1999

**Protect your rights.
Join the Guild.**

Local 3030 UAW

212-791-3400 x108

www.gag.org

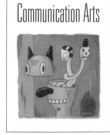
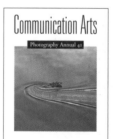
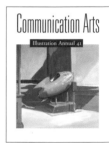

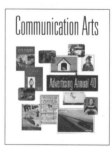
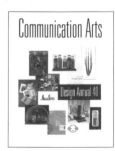